Seeing Species

This book is part of the Peter Lang Media and Communication list.
Every volume is peer reviewed and meets
the highest quality standards for content and production.

PETER LANG
New York • Bern • Berlin
Brussels • Vienna • Oxford • Warsaw

Debra L. Merskin

Seeing Species

Re-presentations of Animals in Media & Popular Culture

PETER LANG
New York • Bern • Berlin
Brussels • Vienna • Oxford • Warsaw

Library of Congress Cataloging-in-Publication Data
Names: Merskin, Debra L., author.
Title: Seeing Species: re-presentations of animals in media & popular culture /
Debra L. Merskin.
Description: New York: Peter Lang, 2018.
Includes bibliographical references and index.
Identifiers: LCCN 2017055810 | ISBN 978-1-4331-5359-4 (hardback: alk. paper)
ISBN 978-1-4331-4756-2 (paperback: alk. paper) | ISBN 978-1-4331-4757-9 (ebook pdf)
ISBN 978-1-4331-4758-6 (epub) | ISBN 978-1-4331-4759-3 (mobi)
Subjects: LCSH: Animals in mass media. | Human-animal relationships.
Classification: LCC P96.A53 M47 2018 | DDC 590—dc23
LC record available at https://lccn.loc.gov/2017055810
DOI 10.3726/b13410

Bibliographic information published by **Die Deutsche Nationalbibliothek**.
Die Deutsche Nationalbibliothek lists this publication in the "Deutsche
Nationalbibliografie"; detailed bibliographic data are available
on the Internet at http://dnb.d-nb.de/.

The paper in this book meets the guidelines for permanence and durability
of the Committee on Production Guidelines for Book Longevity
of the Council of Library Resources.

© 2018 Peter Lang Publishing, Inc., New York
29 Broadway, 18th floor, New York, NY 10006
www.peterlang.com

All rights reserved.
Reprint or reproduction, even partially, in all forms such as microfilm,
xerography, microfiche, microcard, and offset strictly prohibited.

Printed in the United States of America

Lokah Samastah Sukhino Bhavantu
(Hindu prayer for peace)

"May all beings everywhere be happy and free, and may the thoughts, words, and actions of my own life contribute in some way to that happiness and to that freedom for all."

Table of Contents

List of Illustrations ... ix
List of Tables ... xi
Preface ... xiii
Acknowledgements ... xxv

Section 1: Foundations ... 1
   1. Introduction ... 3
   2. Animal Media Studies ... 33
   3. Children and Animals ... 53
   4. Re-presenting Animals in Popular Culture ... 85

Section 2: Case Studies ... 111
   5. Knuffle Bunnies and Devoted Ducklings: The Formation of Gender Identity in Picture Books ... 113
   6. Polarizing Bears: The Semiotic Disconnect ... 135
   7. The Plight of the Prairie Dog ... 157

8. Catty: The Feral Feminine in Media 179
9. Nevermore: Ravens in *Game of Thrones* 205
10. Fables and Foibles as Global Economic Concepts:
    Animals on the Covers of *The Economist* 233

Index 261

Illustrations

Figure 0.1:	*National Geographic*, December 1965.	xvi
Figure 1.1:	The Great Chain of Being.	9
Figure 1.2:	Interspecies Model of Prejudice.	20
Figure 1.3:	Intersecting Axes of Privilege, Domination, and Oppression.	22
Figure 1.4:	Maslow's Hierarchy of Needs.	24
Figure 2.1:	Hegemonic System of Social Control.	36
Figure 2.2:	Althusser's State Apparatus Model.	37
Figure 3.1:	Belsky's Process Model.	65
Figure 3.2:	Five-Month-Old Juliana Interacts With Animal Toys and Real Her Friend, Cora.	66
Figure 3.3:	Friendship.	68
Figure 4.1a:	Petroglyph on Basalt 1. Lake County, Oregon.	89
Figure 4.1b:	Petroglyph on Basalt 2. Lake County, Oregon.	89
Figure 4.2:	A Distinguished Member of the Humane Society.	95
Figure 5.1:	*The Book of the Cat: With Facsimiles of Drawings in Colour* (1903).	119
Figure 6.1:	Polar Bear.	137

Figure 6.2:	Isbjorn (Polar Bear).	141
Figure 6.3:	Maidenform Bra Advertisement (1951).	145
Figure 7.1:	Two Prairie Dogs Sharing Their Food.	158
Figure 8.1:	*Oedipus and the Sphinx.* Gustave Moreau, 1864. Oil on canvas.	186
Figure 8.2:	Tiger.	201
Figure 9.1:	"Not the Least Obeisance Made He." Gustave Doré illustration for the 1884 edition of *The Raven.*	206
Figure 9.2:	Raven.	209
Figure 10.1:	"Tokio Kid Say."	238

Tables

Table 4.1.	Zoological References in Language.	100
Table 5.1.	Titles Analyzed.	126
Table 5.2.	Human Roles.	127
Table 5.3.	Animal Roles.	128
Table 5.4.	Species Representations.	129
Table 6.1.	Polar Bear Facts.	138
Table 7.1.	Prairie Dog Facts.	160
Table 9.1.	Raven Facts.	210
Table 10.1.	Species Re-presented.	248

Preface

The very act of treating people like animals, would lose its meaning if animals were treated well.

—Plous, (2003, p. 510)

Before we can determine how to best treat animals, we must first change how we view them.

—Nussbaum (2006)

The more clearly we see the difference between animals and stones or machines or plastic dolls, the less likely it seems that we ought to treat them the same way.

—Midgley (1998, p. 14)

Auschwitz begins whenever someone looks at a slaughterhouse and thinks: they're only animals.

—Adorno (2016)

"I don't see anything I like," said the visitor to the humane society cattery where I volunteer. On this busy Saturday a gray-haired older gal was looking to adopt a senior male cat, which was encouraging since most people want kittens. And yet her parting words stayed with me. It was the use of the word "thing," rather than "anyone," that made me uncomfortable, as this objectification so precisely represents many people's beliefs about animals.[1] "I don't see anyone I like" would have left me sorry to see her go without a feline companion. The ontological difference is critical to how, when, and if we regard other species as subjects, not objects, as co-participants on the planet. Her languaging should have come as no surprise as anthropocentrism (the belief that humans are the center of the universe with higher moral status and value) is deeply entrenched in America's cultural, economic, political, and legal structures. For example, under U.S. law, domestic animals[2] are considered things; they are classified as property, along with land, cars, houses, and other objects. Where does our thinking of other beings in this detached, impersonal, objectified way come from? Do the mass media contribute to this distancing? When did humans first think about animals as other others? These are questions explored in this book, which has two major themes: first, that classification and representation matter, and second, representation (later written as re-presentation) has implications for and effects on animals and our lives.

The first theme is addressed through an exploration of what is called the human/animal divide, which can be defined as the process of binary classification systems in Judeo-Christian Euro American thought. This eternal and persistent division is expressed in culturally different ways of thinking about animals and multiple methods of re-presenting of them in media and popular culture. Re-presentations include an examination of the underlying psychological processes to Other construction, recognition of the importance of re-languaging and re-imagining how, when, and if we refer to animals other than humans. Through an inter- and multi-disciplinary approach to thinking about animals and their representations readers have the opportunity to examine deep-seated cultural and personal beliefs about our relationships with animals and theirs with us. By this process each reader is encouraged to consider their own questions about animal rights,[3] respect, and responsibility. This book is not meant to be indoctrination into my way of viewing our relationships with animals, rather, is intended to function as a form of media literacy by pulling back the curtain on what is concealed behind contemporary re-presentations of animals and actual practices. For we know that

> Cultural assumptions about nonhuman animals and their moral status relative to humans are as deeply ingrained as any. The long-standing belief that human beings are superior to nonhuman animals and occupy a privileged place in the moral order remains one of the prevailing dogmas of the day. (Engel & Jenni, 2010, p. 60)

The idea that animals should be thought of not only as species with their own interests, desires, preferences, and lives, but also as individuals who do so, is a radical concept in some quarters. The belief that animals are members not only of a species, but also are individuals was first brought to the forefront of global scientific and popular attention in the late 1950s with the work of a young English scientist, Jane Goodall, who studied chimpanzees in the Gombe Stream National Park in the East African nation of Tanzania. At that time, Goodall challenged scientific norms by naming chimpanzees (*Pan troglodytes*), rather than simply assigning them numbers. She recognized and recorded the life ways of individuals such as David Gray Beard, Flo, Fifi, and Passion. Furthermore, she disrupted what human beings had long believed about themselves: that they were the only toolmakers or users. "It was hard for me to believe," she recalls. "At that time, it was thought that humans, and only humans, used and made tools. I had been told from school onwards that the best definition of a human being was man the toolmaker—yet I had just watched a chimp toolmaker in action. I remember that day as vividly as if it was yesterday" (qtd. in McKie, 2010). The chimps' and Goodall's stories gained international attention in part through the cover story of the December 1965 issue of *National Geographic* magazine (See Figure 0.1).

This was followed that same month by a television special that gave viewers a nudge down the path of recognizing the urgent need for empathetic engagement with other species. Dr. Goodall's work was made visible by who she is and what she was doing, a young female scientist embedded in a community of chimpanzees. The exposure was heightened as well because the 1960s was a time when television specials and

Figure 0.1: *National Geographic*, December 1965.
Source: Used by permission, *National Geographic* Creative.

magazines had tremendous visibility and less competition from other forms of communication.[4] It was in fact through the media that Goodall's twin passions for Africa and for chimpanzees were born, "I got my love of animals from the Dr. Doolittle books and my love of Africa from the Tarzan novels," she says. "I remember my mum taking me to the first Tarzan film, which starred Johnny Weissmuller, and bursting into tears. It wasn't what I had imagined at all" (qtd. in McKie, 2010).

The second theme of this book is the implications of media and popular culture re-presentation (language and images) on animal's lived experiences. Media and other social institutions use animals and animality to educate and enrich, however they are also used to advance economic and ideological interests. Typically, animals are thought of more by what they mean to us, in utilitarian, nutritional, and experimental terms. Yet science and personal experience demonstrate that they are more than that. I contend that advertising, news, cinema, television programs, and the Web are carriers of deliberately constructed messages that use animals and their images in ways that directly and indirectly impact their lives. This is complicated by the fact that animals are included in advertising and programming that often has nothing to do with real species. These portrayals come to seem normal and natural, creating a kind of "truth" that serves human interests. In the words of Stuart Hall, re-presentations become narrowed to mean only one thing, they become "naturalized" and closed. Thus

> Whenever you see that, you will think that, whenever you see that, you will think that whenever you see those people, you will assume that they have those characteristics. Whenever you see that event, you will assume it has that political consequence. That's what ideology tries to do, that's what power in signification is intended to do: to close language, to close meaning, to stop the flow. (qtd. in Jhally, 1997, p. 19)

The lens through which this book critiques human relationships with the planet and its inhabitants and the intersections with Othering is "ecological thought" (Morton, 2012, p. 2). Ecological thought is

> ... A virus that infects all other areas of thinking. ... Ecology isn't just about global warming, recycling and solar power—and also not just to do with everyday relationships between humans and nonhumans. It has to do with love, loss, despair, and compassion. It has to do with depression and psychosis. It has to do with capitalism and with what might exist after capitalism. It has to do with amazement, open-mindedness, and wonder. It has to do with doubt, confusion, and skepticism. It has to do with concepts of space and time. It has to do with delight, beauty, ugliness, disgust, irony, and pain. It has to do with consciousness and awareness. It has to do with ideology and critique. It has to do with reading and writing. It has to do with race, class, and gender. It has to do with sexuality. It has to do with ideas of self and the weird paradoxes of subjectivity. It has to do with society. It has to do with coexistence. (p. 2)

This book is my attempt to extend and contribute to Bekoff's (2014) concept of "rewilding our hearts." Rewilding is

> About nurturing our sense of wonder. Rewilding is about being nice, kind, compassionate, empathic, and harnessing our inborn goodness and optimism. In the most basic sense, "rewilding" means to "make wider" or "to make wild once again." This means many things. ... But primarily it means opening our hearts and minds to others. (p. 5)

Rewilding is a "mindset" (Bekoff, 2014, p. 13) that means not only that it is okay to care but more so that "it is essential" (p. 5). It that erases arbitrary borders and boundaries about who is an animal, about appreciating, getting to know, learning to recognize animals in all the ways they inhabit the world, not only for our benefit but for theirs. In addition, in order not to get "stuck in human-constructed theoretical deadlocks" (Jones, 2015, p. 99), I argue for an ethical viewpoint that begins with the premise that other animals have points of view, preferences, and make choices, preferring to live without pain or restriction on natural lifeways, and should be free to enjoy their families and one another's company. After examining what many of those philosophical deadlocks are, we are then free to see animals for who they are and learn to listen to what they have to say and be empathetically entangled with animals "whom we recognize as being already engaged in the pursuit of their own wellbeing and liberation" (p. 98).

This book brings together sociological, psychological, historical, cultural, and environmental ways of thinking about nonhuman animals and our relationships with them. In particular, it uses ecopsychological thinking to locate and identify the connections between how we re-present animals and the impact on their lived experiences in terms of distancing, generating a false sense of intimacy, and stereotyping. Representations of particular species of animals are discussed in terms of the role the media do or do not play in perpetuating status quo beliefs about them and their relationship to and with us. This includes theories and methods such as phenomenology, semiotics, textual analysis, and pragmatism; ethical perspectives include ethic of care, representational ethics, with the goal of unpacking representations of animals in order to learn not only what they says about human beings but also how we regard members of other species. This work is dialectic: "on the one hand critiquing oppressive institutions, practices, and attitudes; on the other, helping to enable the emergence of crushed and hitherto silenced voices" (Donovan, 2011).

For example, wolves are widely re-presented in media almost exclusively as threatening, angry, even evil beings who premeditatively kill each other and us. Furthermore, race and species are intertwined in media re-presentations such as the second *Twilight* movie when it is revealed that Bella's friend, Jacob Black, a Native American youth, can and regularly does, transform himself in to a giant wolf, as do his Quileute friends. Likewise, in a commercial for Volvo, the Little Red Riding Hood theme is modernized showing a stand off in the forest between the trusty automobile and a snarling wolf. The car wins the intimidation stand off. Wolves have been hunted in the U.S. and in Europe to the point of extinction; populations are revived through relocation and breeding programs, and are hunted again. What is the origin of this fear and lack of understanding of the inherent value of this animal's crucial place as a keystone species in the ecological health of the natural world? What are the assumptions that maintain a one dimensional (stereotypical) view of wolves and what purpose do they serve? The answers to these and other questions about entanglements, real and imagined, are urgently needed if activist and conservation groups are to gain traction in changing attitudes and practices.

We urgently need to learn to hear and see animals for who they are, not simply for who *we* are or who *they* are in relation to *us*. This is tricky business, for how can we "atten[d] to the need to hear animals and to make them visible in ways that neither erase[s] difference nor appropriate[s]" them? (Gruen & Weil, 2010, p. 131). My intention is to reveal how social institutions use animals, veil abuse of humans and animals, and how that power is exercised over other beings on the basis of difference, lack of voice, and also "holds that every day practices, those goes-without-saying events, objects, and ways of being are what are perhaps the most significant influences on our lives" (Potts & Armstrong, 2010, p. 3). We must, and the need is urgent, learn to re-vision our relations with other species, to become literate in reading their re-presentations in order to expand what we typically think of as empathy to an enhanced "entangled empathy," which is "an experiential process involving a blend of emotion and cognition in which we recognize we are in relationships with others and are called upon to be responsive and responsible in these relationships by attending to another's needs, interests, desires, vulnerabilities, hopes, and sensitivities" (Gruen, qtd. in Bekoff, 2014). This perspective is advanced by a radical new area of study known as Animal Media Studies (AMS). This interdisciplinary approach uses literacy tools to unpack re-presentations of animals, just as we have done with re-presentations of human beings that are coded in ways that are sexist, racist, or ageist. The growing AMS discipline challenges traditional hierarchical understandings of humans as superior to animals as well as re-presentations in media and popular culture and even the languaging of human/animal relationships that privileges humans often to the disadvantage and disregard of other species. This way of seeing animals, their treatment by humans, and their voices heard is essential for both of our survival, in a world that also belongs to them. Philosopher, architect, and 20th century innovator Buckminster Fuller said, "You never change things by fighting the existing reality. To change something, build a new model that makes the existing model obsolete."

In recent years there has been increased awareness of the role of the media in influencing how/if we think about nature and the environment in general and animals in particular. Ethicists and others have been rethinking the status of animals in the popular imagination and questioning the thinking about them simultaneously as Other and also project on to them our sensibilities, experiences, emotions, and desires (anthropomorphism). This book is an exploration of "the animal question." It challenges dualistic thinking and journeys into the rich territory between the tensions of opposites. As Braidotti (2009, p. 526) notes:

> Humans have long used animals to mark the boundaries between fundamental categories of being and to spell out the social grammar of distinctions among species. This ontological function resulted in the metaphoric habit of composing a sort of moral and cognitive bestiary in which animals refer to values, norms, and morals. I propose that, instead of waxing lyrical about the nobleness of eagles, the deceit of foxes, or the humility of lambs, we acknowledge the centuries-old history and the subtlety of this animal glossary.

In modern industrialized nations we use animals for a variety of things. They function as tools, as loved ones, as food, clothing, adornments, and as adjuncts to our identities. By this I mean that, in addition to all the other roles animals perform for us, they do important symbolic work as well, and always have. From earliest cave drawings to the latest Aflac commercial, animals are used in media primarily to demonstrate something about us, not them.

According to philosopher Martha Nussbaum's capabilities approach, all beings deserve justice and the opportunity to live happy lives. Rather than focus solely on reducing suffering (which is a goal), this views every animal as deserving a happy, healthy life specific to the needs of that species. A feminist ethic of care accompanies this perspective by arguing animals matter not only as species, but that each individual is important because, not in spite of, their particular vulnerabilities, personalities, and characteristics. As a result, humans have a special obligation to them. We need to care about animals as individuals and create worlds in which they can flourish. Mine is a philosophical position that includes but goes beyond preventing suffering, to imagining another kind of world in which nonhuman animals thrive, have agency, and can be themselves in relation to species needs, and not only in relation to us.

Finally, this book is about real animals' essential invisibility and erasure. Animals are routinely laughed at, presented as fools, and used as symbolic stand-ins for human emotions (in greeting cards, comic strips, commercials, and multi-media content). At the same time, we love, admire, cherish, and even worship some animals on the basis of who we think they are. Paradoxically, rather than bringing us closer in understanding them, which is what healthy level of anthropomorphism can do, most re-presentations further distance them from us. One of the consequences is that, in the case of endangered species, repeated exposure in media tends to result in viewers believing animals such as chimps are less endangered than they actually are thus reducing the impact of conservation campaigns and funding appeals. Another example is even animals used symbolically by advocacy groups can fetishize them in ways that are far removed from the animal's actual ways of being, such as the polar bear whose re-presentations are gendered as male and racialized as white. As a teacher and scholar my work has focused on revealing silencing, misrepresentation and the consequences of this in lived experiences of marginalized human beings. In recent years, it has become evident that the embrace of this inquiry includes nonhuman animals—perhaps the most marginalized and voiceless of all.

Organization

This book is organized in to two sections. The first sets the theoretical, philosophical, and psychological context for the book. Chapter 1 introduces central theories and key ideas that contribute to the development of AMS. This includes a brief overview of the religious, philosophical, ethical, moral, and cultural ideologies that inform how, if, when, and whether animals are thought about and how this impacts how they are treated. Using feminist and critical race theories I argue that there are parallels in stereotyping of human beings and animals other than humans.

Chapter 2 is an overview of the development of the specialization in media studies of Animal Media Studies and its contribution to theory and practice.

Chapter 3 looks closely at children's special relationship with animals and the development of empathy. I trace theories of child development and explore the three primary ways children experience the natural world: directly, indirectly (zoos, aquaria), and symbolically (via mediated representations) (Corbett, 2006) in terms of the impact on empathetic understanding. There are psychological, moral, and physical repercussions if a child never experiences animals directly and only knows them vicariously (via media and popular culture).

In industrialized societies symbolic re-presentations of animals are a large part of both children's and adult's experiences with species. This is the focus of Chapter 4. The discussion ranges from re-presentations of animals in prehistoric art etchings to 3-D films, keeping in mind how someone who only knows an animal via representation might think about an animal.

In the second section I explore questions about animal re-presentation focusing on species-specific cases in media content and the implications for law, ethics, moral philosophy, policy, and opinion. Each chapter examines a particular species and a particular media re-presentation in terms of what science tells us about a particular animal, as well as the cultural history of beliefs about the animal and common representations. My hope is that examining specific species in detail serves as an exemplar from which readers will consider other animals' re-presentations. Each chapter critiques a re-presentation and considers how knowing the animal in this way might impact their lived experiences.

Chapter 5, "Knuffle Bunnies and Devoted Ducklings," illustrates many of the ideas in Chapter 3 having to do with how children learn about themselves and animals. How gender, species, and gendered species are shown in children's books is this chapter's focus.

In Chapter 6, "Polarizing Bears," I consider how a ferocious animal, the Polar Bear, is re-presented in a variety of forms of popular culture such as Coca-Cola ads, Nissan Leaf commercials, and stuffed toys. These overly positive re-presentations have implications for how the real animal is viewed and then treated when encountered in the natural world as a species considered to be charismatic megafauna.

Chapter 7, "The Plight of the Prairie Dog," analyzes how documentary films, in particularly Disney's *True Life Adventures*, re-present the prairie dog, an icon of the American west, simultaneously as cute critter and vile rodent.

Chapter 8, "Catty," is an analysis of the substitutability of cats large and small in cosmetics advertising (Maybelline Cat Eyes mascara) and for the Yves St. Laurent fragrance Opium. The study reveals parallels between the exoticization of both in order to sell cosmetics. The conflation of cats and women I call the feral feminine.

Chapter 9, "Nevermore," is a textual analysis of the re-presentation of crows and ravens in the first season of the television series *Game of Thrones*.

Magazines are the focus on Chapter 10, "Bullish about Business," which focuses on the business publication *The Economist*, and the use of animals on the covers of the magazine to communicate something about aspects of the global economy.

Notes

1. The term "animal" is used throughout this book to designate beings of species other than *Homo sapiens* (humans). Although language is a powerful ontological tool for creating distance we too are animals. At times I also use expressions such as "other than human animals," which serves to remind us of our similarities and status as one of many species of animals.
2. Based on the United States Department of Agriculture Animal Welfare Act (11/6/13), "Animals" include "any live or dead dog, cat, monkey (nonhuman primate mammal), guinea pig, hamster, rabbit, or such other warm-blooded animals." Wildlife fall under a separate category. Source: https://www.aphis.usda.gov/animal_welfare/downloads/Animal%20Care%20Blue%20Book%20-%202013%20-%20FINAL.pdf

3. Animal rights is used in the sense that all beings, including animals, have rights to fulfillment of basic needs and interests such as fresh water, food, shelter, companionship, as well as freedom from pain and suffering.
4. At the time the *National Geographic* specials aired, most homes received only three commercial channels, NBC, ABC, and CBS, and one public television channel

References

Adorno, T. (2016). Quoted in J. Pierce. *Run, spot, run: The ethics of keeping pets*. Chicago, IL: University of Chicago Press.

Bekoff, M. (2014). *Rewilding our hearts*. Novato, CA: New World Library.

Braidotti, R. (2009). Animals, anomalies, and inorganic others. *PMLA, 124*(2), 526–532.

Corbett, J. (2006). *Communicating nature* (2nd ed.). Washington, DC: Island Press.

Donovan, J. (2011). The coming of grace. *Tikkun, 26*(1). Retrieved from http://www.tikkun.org/nextgen/the-coming-of-grace

Engel, M. Jr., & Jenni, K. (2010). Examined lives. In M. DeMello (Ed.), *Teaching the animal* (pp. 60–102). New York, NY: Lantern Books.

Gruen, L. (2015, April 28). Interview. Entangled empathy: How to improve human-animal relationships. M. Bekoff in *Huffington Post*. Retrieved from http://www.huffingtonpost.com/marc-bekoff/entangled-empathy-how-to-improve-human-animal-relationships_b_6760696.html

Jhally, S. (1997). (Dir.). *Stuart Hall: Representation & the media*. [Motion picture]. Amherst, MA: Media Education Foundation.

Jones, P. (2015). Afterword. In L. Gruen (Ed.), *Entangled empathy* (pp. 97–104). New York, NY: Lantern Books.

McKie, R. (2010, June 26). Chimps with everything: Jane Goodall's 50 years in the jungle. *The Guardian*. Retrieved from https://www.theguardian.com/science/2010/jun/27/jane-goodall-chimps-africa-interview

Midgley, M. (1998). *Animals and why they matter*. Athens, GA: University of Georgia Press.

Morton, T. (2012). *Ecological thought*. Cambridge, MA: Harvard University Press.

Nussbaum, M. (2013). Talk given at the Chicago Humanities Festival. *Martha Nussbaum on animal ethics*. Retrieved from http://chicagomaroon.com/2013/11/05/chicago-humanities-festival-prof-martha-nussbaum-on-animal-ethics/

Plous, S. (2003). Is there such a thing as prejudice toward animals? In S. Plous (Ed.), *Understanding prejudice and discrimination* (pp. 509–528). New York, NY: McGraw-Hill.

Potts, A., & Armstrong, P. (2010). Hybrid vigor: Interbreeding cultural studies and human-animal studies. In M. DeMello (Ed.), *Teaching the animal* (pp. 3–17). New York, NY: Lantern Books.

Selby (Ed.), *Earthkind: A teacher's handbook on humane education* (pp. 17–32). Stroke-on-Trent: Trentham Books.

Acknowledgements

There are so many individuals to thank for inspiration, guidance, patience, and wisdom that helped this book become a reality. In particular, I am grateful and indebted to the support and encouragement of colleagues, including, but not limited to Dr. Carrie Freeman, Dr. Lori Marino, Dr. Toni Frohoff, Dr. Hope Ferdowsian, and Dr. Debra Durham. Thank you to the support staff at Peter Lang and in particular to Mary Savigar for her enthusiasm for this project and to Kathryn Harrison for helping me see it through. I am obliged to Peter Lang Publishing as well for use of a variation of previous work for Chapter 8.

Many thanks to mural artist Kari Johnson whose public artwork graces the cover of this book. To learn more about Kari's murals, please visit https://www.karijohnsonartist.com/press. Thank you as well to Brooke Rane for photographing Kari's mural.

Above all else, I am most grateful to the many animals I've known who have been my greatest teachers and those whose voices and faces are silenced or invisible. May we do better by them.

Section One

Foundations

Chapter One

Introduction

The use of animals for our purposes without consideration of their interests is so pervasive and our dependence upon it so great, it becomes invisible to us in much the same way that exploitation of women and minorities was invisible for too long.

—Rollin (1989/2011, p. 164)

Dad says people are arrogant about being smarter than animals because we have opposable thumbs but look what we messed up with our opposable thumbs.

—Doyle (2014, p. 87)

Why not animals?

—Light & McKenna (2004, p. 3)

Animals are everywhere. They inhabit our forests, our fields, our imaginations, our dreams, and our stories. Advertisements (Glenn, 2004; Lerner & Kalof, 1999; Spears, 1996), documentaries (Mills, 2010; Pierson, 2005), television programs (Berettini, 2005; Cabeza San Deogracias & Pérez, 2013; Mills, 2010; Pierson, 2005), news stories (Freeman, 2009), social media and video games (Cole & Stewart, 2014), and entertainment films such as *Zootopia* (Beaudine, Osibodu, & Beavers, 2017; Todd, 2016) and *The Secret Life of Pets* are filled with creatures great and small who are used primarily to tell stories about us. They serve as sports team and college mascots, symbols of holidays such as Easter and Thanksgiving, and as national, royal, and familial crests. The oldest known euphemistic term is one that refers to bears, recorded more than 1,000 years ago. It replaced a word that was, in Northern European dialects, never uttered for fear it would invoke the actual animal. Instead, people spoke "of *the honey* eater, *the* licker, or *the grandfather*" (Keyes, 2010, p. 29, ital orig.). And "because the word that 'bear' replaced was never recorded, it remains a mystery" (p. 29). In many cultures, particularly in ancient times, animals were not seen as distinct from what they were named, thus to say a name would be to summon an entity. In this way if one wanted to refer to a tiger, among, for example, the Oraons of India's Chota Nagpur region, they would call them "*long-tailed things*, and similarly, snakes as 'ropes'" (p. 30).

In other ways, animals function as symbolic stand-ins for nations, political parties, stock market behavior, as team mascots, monikers, and for conservation movements. According to Krein (2012, p. 3)

> Everywhere you look in our society, there are animals. Well not *actual* animals, but caricatures of animals selling us mobile-phone plans, toilet paper, cars, interest rates. As projections animals proliferate in the flat-screened zoos of cinema, television, YouTube and screen savers, trapped in Pixar worlds, serving as light relief at the end of the day. In shops you can buy animals cast in clay, plastic, porcelain, and you may hold your new purchase close, cradle it on the way home and place it carefully on the bookshelf, a tiny guardian to watch over your world. Hell, animals are even in our dreams—we wake up talking of lions, snakes and wolves, wondering what they could possibly mean.

But animals are more than "blank screens upon which we project our issues" (Adams, 2001, p. xi). How, what, when, and *if* we think of them as real beings tremendously impacts their lives and ours. They are used by the millions for food, entertainment, clothing, in experiments, and are enjoyed as pets.[1]

The popularity of animals as companions is illustrated by the fact that, in the United States, "more Americans (63 percent or 71 million households) live with a companion animal than have children of their own" (Williams & DeMello, 2007, pp. 231–232). In 2012, that number had increased to nearly 70% (avma.org). In 2015, Americans spent over $60 billion on their pets (Agrawal, 2016). In countries such as India, Brazil, and the Philippines, as economies have improved, dog ownership increased (Bradley & King, 2012). But not all animals are thought of so well or treated as kindly. Why?

A goal of this chapter is to reveal the underpinnings of the human/animal divide as well as the foundation of resistance to seeing the parallels between animals and humans. A kind of "mental vertigo" sets in when questions are raised about which animals are worthy of the status of pet, and which are not, which are live stock, which are wild life, who we eat and who we do not, and why.

Acceptance of eating of dogs and cats in some cultures is another example of moral relativity around animals. These "gastronomic red herrings" are "euphemistic names intended to distract us from [who] we are eating" (Keyes, 2010, p. 153). Giblets, for example "are the inner organs of poultry" (p. 153). While we eat lambs, calves are called "veal," cows are "beef," deer is "venison," and pigs are "pork." Such distinctions "may reflect our ambivalence about eating once-living creatures" (p. 154). Cuts of meat also carry similarly euphemistic names, rather than referring to the actual body part from which they originate. Whereas once human and animal lives (and deaths) were intimately intertwined, over the last few hundred years, in the industrialized west at least, humans have become more distanced from the means of meat production, and production has become largely industrialized. Euphemisms function to fail the actual process of growing animals for food. As a result, we do not have pig chops, but pork chops, for dinner.

These aren't comfortable conversations and distinctions waiver, but "disentangling [discomfort] is the path to relief" (Midgley, 1998, p. 13) for ourselves and for animals. Are we humans, as a species of animal, so clearly different from the others? What is gained or lost by human insistence on superiority of one and inferiority of the other? For centuries, ideologies supported and reified a clear distinction, despite ever growing scientific evidence of more similarities than differences. This chapter ventures to de-center humans and question re-presentations as somehow neutral and not problematic, for as we look at animals, as Berger (1980) reminded us, they are also looking back at us.

What kinds of thinking (ideologies) inform and maintain separation? Are there equivalencies in the ways humans who, for whatever reason, are marginalized and oppressed, and animals? The discussion that follows draws on what Spiegel (1988, p. 31) calls "the dreaded comparison." Spiegel writes

> The parallels of experience are numerous. Both humans and animals share the ability to suffer from restricted freedom of movement, from the loss of social freedom, and to experience pain at the loss of a loved one. Both groups suffer or suffered from their common capacity to be terrified, by being hunted, tormented, or injured. Both have been objectified, treated as property rather than as feeling, self-directed individuals.

This disquieting perspective shines light in to the dark space of shared oppressions. It challenges us to consider if what separates us is more important than what connects us, and if suffering is allowable if the experience happens to other animals. During the early 19th century, for example, laws concerning the treatment and welfare of animals preceded those protecting children. This was not because animals were more highly regarded than children or considered more vulnerable. Rather, it was and remains true that animals had and have economic value (LeBow & Cherney, 2015) and under some laws, are property.[2] Western nations in particular are "habituated to ignoring the interests of animals," or even acknowledging that animals have them (Midgley, 1998, p. 18).

Questions addressed in this chapter include: Who is an animal? What produced and supports a barrier between humans and other beings? What is at stake in maintaining this divide? What theories help unpack this dynamic? And what role do mass media and popular culture play in reifying or challenging the divide?

Who Is an Animal?

The etymology of "animal" is found in the Latin expression *anima* meaning to have breath, and *animalis*, and *animale*, translate to a "living being, being which breathes" (online etymology).[3] Biologically speaking "animals are living entities that are equipped with nervous systems and sensory organs that render them capable of detecting and rapidly responding to stimuli" (Neves-Graca, 2007, p. 44).

Exactly *who* is an animal? This question has challenged philosophers throughout time. Like many words in the English language, "animal" encompasses a vast range of beings (from tiny plankton to blue whales) and can be confusing. Yet, despite the fact that human beings are animals, more specifically mammals, and even more specifically a predator species, we typically refer to other beings as animals, but not ourselves, unless in a sexually aggressive way. Typically, "the animal is defined negatively to the human: it denotes that which the human *is not*" (Morton, 2014, p. 105).

Have you ever thought of yourself as an animal? Despite the central role animals play in all human societies, when the word is used to refer to us, to humans, it is usually in a debasing manner, referencing the worst type of treatment, behavior, or to describe a sexually aggressive person. Particularly in the industrialized West, children are taught that there is a clear, permanent, and nonporous divide between Us and Them (see Chapter 2 for more on this). "Exclusion is, of course, essential to the establishment of any system" (Evernden, 1992, p. 52).

But there were times, not so long ago, in the short time of human evolution, when we saw ourselves in-relation with animals (many cultures still do). In many indigenous cultures, for example, animals are regarded as central to life and not seen as lesser than humans, but by their very nature (and ours) on equal, albeit different, footings. There came a time, however, in Western societies when people began seeing themselves as not-animal and made every effort to reify a deep division intended to keep Us always and forever separate from Them.

The Great Divide

All societies create categories of meaning, behavior, and rules of right-conduct for members. Religion, along with certain forms of spirituality, have proscribed views of the "proper" place of animals. In many belief systems, animals are seen as not having souls, therefore not worthy of consideration or certainly lower in status in terms of moral worth. This is particularly true in Christianity, a belief system in which animals are generally thought to have been created and exist entirely for human use, even with the encouragements of stewardship and husbandry. Some religions modify this with regard to humane treatment, but for the animal the end result is the same. In Christianity, for example, the Great Chain of Being has persevered as model and powerful visual metaphor that inspired universal hierarchical ranking of beings ranking humans as man alone. A 16th century rendition of the model (Figure 1.1), was used to visually organize beings who had been spoken of and written about in religious texts.

Reification of this hierarchy thereby became a way of rationalizing differential treatment. At the top of the ordering is the god figure, underneath are angels. Below the "higher" beings we find humans. According to this structure, male genearativity (God is represented as male) is at the top, which fulfills patriarchal visions of a natural order. Angels are below God, humans (males in particular) are below them, and the animals follow. Animals useful to humans such as goats, chickens, cows, and horses rank about those that are lesser so (wild life), and all rank about the snakes and serpents. This model has historically been used to demonstrate and justify difference as natural, pre-ordained, and thus human/male superiority over all else as the proper nature of power and dominance. The ideology that informed this framework, inherited from Biblical times, came to influence the regard (or lack thereof) for qualities and abilities of other creatures. Belief in placement of higher or lower order has significant implications for humans and other animals. According to philosopher Sam Keen (1991, pp. 60–61) de-humanization strategy is used to establish enemies and to rationalize their disposability:

On the scale of dehumanization, we drop from the midpoint of the subhuman barbarian to the nonhuman, from the savage to the animal ... the lower down in the animal phyla the images descend, the greater sanction is given to the soldier to become an exterminator of pests.

In science, animals have not fared much better. For example, during the 17th century, René Descartes believed animals were mere machines, "subject only to the dictates of biological law" (Birke, 1996, p. 107). Unfortunately, Descartes influenced more than 500 years of science

Figure 1.1: The Great Chain of Being.
Source: 1579 drawing of the great chain of being from Didacus Valades, *Rhetorica Christiana*. Public Domain.

wherein he held that animals were mere automata. Having no souls, unlike humans, they were viewed as thereby incapable of experiencing pain. Some scientists today still believe this, resulting in the torture, suffering (experimentation without the use of anesthetic), and death of millions of animals.

In addition to a lack of soul, the ability to reason has been heralded as a benchmark for difference, and has not been limited to animals. In fact, "in the fairly recent past, women, blacks, the poor, the blind and the dead, as well as animals, have been subject to moral disqualification on the grounds of inability to reason" (Selby, 1995, p. 17). Yet we know today that reason is no simple mode of thought and that, contrary also to Descartes, humans are not simply and only rational, we are also emotional. Each of us, animals and humans, are individuals with complex, interesting, and developed social lives and histories. Some enlightenment thinkers such as Montaigne, Voltaire, Bentham, and Mill, challenged Descartes' line of thought and argued against the use of and justification of reason/rationality, the view that animals are irrational, for if "value and dignity depend entirely on reason, animals cannot matter" (Midgley, 1998, p. 11). In 1789, in *Introduction to the Principles of Morals and Legislation,* Jeremy Bentham wrote

> Other animals, which, on account of their interests having been neglected by the insensibility of the ancient jurists, stand degraded into the class of things. ... The day has been, I grieve it to say in many places it is not yet past, in which the greater part of the species, under the denomination of slaves, have been treated ... upon the same footing as ... animals are still. The day may come, when the rest of the animal creation may acquire those rights which never could have been withholden from them but by the hand of tyranny. The French have already discovered that the blackness of skin is no reason why a human being should be abandoned without redress to the caprice of a tormentor. It may come one day to be recognized, that the number of legs, the villosity of the skin, or the termination of the *os sacr*um, are reasons equally insufficient for abandoning a sensitive being to the same fate. What else is it that should trace the insuperable line? Is it the faculty of reason, or perhaps, the faculty for discourse? ... the question is not, Can they reason? nor, Can they talk? but, Can they suffer? Why should the law refuse its protection to any sensitive being? ... The time will come when humanity will extend its mantle over everything which breathes ...

A belief in cognitive separation also suggested that animals are part of nature whereas humans are not. This thinking has its foundation in the idea that "Humans ... tend to occupy a largely disembodied world of the mind and culture; [whereas] animals are located in a world of 'nature,' of biological determinants, of pure biology" (Birke, 1996, p. 103).

The marked divide, concretized in religious doctrine that places humans "above" all other beings says that we transcend urges whereas animals do not and cannot. The emphasis is not only on difference but also on superiority—that the differences that make us human make us superior. The idea of animal, of inhuman, also "represents the forces that we fear in our own nature, that we are unwilling to regard as a true part of it" (Midgley, 1998, p. 193). The messiness of sex and sexuality, bodily functions, and appetites are not seen as being of the human world, but of the animal. Thus, a person is not viewed as responsible for his or her "animalistic" actions, at most as responding to "seeds that lie hidden in our nature" (p. 193). These parts of ourselves, what might be called instinct, baser instincts, or drives, exist in a liminal zone between who we think we are and who we actually are, under a given set of circumstances. Hence, "the animal [is] the constitutive outside within the human itself" (Oliver, 2009, p. 230).

Bridging

The term "animal" can mean different things based on how it is used and who uses it, "opposed to humans it tends to mean everything we think we are not, or whatever we wish to transcend—the beast within, for example" (Birke, 1996, p. 104). Thus, "good" = human, "bad" = animal. "The crux of our belief," is "in our ability as a species to 'transcend' our proximity to other animals" (p. 104). Then "what do we mean when we speak of 'animal'?" (DeMello, 2010, p. xi). While humans are most definitely not dogs, or horses, or giraffes, they are also not us. Some animals, particularly those closest to us who we refer to as domesticated and call pets (cats, dogs, birds) are often ascribed human characteristics (anthropomorphised), whereas others are placed in other categories (wildlife, farmed animals) so that they might be used by us in ways we generally prefer not to think about too much, for example as lab/experimental animals, livestock, or for entertainment. Some species simultaneously occupy multiple categories, such as rabbits (*oryctralagus cuniculus*) who function simultaneously as pets, meat, and experimental objects. Our language also reveals or conceals animals who are considered, for example, meat. "Our culture," writes Charlotte Wood (qtd. in Krein, 2012) in *Good Weekend*,

> ... is drenched in anthropomorphic slush. But I find most of it troubling because it seems so disrespectful. Denying the creature's essential nature— its very animality—is surely an act not of admiration, but subjugation. To downplay the differences between species is to promote the assumption that "humans will only accept what is like themselves," as American scholar Shelly R. Scott puts it. The more we sentimentalise animals on the one hand, Wood suggested, the more we brutalise them on the other.

There is something of the monstrous seen in animals, which is not believed to exist amongst humans, but insinuates a boundary, however porous, between the two. Boon (2007, p. 33) identifies five distinctions that form the fundamental nature of this divide, of the space between human and non-human:

1. That there are clear distinctions marking "the natural and unnatural"
2. The distinctions "are clear and perceivable"
3. That what is natural (i.e. human) is established by a kind of dominion or preordained source.
4. To be human is a privileged form and thereby natural
5. Being human is comprised of elements "not found in lower forms"

Thus, while animals other than humans are rooted in and forever bound to the biological, according to this ideology, humans are inextricably tied to the social and cultural. As such, the word "animal" also positions those who are not human (or the worst of the worst of humans) as something to be despised, reviled, and treated accordingly. According to the *Oxford English Dictionary* an extended definition of "animal" is "a person without human attributes or civilizing influences;

one who is very cruel, violent, or repulsive." To be attributed with characteristics that are less than human, is to de-humanize, "a psychological process through which others are derogatively likened to 'animals' and perceived as 'less human'" (Costello & Hodson, 2012, p. 2).

Parallels

From the 16th through the 19th centuries, as objects of speculation, ridicule, repulsion, and curiosity, humans were regularly put on display as part of "human zoos, circuses, fairs, ethnic exhibits, freak shows and other spectacles staged [for] the exploitation and dispossession of certain humans by other humans" (Martin, 2013, p. 13). The public exhibition and exploitation of people of color in cities such as Hamburg (1874), Amsterdam (1889), Paris (1889), Chicago (1893) and others, was key to a cultural logic that equated them with animals and viewed characteristics as animalistic. This practice is ancient, found at least as far back as ancient Egyptian exhibitions of "black dwarves" from Sudan and parades of the Roman Empire used to assert superiority and natural domination of others (Blanchard, Boëtsch, & Snoep, 2011, p. 20; see also Tuan, 1984). Columbus brought Amerindians back to Spain for the Queen to see and Cortez similarly captured groups of indigenous people to put on display. Human beings, along with various species of animals, were caged, staged, and displayed as "specimens," "exotics," "monsters," and other variations, "not for what they did, but rather for what they were supposed to be. Beings that were different. Inferior beings. *Others*" (ital orig). (Blanchard, Boëtsch, & Snoep, 2011, p. 16). Treatment was on par with that of animals in similar situations. This contributed to the cultivation of a view of captive beings as expendable objects. Thousands of post cards, photographs, amateur and professional films, and promotional materials remain that attest to this horrifying tool of colonization used to educate and influence public opinion. Saartjie Baartman, The Hottentot Venus of the early 19th century, was exhibited as a freak because of her large buttocks (by European standards). Congolese Pigmy Ota Benga was kidnapped and exhibited with monkeys in the early 20th century. Both are examples of bodies that were defined and identified as abnormal or different, and placed on display for members of majority culture to view. In the United States, in the mid-late 19th century, P. T. Barnum's circuses and Buffalo Bill's Wild West Show, displayed American Indians as tamable "savages," and used terms such as "strange" or "exotic" with descriptions of human animal hybrids (p. 25).

In *Dominance and Affection*, Tuan (1984) discusses efforts to sculpt and control nature, whether through selective breeding of dogs, cultivation of plants, or the keeping of certain groups of humans (black children, dwarves) as child-like pets. The domination served as justification for the keeping of some humans as pets, "reducing [them] to animate nature in order to exploit them economically or to treat them condescendingly as pets" (p. 312), as if it were for their own good. This argument, known as slavery as "a positive good" (Calhoun, 1843, p. 225), was used in the American South by white slaveholders who wanted to conceal the exploitation, suffering, abuse, and loss of agency and individuality of human beings who were seen as incapable of caring for themselves. Hill-Collins (1996) notes, "Certain 'races' of people have been defined as being more body-like, more animal-like, and less god-like than others" (p. 310). Deemed as inferior, they were thus treated as such:

> Blacks, held some pro-slavery writers to be a different species, were subjugated as slaves, saleable units of production whose feelings and interests, like those of the horse and oxen, were of little or no consequence. Oppression of animals, with its markets, auctions, branding, crowded forms of conveyance and treadmill conditions, it has been suggested, provided the prototype for the oppression of black people through slavery. (Selby, 1995, p. 17)

During World War II, Nazi propaganda referred to Jews as *Untermensche*, subhuman, "as leeches, lice, bacteria, or vectors of contagion" (Smith, 2011, p. 15) and as rats (Spence, 2001). At the same time, American propaganda presented Asians as rat-like (see Merskin, 2011; Smith, 2011). These expressions are not and were not purely metaphoric. In the ideology of the times these were literal beliefs that resulted in unimaginably horrific treatment. For "people are more likely to commit violence against a group they do not view as fully human" (Hetey & Eberhardt, 2013, p. 148; see also Bandura, Underwood, & Fromson, 1975; Haslam, 2006) and the more likely violence is seen as acceptable the less another is viewed as deserving of "the moral concern that humans owe each other" (p. 148). Importantly, "human domination over animals may also justify interhuman domination including slavery, genocide, and intergroup prejudices or violence" (Costello & Hodson, 2012, p. 4) (see also Smith, 2011). None of this makes any actual sense and defies scientific or experiential knowledge, but "for some reason we continue to conceive of the universe in a fashion, and we relegate non-human creatures to a lower position" on the scale of consideration and moral regard (Smith, qtd. in Conan, 2011). Furthermore, the persistent, consistent, and corroborated patterns of mass media portrayals predicted by Accumulation Theory (DeFleur & Dennis, 1978) come to make these re-presentations seem normal and natural. For example, "instead of viewing Muslims as people who have been symbolically portrayed as animals they begin in our minds to become animals, imaginatively transposed with images that represent them" (Steuter & Willis, 2009, p. 4).

Thus to "Other" another being is to create difference, on whatever basis, in a way that creates an Us and a Them. It is a dynamic relational process wherein both individual and collective identity are created and affirmed through designation of whatever one is or isn't thus, conversely the Other is or is not. Other denies agency and creates space for "moral distance and detachment that lead[s] to the creation and perpetuation of oppressive practices and institutions" (Cuomo & Gruen, 1998, p. 12). Simultaneously, as Gruen and Weil (2010, p. 128) point out, while Othering designates differences it also, in the case of women and animals, generates "saming" wherein both animals and women are denied the status of person, denied souls. They are paradoxically both denied and yet equated in many ways. For example, as is discussed in Chapter 8, women and cats, particularly big cats, are often seen as parallel when re-presented in art and mass media, in ways having to do with sexuality, allure, elusiveness, and exoticism. In addition to the setting-apart that is endured by those, of whatever species, they are also patronized, i.e. treated like perpetual children in need of care and guidance by those with power. This further reduces one's sense of self. Where do these ideas originate?

In their study of out-group dehumanization, Costello and Hodson (2012, p. 2) note that "dehumanization can result from animalistic-outgroup comparisons" such as comic books, sheet music, newspaper stories, movies, and propaganda posters that presented African Americans as apes or ape-like (Goff, Eberhardt, Williams, & Jackson, 2008; Pieterse, 1995), as "soul-less animals" (Smith, 2011, p. 117). An 1878 anthropology textbook presented this description (Halpin, 1989, p. 287, qtd in Hill-Collins, 1996, p. 140):

> She had a way of pouting her lips exactly like what we have observed in the orangutan. Her movements had something abrupt and fantastical about them, reminding one of those of the ape. Her ear was like that of many apes ... these are animal characters. I have never seen a human head more like an ape than that of this woman.

Further contributing to this view of Africans as other-than-human was the equating of an unbridled sexual appetite with animality, gender, and race. This is evident in a statement by a then-prominent European physician who said, Black women's "animal-like sexual appetite went so far as to lead black women to copulate with apes" (qtd. in Gilman, 1985, p. 212). These attitudes persist, albeit more covertly. For example, a contemporary book on tort law discusses workplace harassment of an African American woman in which coworkers "engaged in offensive behavior and name calling that traded on centuries-old negative images of Blacks as animals, monkeys, and filthy creatures" (Chamallas & Wriggins, 2010, p. 26).

This perspective of certain human beings relegated to higher status while others are treated in physically and psychologically demoralizing ways has its origins in the writings of, among others, Aristotle (350 BCE) whose views justified slavery, oppression of women and animals, and called the ox "the poor man's slave" (*Politics*, book 1, chaps 4–5)

While a full history of the marginalization of women is beyond the scope of this book, a few points are worth mentioning for context. In the mid 19th century, for example, in the United States and in Europe, women were thought to be ruled by biology, gullible to urges whereas men were not. Thus, by extension, women were comparable to animals. This included women's intelligence (thought of as lesser than men's) as well as being innately unable to make rational decisions. The direct impact of biological forces (such as hormones) was thought to make women less intelligent, less capable of sensible decision making, less or more sexual. As such women were considered outside the circle of moral consideration Women were not to be educated (what was the point?) and, whereas men were viewed as strong and rational, women were weak and irrational. Incapable of reason, women were thus to be kept, as property, for the use and often abuse, of men. Much of this view of women has to do with the fear of losing power, and "external power is important ... in so far as it shapes institutions which work to protect the fantasies of the dominant group. Had women been that group, they would no doubt have expressed their own fantasies institutionally in the same way" (Midgley, 1998, p. 78). However, being that men (in systems of patriarchy) are the dominant gender group, there was and is much to be gained by both in reality and symbol, of viewing women as lesser-than. Stereotypes of both women and animals and women as animals are still seen and heard in language (fox, chick, bitch) as well as in cultural re-presentations.

The same arguments have been made about sexual preferences and race. Homosexuality, it was argued, was due to biology (Carroll, 2012, p. 273). Race[4] has been used as justification for differential treatment on the basis of difference, stereotypically asserting some groups are more or less capable of certain things because of race. These arbitrary distinctions are made in order for those with power (economic, social, symbolic) to maintain their positions, which, in the United States, have historically been white and male. As oppressions on the basis of difference, are said to be biological thus, "revolve[s] around the same axis of distain for the body; both portray the sexuality of subordinate groups as animalistic and therefore deviant" (Hill-Collins, 1996, p. 310). This disdain, this seeing women, non-Christians, homosexuals, and people of color as lesser than white men served, and continues to serve, as a foundation for racist, sexist, and classist prejudice, and contributes to legal, cultural, economic, and political discrimination.

The late 19th century American publication *Puck*, for example, presented Irish people as dangerous and animal-like (Curtis, 1971). Niebert (2016, p. 77) notes, "by suggesting that aspects of the oppressed peoples' nature were more like [devalued] other animals, elites and their apologists argued against the creation of social welfare systems, as such programs would only prolong continued existence of 'biologically inferior' humans." To control populations, state sponsored forced sterilization programs, for example, as well as many mental institutions, were created to stop the reproduction of those deemed inferior. Globally these horrors continue. During the Rwandan genocide, for example, Hutus referred to Tutsis as cockroaches (Smith, 2011). Editorial cartoons alluding to U.S. President Barrack Obama referenced a chimpanzee attack (Merskin, 2011). In a study of newspaper stories in which the death penalty was the possible outcome for Black and White defendants, Goff et al. (2008) found that stories using animal associated words such as "predator," "beast," and "animal" more often described Black defendants than White. The word "animal" is "often broadly applied to individual who have committed acts we find particularly loathsome or heinous" (Steuter & Willis, 2009, p. 74). In the post 9–11 speeches of then President George W. Bush, references to Saddam Hussein were animalist, referred to him as scurrying and hiding in his den, and other rodent-like behaviors (Merskin, 2004). This isn't to say that people aren't doing horrible things to one another, they are, but the argument here is that invoking animals as a way of describing the worst of the worst of humans does nothing to help people and ultimately harms our relationships with certain animals who have nothing to do with human conflict. It begs the question then, if animals are the lowest of the low where does that leave them in terms of voice and visibility?

Measuring animal worth by human standards is short-sighted and anthropocentric. Today we might argue that just as humans are not entirely rational (and sometimes quite irrational), and that we can't separate head from the heart in terms of decision-making, animals are similarly complex. If we agree that they are conscience, sentient, can we not also say that they are worthy of consideration? Science yields discoveries almost daily about abilities of, for example, mice to empathize (Langford et al., 2006).

According to Edward Said, "Each age and society recreates its Others" (1985, p. 322), but this does not mean that Othering of one group necessarily ends when these Others are embraced in its divisive and dangerous hold. Historically, women and animals have been particularly

Otherized as property, possession, and playthings. "Our twofold use of words like 'beast' or 'animal' is not just a chance ambiguity that we can set right by policing usage" (Midgley, 2004, p. 198). For it is an odd and disturbing trait of the Western mind, the ability to distance from real suffering, from felt experience, from what is viewed as truth. Rubenstein (1975, p. 30) writes of this construction of difference and distance

> When one contrasts the attitude of the savage [sic] who cannot leave the battlefield until he performs some kind of appeasement ritual to his slain enemy with the assembly-line manufacture of corpses by the millions at Auschwitz, we get an idea of the enormous religious and cultural distance Western man has traversed in order to create so unique a social and political institution as the death camp.

Theoretical Constructs

A useful theory for advancing thinking about parallels in oppression is intersectionality which draws on feminist theories that incorporate an animal rights perspectives. Intersectionality theory predicts/argues that:

1. Underlying systems of oppression are shared and that oppressed groups share in common their marginalization due to a system of patriarchy, hierarchies, and dichotomies.
2. There are links between the oppression of women and the oppression of animals.

Hence, discrimination doesn't occur "along a single categorical axis" (Crenshaw, 1989, p. 140). A Black woman, for example, experiences discrimination not only on the basis of race, sexual orientation, and gender, but also her experience of gender is not the same as is a White woman's. This is the foundation of intersectionality. No identity category is mutually exclusive. For example, a human being is not only male or female, but also of racial or ethnic group, age demographic, sexual orientation, and species. To deny such is to erase and silence. "Race, class, and gender have been the traditional triumvirate of intersectional studies" (Jones, Misra, & McCurley, 2013, p. 1) but it applies to any social status including religion, sexuality, age, and other markers

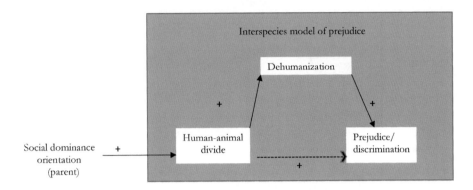

Figure 1.2: Interspecies Model of Prejudice.
Source: Adapted from Costello and Hodson (2012).

of difference, i.e. difference from the group holding the majority of power and resources.

Another model, the Interspecies Model of Prejudice, is useful as it proposes that fundamental beliefs in human/animal divide set the foundation for out-group dehumanization (Costello & Hodson, 2012, p. 4). Persistent beliefs in this divide "allow people to exclude some humans from the realm of humanity by likening them to 'inferior' animals, with these dehumanizing perceptions predicting prejudice and discrimination" (p. 4) (see Figure 1.2).

Thus, to oppress any group is to participate in the oppression of others. As Spiegel writes in *The Dreaded Comparison* (1988, pp. 24–25)

> Any oppression helps to prop up other forms of oppression. That is why it is vital to link oppressions in our minds, to look for the common, shared aspects, and fight against them as one, rather than prioritizing victims' suffering (the "either-or" pitfall). For when we prioritize we are in effect becoming one with the oppressor. We are deciding that one individual or group is more important than another, deciding that one individual's pain is "less important" than that of the next. ... To deny our similarities to animals is to deny and undermine our own power.

Social dominance theory (Sidanius & Protto, 2001) predicts that preference for one's own group and resulting conflict resulte from preferences for social hierarchies and group dominance. Societies such as those in the West that are highly industrialized, urbanized, and modernized and adhere to religious and/or culture beliefs that are hierarchical are thereby likely to endorse structures and behaviors that sustain that model. Individuals with high social dominance orientation (SDO) are "more likely to endorse and engage in the exploitation of non-human animals" (2010, p. 6; see also Hyers, 2006).

In a two-part study manipulating human/animal similarities, Costello and Hodson (2010) found that people whose attitudes toward animals (like us, not like us) influence attitudes toward human immigrants. When subjects felt animals were more like humans, prejudices toward immigrants lessened whereas when the human/animal divide was emphasized, prejudices increased. They concluded "by isolating a powerful origin of dehumanizing perceptions (i.e., the animal–human divide), we targeted and influenced the roots of dehumanization, removing the legitimacy of such perceptions altogether" (p. 18). Emphasized were similarities that resulted in "re-categorization," which "increased immigrant empathy, both of which predicted less prejudicial attitudes toward immigrants" (p. 3). This was the case even among highly prejudicial people.

Clearly, the connection between Us and Them, of whatever species, is powerful as a motivator of attitudes and ultimately behaviors and has a powerful connection to social justice. As the Adorno quote at the beginning of this chapter points out, many human prejudices against other humans can be located in our attitudes toward animals. According to Costello and Hodson (2012, p. 19)

> Children are socialized to endorse perceptions of human superiority over other animals through parental influence, religious teachings, cultural traditions, and/or experiences with industries condoning the exploitation of non-human animals. These socialization practices presumably lead children to endorse the cultural "legitimacy" of dominating, victimizing, or ignoring the plight of non-human animals.

A chart, "Intersecting Axes of Privilege, Domination, and Oppression" (Morgan, 1996) (see Figure 1.3) reveals the many ways in which someone is privileged (or not).

Who is above the line and who below, thus more or less deserving of moral consideration, less likely to experience pain or have emotions,

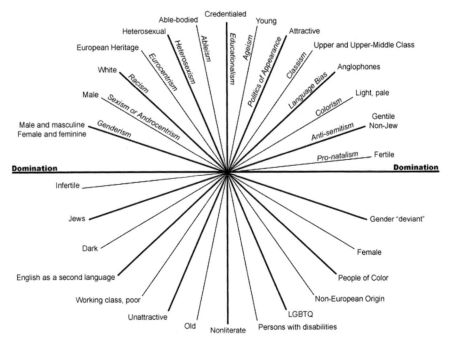

Figure 1.3: Intersecting Axes of Privilege, Domination, and Oppression.
Source: Adapted from Morgan (1996).

be included or excluded from laws and policies, and regarded as in or out-group on the social, economic, and cultural level is indicated on the chart. Since which species one belongs to is also often used to determine who qualifies as one of Us versus one of Them, I have added species to the array of differences.

Considering the conditions of marginalization and mistreatment of other species as parallel in no way demeans human beings. To say that animal marginalization, stereotyping, and discrimination is harmful and has similarities with racism and sexism, in no way makes one more or one lesser, particularly when examining re-presentations of animals other than humans as cultural artifacts. "Like sexism and racism, speciesism is the prejudicial view that there is an ontologically distinct marker, in this case species membership, that adds value to those who belong to the human species and justifies domination of those who don't" (Gruen & Weil, 2010, p. 127). Speciesism is a prejudice "or attitude of bias toward the interests of one's own species and against those of members of another species" for whatever reason (Singer, 1975, p. 6).

How would exclusion on the basis of species membership operate as ideological explanation for species discrimination? Speciesism, as a concept, is tricky. We know that to decide how to treat someone on the basis of race is deplorable. Yet, there are good and sound reasons to treat members of species differently because of different needs as in what a snake versus a lion versus a kangaroo might require. Each species, as well as every individual member of that species, has a unique point of view.

The work that the term speciesism is designed to do is to point out how inclusion/exclusion from morality are determined by which species one belongs. This has parallels with racism: "they all look alike to me," "no dogs or Indians allowed," "Mexicans, they're all the same". Sex, gender, and species are particularly interwoven experiences and designations equating the *seeming* naturalness of women's connections with nature/animals is a deliberate construction in patriarchy, i.e. the dualisms of women/nature/emotions and men/culture/rationality in which women are created as Other.

Duality is defined as "the process by which contrasting concepts are formed by domination and subordination and constructed as oppositional and exclusive" (Plumwood, 1992, p. 31). As such, women are most often associated with nature, whereas men with culture; women as emotional, men as rational and so forth. With women viewed as closer to nature, they are also viewed as closer in status and being to animals, thereby not fully human. Dualist, binary, thinking is a prominent aspect of the Western construction of reality and differences.

It might be difficult to consider embracing animals in the arms of the moral community of humans. Indeed, millions of human beings suffer starvation, torture, abuse, and victimization every day. Shouldn't we be paying attention to them? Are we a species traitor if intellectual, financial, and energetic expenses are given to groups who are not human? That's an argument made many times and is understandable. "The natural preference for one's own species does exist" (Midgley, 1998, p. 104). Furthermore, "all social creatures attend mostly to members of their own species, and usually ignore others" (p. 105). I argue that we must "acknowledge that they, animals and [their] images, matter" (p. 20). It is not necessary to choose one over the other. Rather, being a compassionate human being means cultivating awareness of the naturalness of caring first for others. Believing in ending, or at least not contributing to, suffering, is the goal. The extent of species exclusivity as humans is exceptional, however. If survival is viewed as a competition, which in some parts of the world it is "must we really acknowledge all our long-lost cousins and heave them into the humanitarian lifeboat?" (p. 19). It is an alarming dilemma. In subsistence cultures, indeed, it is necessary to choose one's own survival. However, for those who live in cultures in which concerns are further up Maslow's Hierarchy, things can be different (see Figure 1.4). "Our social life, our interests and our sympathy both can and must extend outside our own species" (p. 19).

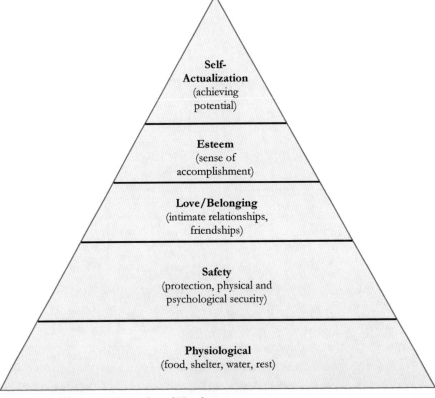

Figure 1.4: Maslow's Hierarchy of Needs.
Source: Adapted from Maslow (1943). A theory of human motivation. *Psychological Review*, 50(4), 370–396. A. Maslow (1954). *Motivation and personality*. New York: Harper & Row.

This encompassing perspective does not deny difference. Living beings are interconnected. Just as humans are not all the same, neither are all animals, or all elephants, or all dogs, or all cows. We need not live in a world of absolute inclusion or exclusion. Rather than take the approach of competition that it's them or us, as it were, for economic resources, "we are incurably members of one of another" (Midgley, 1998, p. 21). While individualism is stressed as a fundamental value, particularly in American culture, it takes group solidarity for individuals to survive and thrive. Thus "lifeboat thinking" (p. 29), that we must rescue humans first in the midst of quickly disappearing resources least the whole ship sink, is supported by a way of thinking that says to think and care about animals is emotional, and therefore not important. This model supports an eco-centric (not ego-centric) circle, drawing on Midgley, of who should be in the boat.

In modern life, despite all of the technology and devices we have for controlling much of the world and our experiences, nature, and nature's inhabitants are largely outside of that sphere of influence and observation. Thus, control requires rather violent means such as "management" of wildlife and/or intentional breeding, along with the creation of language that veils actions (for example, terms such as "culling" as a substitute for "killing"). Deconstructing the Us versus Them dichotomy brings us to a more humane space not only with other animals but also with ourselves and "dissolve[s] the screens of callous habit and reveal[s] hidden injustice" (Midgley, 1998, p. 66).

What Is at Stake?

In her discussion of biology/culture and humans/animals, Birke (1996) suggests that there are two consequences of "the animals/nature versus human/sociality dichotomies" related to admission or exclusion from the moral community. First, there is a natural human tendency to separate ourselves "from less worthy 'others' which 'is a trait linked to … global domination' regardless of species" (Birke, 1996, p. 106). Who is excluded or included can and does shift, yet all the while a boundary is maintained between who is one of Us and who is one of Them. "Nature [which includes animals] remains firmly outside" (p. 106).

Thus, if biology is used as the basis of exclusion it becomes an easy way to dismiss and discriminate others, on whatever basis. This rationalist view says animals fall outside the moral sphere because "morality is a contract between rational beings" and, animals are not rational, they are thus not included in the circle of inclusion (Midgley, 1998, p. 42).

Second, explaining difference in terms of biology is reductionist and "if reductionism impoverishes our understanding of human behaviour, then surely it must also do so with regard to animal behaviour" (Birke, 1996, p. 107). There is no doubt that humans possess (or develop) skills and characteristics that appear to be unique to our species, just as other species do, for example, the heightened sense of smell and hearing in dogs (Horowitz, 2010) and the ability to echolocate in bats or dolphins (Moss & Vater, 2004). This doesn't mean these are traits exclusive to that species, as a biological determinist view holds.

What Role Do Mass Media and Popular Culture Play in Reifying the Divide?

Our job, as stewards of the planet, is to be literate in these re-presentations in order to reveal the deeper meanings behind them, to pull back the curtain as in *The Wizard of Oz*. As fellow beings, and as professional communicators, we have an ethical responsibility to consider who is re-presented, under what circumstances, and with what effect. Knowledge of the impact these re-presentations on others and ourselves who share this planet is crucial. Professional communicators view the media and its ancillary services such as public relations and advertising as having power, power to frame, to include or exclude, to set the agenda for what citizens see, hear, and thus know. By taking a close look at the stories we are told and tell about certain animal, their contemporary conditions and treatments can be seen more clearly as well as how ways of thinking of animals other than humans informs language, thought, and politics. For example, in order to maintain the conditions within which many animals are born, raised, and kept (which is the foundation of huge economic industries such as the production of meat, dairy, and leather) corporations obscure the means of production making divisions appear natural and normal.

Borrowing from Goffman's (1979) classic study of gender advertisements, we should be asking of all media re-presentations, "why don't these ads [television programs, movies, magazines] look strange to us?" Careful consideration of how animals are seen, not seen, re-presented, or rendered invisible can help us understand how and why all re-presentations matter. Just as stereotypes of marginalized human beings are informed by fear-based, uninformed generalizations and suppositions, animals, when rendered symbolically give rise "to the unconscious desires, fears, and tensions that underlie the conscious patterns of human behavior" (Campbell, 1968, p. 219). An understanding of the power of media helps us understand "the deep forces that have shaped [hu]man destiny and must continue to determine both our private and our public lives" (p. 220). In addition, "*everything* in social and cultural life is fundamentally to do with *power*. Power is at the centre of cultural politics. It is integral to culture. *All signifying practices*—that is, all practices that have meaning—involve relations of power" (Ital. Orig) (Jordan & Weedon, 1994, p. 11). The primary determinant of difference is power.

In the next chapter, power, and its articulation in differences, distinctions, stereotypes, privilege, and class are discussed in detail as part of a revolutionary new discipline: Animal Media Studies (AMS). In the last decade or so, this hybrid discipline has arisen bringing together areas, interests, and studies that explore the intersectional parallels in oppressions between all beings. At its core AMS examines how cultural texts, in the form of media and popular culture, function, on the one hand, as tools for the construction, maintenance, and perpetuation of stereotypes about species and on the other, and as powerful liberatory mechanisms that can inspire and motivate social change in attitudes toward and treatment of animals other than humans.

Notes

1. The term "pet" is used in this book, as it is commonly understood. However, a more relational term is companion species or guardians and these words are also used. For a discussion on the power dynamics and objectification inherent in the term "pet" see McKenna (2013).

2. Laws protecting children were based almost entirely on those designed for animal protection. For more on this see LeBow and Cherney (2015).
3. The term "animal" is used in this book to identify other than human species. This is not intended to separate humans from other species, but for ease of writing. In fact, one goal of this book is to challenge that divide.

References

Adams, C. (2001). Foreword. In S. Baker (Ed.), *Picturing the beast* (pp. xi–xiii). Champaign, IL: University of Illinois Press.

Agrawal, T. (2016). Pets are comforting, but shares of pet-focused companies may not be. Reuters. Retrieved from http://www.reuters.com/article/us-stocks-pets-idUSKCN0VO1FV

"Animal." Retrieved from http://www.etymonline.com/index.php?term=animal

"Animal." *Oxford English Dictionary*.

Aristotle (350 BCE). *Politics* (B. Jowett, Trans.). Retrieved from http://classics.mit.edu/Aristotle/politics.1.one.html

Bandura, A., Underwood, B., & Fromson, M. E. (1975). Disinhibition of aggression through diffusion of responsibility and dehumanizations of victims. *Journal of Research in Personality*, 9(4), 253–269.

Beaudine, G., Osibodu, O., & Beavers, A. (2017). Disney's metaphorical exploration of racism and stereotypes: A review of *Zootopia*. *Comparative Education Review*, 61(1), 227–234.

Berettini, M. L. (2005). Danger! Danger! Danger! Or when animals might attack: Adventure activism and wildlife film and television. *Scope: Online Journal of Film Studies*. Retrieved from http://pdxscholar.library.pdx.edu/cgi/viewcontent.cgi?article=1006&context=ta_fac

Berger, J. (1980). *Why look at animals? About looking*. New York, NY: Pantheon.

Birke, L. (1996). Animals and biological determinism. In S. Jackson & S. Scott (Eds.), *Feminism and sexuality: A reader* (pp. 101–109). New York, NY: Columbia University Press.

Blanchard, P., Boëtsch, G., & Snoep, N. J. (2011). *Exhibitions: L'Invention du sauvage*. Branly: Musee du Quai.

Boon, K. A. (2007). Ontological anxiety made flesh: The zombie in literature, film, and culture. In N. Scott (Ed.), *Monsters and the monstrous: Myths, and metaphors of enduring evil* (pp. 33–44). Amsterdam: Rodopi.

Bradley, T., & King, R. (2012, November 13). The dog economy is global—But what is the world's true canine capital? *The Atlantic*. Retrieved from https://www.theatlantic.com/business/archive/2012/11/the-dog-economy-is-global-but-what-is-the-worlds-true-canine-capital/265155/

Cabeza San Deogracias, J., & Pérez, J. (2013). Thinking about television audiences: Entertainment and reconstruction in nature documentaries. *European Journal of Communication*, 28(5), 570–583.

Calhoun, J. C. (1843). *Speeches of John C. Calhoun: Delivered in the congress of the United States*. New York, NY: Harper & Brothers.
Campbell, J. (1968). *The hero with a thousand faces*. New York, NY: New World Library.
Carroll, J. L. (2012). *Sexuality now: Embracing diversity*. Belmont, CA: Cengage.
Chamallas, M., & Wriggins, J. B. (2010). *The measure of injury: Race, gender, and tort law*. New York, NY: NYU Press.
Cole, M., & Stewart, K. (2014). *Our children and other animals: The cultural construction of human-animal relations in childhood*. London: Ashgate.
Conan, N. (2011, March 29). "Less than human": The psychology of cruelty. *Talk of the Nation*. National Public Radio. Retrieved from http://www.npr.org/2011/03/29/134956180/criminals-see-their-victims-as-less-than-human
Costello, K., & Hodson, G. (2010). Exploring the roots of dehumanization: The role of animal-human similarity in promoting immigrant humanization. *Group Processes & Intergroup Relations, 13*(1), 3–233.
Costello, K., & Hodson, G. (2012). Explaining dehumanization among children: The interspecies model of prejudice. *British Journal of Social Psychology, 53*(1), 1–23.
Crenshaw, K. (1989). Demarginalizing the intersection of race and sex: A black feminist critique of antidiscrimination doctrine, feminist theory, and antiracist politics. *University of Chicago Legal Forum, 1989*(1), 139–167.
Cuomo, C. J., & Gruen, L. (1998). On puppies and pussies: Animals, intimacy, and moral distance. In B.-A. Bar On & A. Ferguson (Eds.), *Daring to be good: Essays in feminist ethico-politics* (pp. 129–142). New York, NY: Routledge.
Curtis, L. P. (1971). *Apes and angels: The Irishman in Victorian caricature*. Washington, DC: Smithsonian Institution Press.
DeFleur, M. L., & Dennis, E. (1978). *Understanding mass communication: A liberal arts perspective*. New York, NY: Houghton Mifflin.
DeMello, M. (2010). Introduction to human-animal studies. In M. DeMello (Ed.), *Teaching the animal* (pp. xi–xix). New York, NY: Lantern Books.
Doyle, B. (2014). *Children & other wild animals*. Corvallis, OR: Oregon State University Press.
Evernden, L. N. N. (1992). *The social creation of nature*. Baltimore, MD: John Hopkins.
Freeman, C. P. (2009). This little piggy went to press: The American news media's construction of animals in agriculture. *The Communication Review, 12*(1), 78–103.
Gilman, S. (1985). Black bodies, white bodies: Toward an iconography of female sexuality in late nineteenth-century art, medicine, and literature. *Critical Inquiry, 12*(1), 205–243.
Glenn, C. B. (2004). Constructing consumables and consent: A critical analysis of factory farm industry discourse. *Journal of Communication Inquiry, 28*(1), 63–81.
Goff, P. A., Eberhardt, J. L., Williams, M. J., & Jackson, M. C. (2008). Not yet human: Implicit knowledge, historical dehumanization, and contemporary consequences. *Journal of Personality and Social Psychology, 94*(2), 292–306.
Goffman, E. (1979). *Gender advertisements*. New York, NY: Harper & Row.
Gruen, L., & Weil, K. (2010). Teaching difference. In M. DeMello (Ed.), *Teaching the animal* (pp. 127–142). New York, NY: Lantern Books.

Halpin, Z. T. (1989). Scientific objectivity and the concept of "the Other." *Women's Studies International Forum, 12*(3), 285–294.

Haslam, N. (2006). Dehumanization: An integrative review. *Personality and Social Psychology Review, 10*(3), 252–264.

Hetey, R. C., & Eberhardt, J. L. (2013). The interplay of mechanistic and animalistic dehumanization in the criminal justice system. In P. G. Bain, J. Vaes, & J. P. Leyens (Eds.), *Humanness and dehumanization* (pp. 147–166). New York, NY: Routledge.

Hill-Collins, P. (1996). Black women and the sex/gender hierarchy. In S. Jackson & S. Scott (Eds.), *Feminism and sexuality: A reader* (pp. 307–313). New York, NY: Columbia University Press.

Horowitz, A. (2010). *Inside of a dog: What dogs see, smell, and know.* New York, NY: Scribner.

Hyers, L. (2006). Myths used to legitimize the exploitation of animals: An application of social dominance theory. *Anthrozoos, 19*, 194–210.

Jordan, C., & Weedon, G. J. (1994). *Cultural politics.* Malden, MA: Blackwell.

Keen, S. (1991). *Faces of the enemy: Reflections on the hostile imagination.* New York, NY: Harper Collins.

Keyes, R. (2010). *Euphemania.* New York, NY: Little Brown.

Krein, A. (2012, March). Us and them: On the importance of animals. *The Monthly.* Retrieved from https://www.themonthly.com.au/importance-animals-admin-4738

Langford, D. J., Crager, S. E., Shehzad, Z., Smith, S. B., Sotocinal, S. G., Levenstadt, J. S., … Mogil, J. S. (2006). Social modulation of pain as evidence for empathy in mice. *Science, 312*, 1967–1970.

LeBow, E. W., & Cherney, D. J. (2015). The role of animal welfare legislation in shaping child protection in the United States. *International Journal of Education and Social Science, 2*(6), 36–44.

Lerner, J. E., & Kalof, L. (1999). The animal text: Message and meaning in television advertisements. *Sociological Quarterly, 40*(4), 565–586.

Lewis, G. (2009, December 10). Chihuahuas crowding California shelters. *NBC News.* Retrieved January 10, 2015 from http://www.nbcnews.com/id/34352750/ns/healthpet_health/t/chihuahuas-crowding-california-shelters/#.VL2NwcY02CI

Light, A., & McKenna, E. (2004). Introduction: Pragmatism and the future of human-nonhuman relationships. In E. McKenna & A. Light (Eds.), *Animal pragmatism* (pp. 1–18). Bloomington, IN: Indiana University Press.

Martin, L. (2013). Preface. In P. Blanchard, G. Boëtsch, & N. J. Snoep (Eds.), *Human zoos: The invention of the savage* (p. 13). Exhibition book. Paris: Musée du Qual Branly.

Maslow, A. (1943). A theory of human motivation. *Psychological Review, 50*(4), 370–396.

Maslow, A. (1954). *Motivation and personality.* New York, NY: Harper & Row.

McKenna, E. (2013). *People, pets, and pragmatism.* New York, NY: Fordham.

Merskin, D. (2004). The construction of Arabs as enemies: Post-September 11 discourse of George W. Bush. *Mass Communication and Society, 7*, 157–175.

Merskin, D. (2011). *Media, minorities, and meaning: A critical introduction*. New York, NY: Peter Lang.
Midgley, M. (1998). *Animals and why they matter*. Athens, GA: University of Georgia Press.
Midgley, M. (2004). *The myths we live by*. London: Psychology Press.
Mills, B. (2010). Television wildlife documentaries and animals' right to privacy. *Continuum, 24*(2), 193–202.
Morgan, K. P. (1996). Describing the Emperor's new clothes: Three myths of education (in)equality. In A. Diller (Ed.), *The gender question in education: Theory, pedagogy & politics* (pp. 105–122). Boulder, CO: Westview.
Morton, S. (2014). Troubling resemblances, anthropological machines, and the fear of wild animals: Following Derrida after Agamben. In L. Turner (Ed.), *The animal question in deconstruction* (pp. 105–123). Edinburgh: Edinburgh University Press.
Moss, C., & Vater, M. (2004). *Echolocation in bats and dolphins*. Chicago, IL: University of Chicago Press.
Neves-Graca, K. (2007). Animals. In P. Robbins (Ed.), *Encyclopedia of environment and society*. New York, NY: Sage.
Niebert, D. A. (2016). Origins of oppression, speciesist ideology, and the mass media. In N. Almiron, M. Cole, & C. P. Freeman (Eds.), *Critical animal and media studies* (pp. 74–88). New York, NY: Taylor & Francis.
Oliver, K. (2009). *Animal lessons: How they teach us to be human*. New York, NY: Columbia University Press.
Pierson, D. P. (2005). "Hey, they're just like us!" Representations of the animal world in the Discovery Channel's nature programming. *The Journal of Popular Culture, 38*(4), 698–712.
Pieterse, J. N. (1995). *White in black: Images of Africa and blacks in western popular culture*. New Haven, CT: Yale University Press.
Plumwood, V. (1992). Feminism and ecofeminism: Beyond the dualistic assumptions of women, men, and nature. *The Ecologist, 22*(1), 8–13.
Rollin, B. (1989/2011). *The unheeded cry*. New York, NY: Oxford University Press.
Rubenstein, R. L. (1975). *The cunning of history*. New York, NY: Harper & Row.
Said, E. W. (1985). *Orientalism*. Harmondsworth: Penguin.
Selby, D. (1995). *Earthkind: A teachers' handbook on humane education*. Stoke-on-Trent: Trentham Books Limited.
Sidanius, J., & Protto, F. (2001). *Social dominance: An intergroup theory of social hierarchy and oppression*. Cambridge: Cambridge University Press.
Singer, P. (1975). *Animal liberation*. New York, NY: Harper's.
Smith, T. L. (2011). *Less than human: Why we demean, enslave, and exterminate others*. New York, NY: Macmillan.
Spears, N. E. (1996). Symbolic role of animals in print advertising: Content analysis and conceptual development. *Journal of Business Research, 37*(2), 87–95.
Spence, N. C. (2001). The human bestiary. *The Modern Language Review, 96*(4), 913–930.
Spiegel, M. (1988). *The dreaded comparison: Human and animal slavery*. New York, NY: Heretic Books.

Steuter, E., & Willis, D. (2009). *At war with metaphor: Media, propaganda, and racism in the war on terror.* Lexington, KY: Lexington Books.

Todd, K. (2016, May 5). Real predators don't eat popsicles. *High Country News.* Retrieved from http://www.hcn.org/issues/48.8/real-predators-dont-eat-popsicles

Tuan, Y.-F. (1984). *Dominance & affection: The making of pets.* New Haven, CT: Yale University Press.

Williams, E., & DeMello, M. (2007). *Why animals matter: The case for animal protection.* Amherst, NY: Prometheus.

Wood, C. (2012, March). In Krein, A. (2012, March). Us and them: On the importance of animals. *The Monthly.* Retrieved from https://www.themonthly.com.au/importance-animals-admin-4738

Chapter Two

Animal Media Studies

If I am to expect others to respect my life, then I must respect the other life I see, however strange it may be to mine. ... Ethics in our Western world has hitherto been largely limited to the relations of man to man. But that is a limited ethics. We need a boundless ethics which will include animals also.

—(Albert Schweitzer)

To the degree that we come to understand other organisms, we will place a greater value on them, and on ourselves.

—Wilson (1984)

To cause animals to suffer cannot be defended merely on the grounds that we like the taste of their flesh, and even if animals were raised so that they led generally pleasant lives and were 'humanely' slaughtered, that would not insure that their rights, including their right to life, were not violated.

—Regan (1982, p. 1)

Are media theories only meant to apply to humans? Do media theories predict effects that would be useful to understanding other animals and our relationships with them? Is there a connection between studying media and thinking about nonhuman animals? This chapter explores these questions as well as presents a media studies perspective for thinking about how critiques of human use of other animals are consistent with those applied to similar analyses of gender, race, ethnicity, sexuality, disability, age, and other markers of difference.

This chapter is an introduction to the development of a radical, new, interdisciplinary area subfield, Animal Media Studies (AMS), within the context of cultural and media studies. The goal is to illustrate how AMS grew out of the fertile soil of other social justice-oriented disciplines which have, over time, revealed the multiple ways patriarchy and power, particularly as expressed through economic interests, function to maintain the status quo. This review sets the foundation for the chapters that follow. The following sections provide a brief overview of the development of the fields of Cultural Studies and from that, Media Studies, and from that, Animal Media Studies.

Background

Cultural Studies, the foundation out of which Media, and, as is discussed later in this chapter, AMS was built, was first labeled a field in the early 1960s in England by Stuart Hall and Richard Hobart. Named the Birmingham School, Hall and Hobart created a center that brought together what had been rather abstractly dealt with in disciplines such as language, literature, history, and the fine arts, with the concept of culture. Hall and Hobart were concerned with "questions of culture," i.e. "the changing ways of life of societies and groups" engaged with the "networks of meaning" (Hall, 2006, p. 1). In other words, they brought scholarly attention to taking seriously the implications of everyday life, i.e. those moments and artifacts located at "the dirty crossroads where popular culture intersects with the high arts" and where "power cuts across knowledge" (p. 1). Hall's work focused on race and social class and the cultural production of texts and meaning by audiences. This fine-tuning and critical approach to thinking about cultural meaning production and symbolic representation represented a "turn" in studying culture.

A "turn" is the expression used when discussing a shift in points of view away from dominant methodologies and ways of seeing to multipersectival ones. A cultural turn in social sciences and the humanities began in the 1970s. It was a marked redirecting from a positivist epistemological view toward an emphasis on meaning. Similar "turns" took place in other disciplines where lessons learned from the past were revisited and added to, but with new understandings. For example, what is known as the linguistic turn "insisted that we have no access to unmediated experience or knowledge but only to representations that are them- selves [sic] fraught with linguistic and ideological baggage" (Weil, 2013, p. 5). As Frederic Jameson wrote:

> The very sphere of culture itself has expanded, becoming coterminous with market society in such a way that the cultural is no longer limited to its earlier, traditional or experimental forms, but it is consumed throughout daily life itself, in shopping, in professional activities, in the various often televisual forms of leisure, in production for the market and in the consumption of those market products, indeed in the most secret folds and corners of the quotidian. Social space is now completely saturated with the image of culture. (1998, p. 111)

Most particularly the turn in media studies to a multi-cultural way of knowing and locating meaning construction, most notably in the work of Hall (2013) and others, brought terminology and concepts such as power, hegemony, ideology, and agency to light using modern mediated examples. When thinking about representation Hall (1997) noted

> ... the word *representation* or *re*presentation does sort of carry with it the notion that something was there already and, through the media, has been *re*presented. ... what we're talking about is the fact that in the notion of representations is the idea of *giving meaning*. So the representation is the way in which meaning is somehow given to the things which are depicted through the images or whatever it is, on screens or the words on a page which *stand for* what we're talking about.

Who has control over discourse, how we consent to mainstream ideas that support the status quo, and whether or not we have means of resisting are all key components of this critique. Media studies scholars within the cultural approach typically look at human differences, group processes, audience reception, content creation (encoding) and above all, keep eye and ear to the meaning people make (decoding), with and from media and how that meaning becomes naturalized. Within this approach, scholars investigate not only what media do to us but also what we do to media, the "we" being broadly and deeply defined. Furthermore, the media, as a social institution (akin in power to family, religion, education, economics, and politics), are interrogated as creating, sustaining, and distributing mainstream ways of thinking. Scholars with this perspective conduct research designed to reveal how meaning is generated with an eye to the power dynamics and the epistemological framework that creates it.

At the core of this revolutionary discipline are the concepts of hegemony and ideology (see Figure 2.1). Hegemony is a method of social control that relies on the influence of thought, rather than the threat of physical force, to gain compliance from citizenry. The result is the sense of voluntary consent and participation in the system that is gained through ideas taught (ideologies) by private domain social institutions such as education, religion, and mass media. The Ideological State Apparatus (ISA) gains consent and participation in mainstream society through ideology, described below, where people fear rejection,

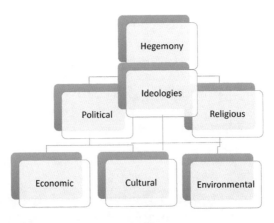

Figure 2.1: Hegemonic System of Social Control.

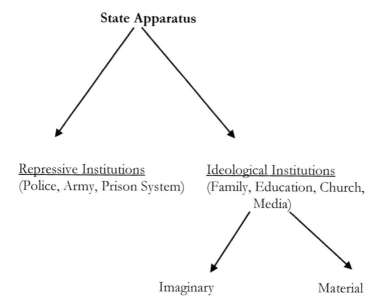

Figure 2.2: Althusser's State Apparatus Model.

standing out, or being otherwise marked for holding opposing ideas to the dominant system (Althusser, 1970).

The ISA contrasts with the Repressive State Apparatus (RSA) which is a system of social control that is gained on the basis of physical intimidation through governments, courts, military action, abusive government policies and interventions that function as a single entity (Figure 2.2).

An example of ISA in relation to animals is the way a species of animal is thought about through the telling of folk stories, fairy tales, in cartoons, movies, stuffed toys, and other "soft" mechanisms of generating a consistent narrative about the animal. Bears, for example, are constructed as playful, familial, and friendly on the one hand, but also, in more adult programs and stories, as fearful, fearsome, and dangerous. An RSA example is the Department of Fish and Wildlife's "managing" of bear populations through controlled breeding or culling (killing) programs, the local, government-employee "dog catcher," and other official groups use fines, captures, and other means of gaining consent and control.

Central to hegemony is the creation, maintenance, and perpetuation of ideologies. An ideology is a system of ideas, beliefs, values, and attitudes that function as the ISA. We all learn and adhere to ideologies that are political, economic, cultural, social, and environmental. In the United States, for example, the dominant political ideology is that the best form of government is democracy. The economic ideology is capitalism, religious is Christianity, and the most common environmental ideology is utilitarian and anthropocentric. This last ideology is one of human exceptionalism puts human beings first and animals second, viewing animals as ours to use as we see fit. This might be very utilitarian or conservationist, but nevertheless puts animals in the position of being property and belonging to us. This view is supported by religious views, policies, laws, and other practices that weave a seemingly seamless web of identity construction of animals as Others.

The ideology most associated with dominant beliefs toward animals can be captured under the term "environmental ideology," meaning "a way of thinking about the natural world that a person uses to justify actions toward it" (Corbett, 2006, p. 26). In a global study of people's attitudes toward nature Kellert (1996, p. 6), identified a taxonomy of nine basic values (sense of worth) about nature and animals that are prevalent in American society. These values and interests are utilitarian, naturalistic, ecologistic-scientific interests, aesthetic, symbolic, dominionistic, humanistic, moralistic, and negativistic, and are briefly described below:

1. "A *utilitarian* interest in pragmatically exploiting wildlife and nature" (p. 6). This conventional value system sees using animals for material human benefits as the normal order of things. For example, the view that animals exist to provide humans with food, medicine, clothing, work as tools, experimental objects, keeping animals as pets, training animals, and so forth.
2. "*Naturalistic* interest in experiencing direct contact with wildlife and the outdoors" (p. 6). This very ancient value is one of the simple pleasures found in being in nature and experiencing the presence of animals.
3. "*Ecologistic-scientific* inclination to understand the biological functioning of organisms and their habitat" (p. 6). The ecologist focuses on interdependence of beings and the scientific value, which also focuses on patterns and functions, focuses on morphology and biological processes.

4. "*Aesthetic* attraction for nature and animals" (p. 6). The beauty of a mountain, the awe-inspiring experience of a breaching whale, the laughter at a dolphin's playful leaps, the beauty of a lion's mane, all inspire admiration and give pleasure to different people in different ways.
5. "A *symbolic* use of nature for communication and thought" (p. 6). For as long as human beings have been expressing themselves they have been re-presenting animals. Sometimes purely for aesthetic reasons, as described above, and also as symbolic stand-ins for human emotions, values, and concepts by way of metaphoric expression.
6. *Dominionistic* interest in exercising mastery and control over wildlife. The idea that nature and animals are to be subdued is a long standing view.
7. "*Humanistic* affection and emotional bonding with animals" (p. 6). This view is often seen with companion animals who become close emotional intimates with and for people and are seen as being similar to people.
8. "*Moralistic* concern for ethical relations with the natural world" (p. 6). This view holds that we are all connected, that there is an important, vital, and dynamic interrelationship between all beings, and while this view holds many of the same perspectives as the humanistic, it holds more that there are rights and wrongs in terms of how humans treat other species.
9. "*Negativistic* avoidance of animals and the natural environment for reasons of fear, dislike, or indifference" (p. 6). Whereas the other eight are generally positive views of animals, the negativistic holds certain sense of dread and avoidance toward nature and animals, seeing them as threats to be avoided.

These ideologies are not mutually exclusive. They reveal values which are useful in ascertaining one's own attitudes toward animals as well as those held in different cultures. An individual might simultaneously hold a different value when it comes to different components of nature. For example, one person might aesthetically appreciate photographs of lions in the wild while also hunting them (dominion). Or, another might support experimenting on animals for research (utilitarian) but also keep a rabbit as a pet (humanistic). The development of an awareness of these changing and changeable, sometimes contradictory and paradoxical attitudes and actions toward animals, became clear to scholars who saw parallels between re-presentations of animals and those of marginalized human beings and the impact visibility or invisibility has on lived experiences. This consciousness led to a turn within a turn, if you will, as Cultural Studies yielded Media Studies, which generated the subfield of Animal Media Studies. In "A Report on the Animal Turn," Weil (2013, p. 1) notes:

> Theory has gone to the birds ... and to apes, dogs, and horses. The recent explosion of writing and teaching on animals has recharged those questions of identity and difference, of power and its effects that have embroiled academic theory over the past quarter century.

The Animal Turn in Media Studies

In the midst of the movement to unpack the tropes of race (dominant: white), sex (dominant: male), sexuality (dominant: heterosexual) that are contained in media, other scholars examined content that contained or reflected nonhuman animals to ascertain whether the re-presented was consistent with the lived. Simultaneously they began seeing the connection between oppression of human beings and other species and exclusion from moral consideration on the basis of species membership.

The animal turn in media studies is thereby a reaction to the anthropocentrism inherent in language, verbal and visual. Or what is narrowing of interpretations and meaning-making so that it fits the hierarchical structure that a maintains a clear demarcation between Humans and Other Animals. This requires *critical* empathy, defined as a "conjunction of affect and critical awareness [that] may be understood to constitute the basis of an empathy grounded not in affinity (feeling for another insofar as we can imagine being that other) but on a feeling for another that entails an encounter with something irreducible and different, often inaccessible" (Bennett, 2005, p. 10).

In his classic essay *The Animal that Therefore I am*, Derrida (2002) speaks to being naked in front of his cat. What does the cat see? Is shame a purely human invention? Derrida does not deny his cat is a cat, nor does he view Cat as another category for humanness, as a projection of our values on to the animal. Rather, he argues that we must recognize the damage done to animals through human projection. Is a cat (or a dog or a horse) naked? They wear no clothing, but, why would they? He makes it clear he is talking about a real cat, not an imaginary one

> Before the cat that looks at me naked, would I be ashamed *like* an animal that no longer has the sense of nudity? Or on the contrary, *like* a man who retains the sense of his nudity? Who am I therefore? Who is it that I am (following)? Whom should this be asked of if not of the other? And perhaps of the cat itself? (p. 374)

Three theoretical movements contributed to this animal turn: linguistic, post-or counter-linguistic, and ethical (Weil, 2013). The human-animal/animal human is given, but there is also the question of how to capture animal perspectives now that there is agreement that they have them. Without shared language this is difficult, but similar to ascertaining the interests and needs of prelingual children or those with disabilities, it is possible. To truly advance the academic as well as the activist, the *voices* of the oppressed needed to be brought in. With human beings this is not without challenges, for some, doing so with other species who do not share our way of communication seems impossible. This also is changing and the role of allies and advocates cannot be overestimated (Merskin, 2010; Merskin & Durham, 2015). The many skills and resources of activists, academics, and activist-academics can be used to "draw out what the animals cannot tell us" and "give words to the wordless, and voice to the voiceless" (Safina, 2002, p. 98).[1]

Nussbaum's (2003) Ten Core Entitlements, viewed through a legal and philosophical lens, considers nonhuman animals as primary subjects of justice, as individuals (rather than in aggregate), and to whom humans have responsibility. The Entitlements are:

- Life
- Bodily Health
- Bodily Integrity
- Senses, imagination, and thought
- Emotions

- Practical reason
- Affiliation
- Other species
- Play
- Control over one's environment

For Nussbaum, and many in the AMS field, these rights are not the end but rather starting points for how other animals ought to be regarded and cared for. Nonhuman animals, as subjective beings, aren't "just like us" if we think of them only collectively, rather they are individuals, each with his or her own preferences, particularities, cultures, and histories. Just as de-centering Eurocentrism is needed for thinking about all peoples as individuals, so de-centering the human, the anthropo, is required to best empathize with, and understand, colonial and subjected histories of other species. This brings with it a mistrust of the grand/master narratives that have defined relationships in the past and continue to inform mainstream re-presentations of the present.

Animal Media Studies

Akin to the intersectional social justice approach of feminist and critical race studies, AMS scholars ask questions such as: How do animals figure in human identity? How do humans figure in animal worlds? Why the consistent insistence on a boundary? How do deeply entrenched stereotypes figure in to the treatment of real animals? Building on concepts found in conservation psychology (Clayton & Myers, 2009; Mascia et al., 2003; Saunders, 2003), research in AMS thereby addresses topics such as:

> How and why humans care about animals.
> How humans develop beliefs and knowledge about animals.
> How humans behave toward animals.
> How and why humans re-present animals.
> What humans learn from these re-presentations.
> How these re-presentations impact animals and humans.
> How Human-to-animal relations are relevant to conversation.
> The importance of the relationship between humans, animals, and social institutions.

Unlike animal studies, AMS does not focus on animal behavior (per se), biology, or morphology. Nor is it a study of human-animal interactions per se (except for symbolic). Rather, AMS draws on the knowledge of disciplines such as environmental studies, ethnic studies, women and gender studies, media and cultural studies to interrogate questions such as how do re-presentations of animals other than humans impact the lives of real animals? And what can we learn about ourselves when looking at and thinking about other animals? Finally, how can this knowledge be used in service of animals other humans?

While Singer (1975) and Regan (1982) are considered the "fathers" of animal rights and welfare, many "mothers" made the connections long before. In fact, feminism has long recognized intersectionality (see Chapter 1) and its application beyond the human. For example, 1960s and 1970s vegetarian and vegan collectives produced publications about the connections between the oppression of all groups. Moore Lappé's (1971) *Diet for a Small Planet* and Ruether's (1974) *New Woman, New Earth* made powerful arguments and provided inspiration for what became known as ecofeminism. In the 1980s, both men and women in the ecofeminist movement elevated the argument that nonhuman animals are sentient beings. Critiques of animal treatment in the wild and as subjects of experimentation and food production became part of the literature for what would become AMS.

In the 1980s, Kheel, and in the 1990s, Adams, Gaard, Kappeler, and others brought attention to images and words as a form of discursive violence. New terminology, such as *misothery* (hatred/contempt and animal) was introduced to accompany existent *misogyny* (Mason, 1997, p. 215) and *speciesism* to other isms (Ryder, 1970). Speciesism, described in Chapter 1, as do other isms (age, hetero, sex, race) is a symptom of oppression, a prejudice, that is a "composite of interspecies injustices within material institutions, discursive regimes, and embodied effects" that "systematically, non-criminally, sacrifices the lives of and interests of animals" (Weitzenfeld & Joy, 2014, p. 20).

Whereas the humanities and social sciences are often criticized for the lack of real world vision or application, the practical implications of ecofeminism and the interconnectedness between sex, race, gender, sexuality, and species is an important distinction of this work. Adams'

(1990/2001) scholarship on the connection between violence against women, for example, and killing of companion species has informed courts, shelters, law, and policy (Adams & Gruen, 2014). That nonhuman animals are caught in a hierarchical structure that also privileges certain charismatic species over others becomes increasingly clear. Jones (quoted in Adams & Gruen, 2014) writes:

> We understand that the currently dominant gender system—which both feminist and trans activists critique, albeit in different ways—is a product of the same European mania for pseudoscientific categorization that brought us the conceptions of race and species that are central to racism and speciesism. We know that taking that diversity into account can lead to new ways of thinking about both gender and sexuality. (p. 24)

With goals consistent with critical race theory (discussed in Chapter 1), ecofeminism, animal welfare, and in some cases animal rights movements, AMS, as a cross-disciplinary field provides the context within which we can recognize shared histories of oppression. The classificatory system that dichotomizes in group/out group, insider/outsider, human/animal, has parallels in white/ not white, men/women, heterosexual/homosexual visibilities and invisibilities. AMS also considers nonhuman animals as beings in their own right, with preferences, interests, and purposes beyond which humans assign them. Ultimately, AMS scholars interrogate the power dynamics that underlie our relationships with other species.

In the opening sentence of the classic book, *Dominance & Affection: The Making of Pets*, Tuan (1984, p. 1) states, "any attempt to account for human reality seems to call for an understanding of the nature of power." However, he notes, if we only look at domination (whether conscious or subconscious) we miss an important part of what sustains that relationship—that there is someone on the other side of the gaze, who, for whatever reason, is cooperating. Furthermore, the power might in fact be motivated by affection: "affection is not the opposite of dominance; rather it is dominance's anodyne—it is dominance with a human face" (pp. 1–2). Breaking apart dualisms to reveal the continuum that exists in all human beliefs, attitudes, and behaviors is another shared goal of the many disciplines that are part of AMS. Linné (2016, p. 253) posits that the media function as a space "where the norms of human and other animal relations are constructed" and that there are two dimensions to this space. The first "concerns animals' visibility and invisibility" (p. 253). Animals seem to be everywhere but what we see are their re-presentations and these re-presentations in visual culture are often distorted and far removed from true visibility. As such, these animals are "at the same time the center of visual attention, and wholly absent" as they bear no real likeness to real beings (Malamud, 2012, p. 39). The "animals" we see in media are there to say something about us, to serve our purposes, and have any individuality blurred into a mass of sameness and lack of identity to function as part of the human food production system or wildlife management paradigms.

The second dimension of media space in which human/animal relations occur "concerns proximity and distance" (Linné, 2016, p. 253). As is discussed in later chapters the *sense* that we are in relation to animals by virtue of their seeming high numbers in re-presentations blurs the real conditions of their lived experiences. Just as Marx articulated consumer capitalism focuses on alienating citizens from the means of production when it comes to knowing the full process of how a product is created and distributed, we are symbolically connected to that which appears to be real animal and yet nothing could be further from the truth.

If we only know other animals based on mediated re-presentations, they mostly appear happy and healthy. However, behind these cheerful cows, plump pigs, dancing dogs, and corporate monkeys, billions of nonhuman animals are tortured and killed and served to us as the objects of laboratory experimentation, as laborers, in entertainment, as clothing, as pets, and as food. The uneven application of dominance/affection in this one-way relationship has a significant impact on the future of our own species as well as theirs. As was noted in a 2013 call for papers related to animal geographies:

> [The] ambivalent material-semiotic entanglements between humans and animals are both at stake and implicated in contemporary ecological crises, bringing a critical urgency to the task of rethinking dominant orders (capitalist, species, juridico-political, scientific) that structure human-animal relations. (https://animalvisions.wordpress.com/)

But can we think in to the experiences of other animals without overly projecting our own interests, desires, and needs on them, "while fostering coalitions in which felt solidarity in conjunction with respectful recognition of difference spark[s] innovative responses to intersecting problems?" (Jones, 2014, p. 100). Sprinkling our entangled inter-relationship with just the right amount of anthropomorphism can carry us closer to, rather than further from, shared empathy without polluting the symbolic stew with too much saccharine of us-ness, the ideology that all other beings' interests are subordinated to ours (human-animal dualism). Owning human privilege in a world constructed to maintain that position is central.

This is not to argue we are the same, but rather that we honor and respect difference. Finding ways of relating to nonhuman animals that are about their interests, not just ours, is called "critical anthropomorphism" (Weil, 2013, p. 44). Those whose work focuses on the lived conditions of human beings often argue that, with so much human suffering in the world, attentions should be directed there. AMS scholars don't deny human disadvantages, rather argue that by widening the circle of compassion benefits all beings. This is not an either/or situation. There is little to be gained, for humans or animals, by engaging in "the Oppression Olympics" (Jones, 2014, p. 100). Rather, this radical interdisciplinary field argues that *all* systems of oppression must be confronted, all social and cultural institutions interrogated, including the media.

Re-presenting Other Animals

An AMS view argues that the same ideology about hierarchical (de) valuation on the basis of species informs what media are made, what content they contain, and what hegemonic message they express. Typically, nonhuman animals in media function as boundary objects, as the limit test, between what humans are and are not. As we learn more about them the line is continuously drawn and redrawn to maintain difference. AMS interrogates systems of power and domination between humans and other species, recognizing that re-presentation plays an important role in establishing and maintaining this dynamic. One of the criticisms leveled at scholars who examine the human-animal binary is that the work makes no connection to nonhuman animal's lived experiences, speaking particularly in fields of animal studies (hard sciences) and human-animal studies (humanities), "most scholars in these fields speak about animals not as individuals but as objects, with nary a mention of the torture and murder inflicted upon nonhumans by the billions each year" (Nocella, Sorenson, Socha, & Matsuoka, 2014, p. xxiv). AMS scholars, while often studying representational systems and how animals are objectified and communicated about rather than with, almost always make the connection between image and reality. Similar to the erasure and/or stereotyping of human groups in media, it is the seamless naturalness of that makes representations so powerful—"[they] appeal[r] to be something which is simply *available*, out there in the culture" (Baker, 1993/2001, p. 43).

A concern of many AMS scholars is what Adams (1990/2001, p. xii) describes as the absent referent, the space of "slippage inherent between the reality of animals and their representations" because it is here where, particularly in modern industrialized societies, we loose sight of the real in the re-presented.

This disconnection has consequences for the lived experiences of animals in the world, animals who are fast disappearing. The greatest concern is the blurring of the real and the representational, with no return to the real.

Sports teams, for example, might have animal as the symbol on sports paraphernalia and still walk a *real* version on to the field. And yet there is a fundamental disconnect or at least contradiction evident in the treatment of real animals. For example, the Washington State cougars team offers stuffed toys resembling cougars for sale in gifts shops, and emblazons cougar images on t-shirts, coffee mugs, and banners, yet, simultaneously, a few miles away, real mountain lions are killed for sport. In order to venture into this relatively new area of inquiry, at least in the media studies field, we must "hol[d] questions open and … Resis[t] popular visual culture's tendency to jump to neat answers, pictorial clichés, and thus to conceptual closure" when attempting to understand what is happening (Baker, 1993/2001, p. xvii).

Similarly, collectively understood emotions, when applied to another species, typically go without question. They don't require explanation because they are so deeply ingrained in our psyches. The hegemony of a vision of the animal is therefore part of "everything we do, including writing, [and] is shaped by our long evolutionary history of interactions with other animals and our present lived interdependence with them" (Benson, 2011, p. 4).

A view of the view of the intersections between race, gender, sexuality, and species as a philosophical, legal, and political tool is likely the most powerful tool used in AMS. That we are connected, that oppression, drawing on Dr. Martin Luther King, in any form, is related to oppression in all forms, motivates many AMS scholars. Thus, the toolbox of theories and methodologies available to cultural media studies scholars can be employed, and should be employed, to unpack the deeply anthropocentric in communication theory.

Several traditional media studies theories are useful in revealing the linguistic and imagistic anthropocentric bias in communications. Uses and gratifications theory, for example, can help us understand the functions served by cat videos on the Internet. Content and textual analyses of news and other media coverage of human/animal interactions are useful in determining tone, perspective, and risk based on newspaper coverage of, for example, a black bear attack (Gore, Siemer, Shanahan, & Scheufele, 2005), urban fox attacks (Cassidy & Mills, 2012; Stewart & Cole, 2016), or sharks (Muter et al., 2013). Studies have also examined media framing of animals in agriculture (Freeman, 2009), farmed animals (Freeman, 2014), animals who are experimented upon (Kruse, 2001), and companion species (Cudworth & Jensen, 2016). Rhetorical and discourses analyses at Disney animal parks (Scott, 2007), zoos (Milstein, 2009, 2012), whale tours (Milstein, 2011), aquaria and circuses offer important interrogations of what appear to be "natural" re-presentations of animals.

To undo dichotomous assumptions and disrupt the dominant speciesist ideology by including animal voices in the many perspectives professional communicators, activists, and scholars bring to their worlds and to ours will only help us all. As AMS moves forward we can take a lesson from the humanities and the social sciences who have been criticized for using marginalized human beings as theoretical test cases, for not caring about individuals, rather using groups to pursue theoretical and pedagogical gain. As Haraway (2003) reminds us in *The Companion Species Manifesto*, "Dogs are not surrogates for theory, they are not here just to think with. They are here to live with" (p. 5). Similarly, AMS scholars bear reminding that it is the embodied capacities of animals, their "significant otherness," that must be remembered when we critique representations in media and communications. "Ethical relating" (p. 50) will thus serve to care for them, for us, and for the planet. We find them fascinating, disgusting, appealing, exotic, erotic, fearsome, and funny. They symbolically stand-in-for us, teach about morals, values, and behaviors (Baker, 1993/2001; Fudge, 2004). We use them, but it is more complex than that. For they also exist as real beings in the world, full of desires, fears, goals, and perspectives.

How do we get at the ideological elements that inform contemporary (dis)regard for species other than humans? By examining from whence we came: childhood. That is the topic of the next chapter in which influences on child development are explored in terms of attitudes toward animals and the influence of symbolic/mediated culture on perceived knowledge of the natural world.

Note

1. For more on this see The Society of Professional Journalist's code of ethics (http://www.spj.org/ethicscode.asp), particularly the section "Seek the Truth and Report It." And, for a style guide for respectful and accurate information see animalsandmedia.org.

References

Adams, C. (1990/2001). *The sexual politics of meat*. New York, NY: Continuum.
Adams, C., & Gruen, L. (2014). *Ecofeminism: Feminist intersections with other animals & the earth* (pp. 1–5). New York, NY: Bloomsbury.
Althusser, L. (1970). Ideology and ideological state apparatuses. In L. Althusser (Ed.), *Lenin and philosophy and other Essays*. New York, NY: Monthly Review Press.
Baker, S. (1993/2001). *Picturing the beast*. Champaign, IL: University of Illinois Press.
Bennett, J. (2005). *Empathetic vision*. Stanford, CA: Stanford University Press.
Benson, E. (2011). Animal writes: Historiography, disciplinarity, and the animal trace. In L. Kalof & G. M. Montgomery (Eds.), *Making animal meaning* (pp. 3–16). Lansing, MI: Michigan.
Cassidy, A., & Mills, B. (2012). "Fox tots attack schock": Boundary breaching. *Environmental Communication, 6*(4), 494–511.

Clayton, E., & Myers, S. (2009). *Conservation psychology: Understanding and promoting human care for nature*. New York, NY: Blackwell.

Corbett, J. (2006). *Communicating nature*. Washington, DC: Island Press.

Cudworth, E., & Jensen, T. (2016). Puppy Love? Animal companions in the media. In N. Almiron, M. Cole, & C. P. Freeman (Eds.), *Critical animals media studies: Communication for nonhuman animal advocacy* (pp. 185–204). New York, NY: Routledge.

Derrida, J. (2002). The animal that therefore I am (more to follow). Trans. D. Willis. *Critical Inquiry, 28*(2), 369–418.

Freeman, C. P. (2009). This little piggy went to press: The American news media's construction. *The Communication Review,12*(1), 78–103.

Freeman, C. P. (2014). *Framing farming: Communication strategies f or animal rights*. Amsterdam: Rodopi Press.

Fudge, E. (2004). *Animals*. London: Reaktion Books.

Gore, M. L., Siemer, W. F., Shanahan, J. E., & Scheufele, D. A. (2005). Effects on risk perception of media coverage of a black bear-related human fatality. *Wildlife Society Bulletin, 33*, 507–516.

Hall, S. (1997). In S. Jhally (Dir.). *Stuart Hall: Representation & the media*. [Motion picture]. Amherst, MA: Media Education Foundation.

Hall, S. (2006). The origins of cultural studies. [Motion Picture]. S. Jhally (Dir.). Northampton, MA: Media Education Foundation.

Hall, S. (2013). *Representation: Cultural representations and signifying practices*. Thousand Oaks, CA: Sage.

Haraway, D. (2003). *The companion species manifesto*. Chicago: Prickly Paradigm Press.

Jameson, F. (1998). *The cultural turn: Selected writings on the postmodern, 1983–1998*. Brooklyn, NY: Verso.

Jones, P. (2014). Quoted in C. J. Adams & L. Gruen (Eds.), *Ecofeminism: Feminist intersections with other animals & the earth*. New York, NY: Bloomsbury.

Kellert, S. (1996). *The value of life: Biological diversity and human society*. Washington, DC: Island Press.

Kruse, C. R. (2001). The movement and the media: Framing the debate over animal experimentation. *Political Communication, 18*(1), 57–87.

Lappé, F. M. (1971). *Diet for a small planet*. New York, NY: Ballantine.

Linné, T. (2016). Tears, connections, action! Teaching critical animal and media studies. In N. Almiron, M. Cole, & C. P. Freeman (Eds.), *Critical animal and media studies: Communications for nonhuman animal advocacy* (pp. 251–264). New York, NY: Taylor & Francis.

Malamud, R. (2012). *An introduction to animals and visual culture*. New York, NY: Springer.

Mascia, M. B., Brosius, J. P., Dobson, T. A., Forbes, B. C., Horowitz, L., McKean, M. A., & Turner, N. J. (2003). Consertation and the social sciences. *Conservation Biology, 17*(3), 649–650.

Mason, J. (1997). *An unnatural order: Why we are destroying the planet and each other*. New York, NY: Continuum.

Merskin, D. (2010). Hearing voices: The promise of participatory action research for animals. *Action Research, 9*(2), 144–161.

Merskin, D., & Durham, D. (2015). Expanding reach and justice with PAR: Working with more than humans. In H. Bradbury (Ed.), *The Sage handbook of action research* (3rd ed.). London: Sage.

Milstein, T. (2009). "Somethin" tells me it's all happening at the zoo': Discourse, power, and conservationism. *Environmental Communication, 3*(1), 24–48.

Milstein, T. (2011). Nature identification: The power of pointing and naming. *Environmental Communication, 5*(1), 3–24.

Milstein, T. (2012). Banging on the divide: Cultural reflection and refraction at the zoo. In E. Plec (Ed.), *Perspectives on human-animal interaction: International communication* (pp. 162–181). London: Routledge.

Muter, B., Gore, M. L, Gledhill, K. S., Lamont, C., & Huveneers, C. (2013). Australian and U.S. news media portrayal of sharks and their conservation. *Conservation Biology, 27*(1), 187–196.

Nocella, A. J., Sorenson, J., Socha, K., & Matsuoka, A. (2014). The emergence of critical animal studies. In A. J. Nocella, J. Sorenson, K. Socha, & A. Matsuoka (Eds.), *Defining critical animal studies* (pp. ix–xxxvi). New York, NY: Peter Lang.

Nussbaum, M. (2003). Capabilities as fundamental entitlements: Sen and social justice. *Feminist Economics, 9*(2/3), 33–59.

Regan, T. (1982). *All that dwell therein: Animal rights and environmental ethics*. Los Angeles, CA: University of California Press.

Ruether, R. (1974). *New woman/new earth*. New York, NY: Seabury.

Ryder, R. D. (1970). *Speciesism*. Leaflet. Oxford: Oxford University Press.

Safina, C. (2002). *Eye of the albatross: Visions of hope and survival*. New York, NY: Henry Holt.

Saunders, C. D. (2003). The emerging field of conservation psychology. *Human Ecology Forum, 10*(2), 137–149.

Scott, S. R. (2007). Conserving, consuming, and improving on nature at Disney's Animal Kingdom. *Theatre Topics, 17*(2), 111–127.

Singer, P. (1975). *Animal liberation*. New York, NY: Harper's.

Stewart, K., & Cole, M. (2016). The creation of killer species: Cultural rupture in representations of "urban foxes" in UK newspapers. In N. Almiron, M. Cole, & C. P. Freeman (Eds.), *Critical Animals Media studies: Communication for nonhuman animal advocacy* (pp. 124–137). New York, NY: Routledge.

Tuan, Y-F. (1984). *Dominance & affection: The making of pets*. New Haven, CT: Yale University Press.

Weil, K. (2013). *Thinking animals: Why animal studies now?* New York, NY: Columbia University Press.

Weitzenfeld, A., & Joy, M. (2014). An overview of anthropocentrism, humanism, and speciesism in critical animal theory. In A. J. Nocella II, J. Sorenson, K. Socha, & A. Matsuoka (Eds.), *Defining critical animal studies* (pp. 3–27). New York, NY: Peter Lang.

Wilson, E. O. (1984). *Biophilia*. Boston, MA: Harvard University Press.

Chapter Three

Children and Animals

Living animals are central presences to young children.
—Myers (2007, p. 6)

Animals are such agreeable friends—they ask no questions; they pass no criticisms.
—Eliot (1857/2015)

For at least the last hundred years, American cultural images weave child and animal into the same cloth.
—Melson (2001, p. 18)

The childhood landscape is learned on foot, and a map is inscribed in the mind—trails and pathways and groves—the mean dog, the cranky old man's house, the pasture with the bull in it—going out wider and farther. All of us carry within us a picture of the terrain that was learned roughly between the ages of 6 and 9.
—Snyder (1990, p. 26)

Wide-eyed with wonder and whimsy, a child encounters an animal. Seeing someone or something for the very first time is a rare and precious moment not only as we develop, but also throughout our lives. "Just think about the light a child shows upon seeing a chipmunk or a family of ducklings paddling across a pond, or the sheer joy expressed when a colorful butterfly flits past" (Selly, 2014, p. 2). Do you remember the first time you cuddled a kitten? Petted a puppy? Or as an adult, the first time you saw, in person, an animal you had only read about in books, seen in movies, or on television programs? Universally animals matter to children and in the presence of them, children are "calmer, more curious, and more joyful" (p. 2) and no doubt adults are too. But why?

This chapter contributes to the call for "a more rounded picture of children's lives," which is one that includes animals (Tipper, 2011, p. 149). Interactions with animals are one of the many everyday encounters that are taken for granted because they are so common, yet are simultaneously some of the most important in their and our lives:

> The fact that pets are important to young children is often noted by researchers but rarely explored in any depth, possibly because it is seen as trivial and essentially childish. This in turn may enable adults to trivialize other expressed wishes or views from children. (Morrow, 1998, p. 49)

In this chapter we explore the human/animal connection on a physiological level. What is it that children seem to "get" about other species that they are then expected to outgrow as young adults? What ways do they learn about animals and what impact does first person versus vicarious learning have on the development of attitudes about animals and the likelihood of being an empathetic individual? Answers to these questions, as well as a review of literature related to children's developmental phases are presented in the following sections.

The Connection

If you are a parent, have younger siblings, or recall your own childhood experiences, there is undeniably something special felt or witnessed when children interact with animals. That humans and animals have been in relationship for thousands of years is well documented (see Chapter 1 for more on this). It can be argued that we deeply sense this ancient bond, even in modern times. Animals provide comfort to us in times of sorrow, are companions in everyday life, and help us do our work in the world by serving as guides, to those who are unsighted or Deaf, aid in police investigations or war, work search and rescue operations, herd sheep, retrieve, and have finely attuned skills that are helpful in different forms of therapy.

There is evidence that being in relationship with animals, particularly companion species, has physical benefits for people of all ages in terms of, for example, boosting immunity and lowering blood pressure (O'Haire, 2010), and increasing the likelihood of surviving coronary heart disease (Beck & Katcher, 2003). According to an annual Australian study, the National People and Pets Survey, animals have a place in medicine and in mental well-being. This study was the first of its kind to examine the relationship between pet keeping and human health and revealed that people who share their homes with cats and dogs tend to have more positive mental health, make fewer doctor visits, have less trouble sleeping, and are less likely to be on medication for heart issues (Headey, 1999). And the animal need not only be the four-footed cuddly type. Insect pets such as crickets also have positive effects on mental health of the elderly (Ko, Youn, Kim, & Kim, 2016). This has significant financial benefits as well to individuals and institutions.[1]

Individuals at an Alzheimer's facility, for example, were better able to focus their attention when they "dined in front of aquariums with brightly colored fish" and as a result "they ate more, got better nutrition and were less prone to pacing. They were also more attentive and less lethargic" (Oaklander, 2017). Hence, to ignore the importance of these relationships, or to dismiss them as immature or silly, is to miss something very important in the imaginative and moral development of children and children as eventual adults. Oddly, children's relationships with animals and their experiences are "conspicuously absent" from, and are amongst the least researched aspects of, their development (Tipper, 2011, p. 148; see also Myers, 2007).

Studies of children and animals tends to look at their dynamics in two ways: (1) research that looks at the impact of companion species on children's development, and (2) research that examines the impact of the use of animals for species-specific therapies such as dolphin, horses, and dogs (i.e. Animal Assisted Activities (AAA) and Animal Assisted Therapy (AAT)) (Endenburg & van Lilith, 2011). A developing body of research examines the impact on animals themselves, i.e. of using them to reduce our stress and the related animal welfare issues that can result from putting them in stressful situations such as providing comfort following natural disasters, accidents, or work in war situations (Dodman, 2016).

A difficulty in conducting studies on the nature of the relationship between animals and children is that the encounters are often artificial, taking place in a lab or classroom setting, for example, both being unnatural and temporary constructions. Nevertheless, there is sufficient research to demonstrate what many of us already know intuitively: animals matter, they enhance our lives in a multitude of ways and they have emotions, needs, and wants not unlike our own. For anyone who has spent time with other species, or witnessed the interactions between little humans (i.e. children) and little animals, an almost magical something goes on. They touch, kiss, talk to, and hold them. Long ago, psychologist Sigmund Freud (1913/1950, pp. 126–127) noted this connection:

> Children show no trace of the arrogance, which urges modern adult civilized men to draw a hard-and-fast line between their own nature and that of all other animals. Children have no scruples over allowing animals to rank, as their full equals. Uninhibited as they are in the avowal of their bodily needs, they no doubt feel themselves more akin to animals than to their elders, who may well be a puzzle to them.

The value of animals to learning was identified more than 40 years ago in the Northern Italy town of Reggio Emilia, where a set of progressive schools was created with the pedagogical focus on each child's individual abilities, emotional, psychological, and moral development in an effort to and "challeng[e] false dichotomies [such as] art versus science, individual versus community, child versus adult ... " (Gardner, 1998, p. xvii). This program recognized the importance of connecting children and animals. The approach requires two teachers always present in the classroom. Thus the environment, the space of the classroom is viewed as a "the third educator" of children at school, contributing, in addition to cognitive and social learning, to "a sense of well being and security" (Malaguzzi, 1984, qtd. in Gandini, 1998, p. 177). Animals are a "fourth educator" in Malaguzzi's pedagogical array (Bone, 2013, p. 57). Given that animals are everywhere in the world of children, from classroom experiences to learning materials such as characters in stories and games, that they are also co-learners in the classroom just makes good sense.

These findings have important pedagogical implications not only for science education but also for understanding the development of empathy, discussed in detail later in this chapter, amongst children and for future regard for animals, as "the non-human environment, far from being of little or no account to human personality development, constitutes one of the most basically important ingredients of human psychological existence" (Searles, 1960, p. 6). This dynamic directs the next section of this chapter which explores the significance and quality of the child and animal connection.

Animals in Children's Lives

Children are not ashamed to talk about the animals in their lives, they do not, as adults might, worry what someone would think of them for speaking about a close connection with other beings (Cole & Stewart, 2014; Tipper, 2011). Children's relationships with animals are different from those they have with adults and figure in to their self-reports as very important family members and friends. These relationships are

> Situated, emplaced, embodied, relational engagements with animals are a part of what it means to live as a child and attending to them may well enhance our understanding of children's everyday experience. If we wish to fully understand how children engage in relationships, or experience issues such as place, generation, embodiment and discipline or rules, then we need to attend to animals. (p. 160)

Trans-species friendships might seem more natural to children in part because animals are more like peers in terms of autonomy or power (or lack thereof), and size. This is particularly so when children are very young and have few language skills and share nonverbal forms of communication with pets in "the language of gesture, grunt, and howl" (Melson, 2001, p. 19). In addition,

> The structural and social realities of being a child seem also to shape children's relationships with animals. Children's particular access to power, authority and knowledge may mean that children may frame their understandings of relationships with animals in terms, which resonate with their everyday experience of relationships, e.g. highlighting rules, disrespect and disobedience and hierarchies of age. (Tipper, 2011, p. 160)

Part of "becoming" an adult is the experience of childhood. Who and what comprises that life period warrants serious consideration. This includes listening to and analyzing the voices of children themselves (James, Jenks, & Prout, 1998, pp. 207–208). Children seem to have a particularly strong attraction, perhaps even instinct, to connect with other species and "tak[e] them in to their hearts as comrades and companions" (Dancy, 2011, p. 169). One reason children are attracted to animals, such as dogs, cats, rabbits, and birds, is because they too are small and vulnerable, and who don't have the same communication abilities as adults. "Many a parent, educator, or interested adult has observed the plain delight, intense interest, and strong feelings animals invoke in young children. This phenomenon alone provokes curiosity. But beneath this sturdy fact, what is going on?" (Myers, 2007, p. xiii). This experience is part of learning to externalize and to see others as having lifeworlds of their own. This is evident in children's

> natural attraction ... to animals ... a predisposition to attune to animals and other living things [that] is part of the human evolutionary heritage ... children [are] born assuming a connection with other living things ... Every human child begins life situated in what adults call "the animal world." (Melson, 2001, p. 20)

In interviews with 49 children, Tipper (2011, p. 158) found "children readily expressed affection for animals, spoke about them as individuals, friends, and kin. Not only were children unashamed of these connections, but they spoke at length about animals and frequently reoriented the interview discussion towards [them]." Furthermore, by listening to children's own accounts, Tipper found that, to children, animals "matter in their own right," and are seen as individuals (p. 158).

Making (and Breaking) "the Connection"

As we mature we're told to leave the silly, sassy, playful, sides of ourselves behind, and embrace the serious. Animal friendships, come to be perceived "as trivial or essentially childish" by adults (Morrow, 1998, p. 49). Why is it that to be mature means to no longer be in touch with animals as they are in the world or the animal in us? In part the answer lies in the long held view that children and animals are regarded as simple beings who are closer to nature. To be part of so-called civilized society, argued Freud (1930) means to abandon the natural, the "uncivilized" parts of the self. Fawcett (2002, p. 133) notes

> It is perplexing ... that as more live animals disappear we continue to inundate children with animal symbolism. We give them stuffed animals to cuddle up beside before they go to sleep, live animals as companions, elaborate zoo visits, endless animal allegories, stories, movies, and cartoon animals to teach them implicit morals and values while entertaining them. Then, as these humans "grow up" we encourage them to separate from animals, to disappear animalness from their lives.

Curiously, this sense of animal connections as insignificant continues to the present day, even in contemporary child rearing literature. For example, in the 2011 book *You Are Your Child's First Teacher*, the author writes (drawing on a 1946 guide by von Heydebrand), that it is best *not* to give young children realistic animal toys because

> when animals are taken out of their normal postures, dressed up in clothes, and made to imitate people, the image of the human being is also brought down to a lower level. Respect for our unique position in relation to the rest of the animal kingdom is worth fostering in a culture that tends to reduce the human being to animal or mechanistic levels. (Dancy, 2011, p. 170)

This view is representative of the hegemonic structure described in Chapter 2, and continually reinforces, a hierarchical relationship to nature and animals, a view that has thus far not served either of us well. These relations of hierarchy are particularly problematic when manifested in abuse, discussed later in this chapter. Catharine MacKinnon (2004, p. 264) argues, "in spite of the evidence that men socially dominate women and people dominate other animals, the fact that relations of domination and subordination exist between the two is widely denied." Sometimes this dynamic is concealed behind language and acts viewed as loving or protective, but in reality "women are the animals of the human kingdom, the mice of men's world" (p. 265). Children conceivably are amongst the status of women as well in terms of regard.

The child, as closer to and in a state of nature, is regarded as idealized and problematized. Thus, until they mature, children are often thought of as little animals. Bataille (1976/1992, qtd. in Melson, 2001, p. 35) asked "what are children if not animals becoming human?" As such they represent little noble savages, romanticized projections of the "uncivilized" self:

> The idea that children like animals emerged in tandem with the idea that children are like animals: sometimes wholesome and innocent, yet also potentially wild, uncivilized, Dionysian creatures disposed towards mindless violence. (Tipper, 2011, p. 147)

It is from this construction that the idea of children as endlessly demanding and desiring little beasts emerges, creatures who are wild, untutored creatures who must be "trained" if they are to be successful in a "civilized" society. This means leaving behind connections with nature. Unfortunately, many children who are naturally drawn to animals and might even pursue careers related to them, are frustrated at this point when told they should pay attention to more "serious" aspects of life. What theories might explain the value of nature and animals to children's physical and psychological development? That is the subject of the next section.

Is the Connection Natural?

Two of the most often cited theories for predicting the reason for and impact of human/animal relationships are (1) Biophilia, and the (2) Social Support hypotheses. Biophilia, a term popularized by Edward O. Wilson (1984, p. 1), is "the innate tendency to focus on life and lifelike process." Wilson (1984) asserts that within every living being exists a desire to connect with other living beings. Humans are attracted to the new, the novel, the different but no matter the pull of the exotic or other worldly, we naturally want to associate, to affiliate, with nature, and doing so is crucial to healthy psychological and physical development. In fact, "we learn to distinguish life from the inanimate and move toward it like moths to a porch light" (Wilson, 1984, p. 1).

Disconnection from nature, which has been increasing over time, particularly for those who live in industrialized, urbanized, and modernized societies, comes at a significant emotional, physical, and environmental price. Loss of connection to one another was predicted more than 100 years ago by sociologists such as Durkheim (1897/1951) who argued that increased occupational and social specialization would lead to psychological alienation, weakening social bonds, a condition he termed *anomie*. While an anomic individual is not integrated in to society he or she is disconnected from nature. Furthermore, in consumer-oriented societies, "the more one has, the more one wants, since satisfactions received only stimulate instead of filling needs" (Durkheim, 1897/1951, p. 258). Psychological disconnect from our relationship with the planet and the other beings who share it with us, similarly leads to "a deprived and diminished existence" (Kellert, 1996, p. 9) and less concern for it and each other.

Support for the Biophilia Hypothesis comes from a variety of fields, contributing to its usefulness as a framework for studying human relationships with nature, animals, and their import (Kahn, 1997). For example, landscape features people find calming, reassuring, and aesthetically pleasing in paintings, photography, and in person experiences reveal our natural affinity to particular spaces. The Savanna Hypothesis predicts that, because of our evolutionary origins, human beings are drawn to landscapes and environments that resemble grasslands and open territory (Ulrich, 1993). Research supports this as natural settings in real life or in the media are shown to reduce stress, lower blood pressure, and speed surgical recovery, thus the positioning of photographs and paintings of outdoor spaces in waiting and hospital rooms, doctor's offices, prisons, and mental hospitals (Ulrich, 1993). Even the presence of an aquarium is soothing (DeSchriver & Riddick, 1990). Hence, "viewed as an essential bond between humans and other living things, the natural environment has no substitutes" (p. 203).

In terms of human evolution, being in relationship with animals enhances the likelihood of human survival because animal behavior can indicate impending dangers or threats to safety (Wilson, 1984, 1993). Dogs (and to an extent llamas and other vigilant species) alert us when something might be amiss. Today, companion species primarily provide calming effects, reduce anxiety, and enhance well being. Studies of both young children (Friedman, Katcher, Lynch, & Messent, 1983) and undergraduate students (Wilson, 1991) show reduction in anxiety (measured by reductions in blood pressure) when a dog is present. This effect seems to apply whether the actual animal is there or simply images of animals viewed. It's no surprise then that animals are so often present in films, television programs, advertising, and popular culture even if the product or story or plot has nothing to do with them (see Chapter 4 for more on this). If an animal is shown in a scene or in a picture, research participants describe the people in the scene "as friendlier, happier, and less threatening than the same people in scenes without animals" (O'Haire, 2010, p. 2).

This finding was demonstrated in what is called the Thematic Apperception Test (AAPT) (Murray, 1943) in which two sets of pictures were shown to study participants. One set included animals and the other did not. Replications show this to be consistently part of situations that are perceived as less stressful, resulting in a calming sense of well being (Friedmann, 1995).

The second theory that predicts animal/human intersections will be beneficial is the Social Support Hypotheses. Social support is knowing that there are others to whom you can relate, who provide companionship, i.e. reduce loneliness and, as a result, contribute to an overall sense of well being. This is true of both children and adults. As we grow up, knowing we have friends, feeling like we matter to someone, are loved and not alone, are critical contributors to psychological and physical health. We form similar attachments to companion animals who also provide a bridge to other people. Whether the person is ill, young or old, the psychological results clearly influence the physical benefits.

The disappearance of real animals in the world and in everyday experiences of children (except those who are controlled such as pets), impacts their moral development, particularly in terms of empathy. As discussed in Chapter 2, empathy is the capacity to feel what another being feels.

Furthermore, relegation of interactions with animals to the realm of the childish, romantic, trivial, thus unimportant to adulthood supports a capitalist system built on mass production of animals for consumption, who are intentionally kept out of view of the critical, empathetic eye. But "in the actual lives of children, the animal is a whole and compelling presence" (Myers, 2007, p. 2). They relate to animals as subjective others, seeing behavior in ways similar to their own, not in overly anthropomorphic sense, but in a kind of kinship where other animals love one another, play, make homes, raise their families, and have feelings. There is a pattern to this relating:

> Young children demonstrate finely attuned sensitivities to certain basic and somewhat variable qualities of animals as interactants, even as the children also show certain biases as intersubjective and linguistic young humans. We repeatedly find a small set of core traits of animals (including humans) uniting a whole range of animal-related activities of children. (Myers, 2007, p. 4)

The traits Myers (2007) speaks of are:

1. *Agency* ("the animal moves on its own and can do things like bite, crawl, look around")
2. *Codependence* ("the animal is easily experienced as an organized whole")
3. *Affectivity* ("the animal shows emotions ... and many different qualities of feeling")
4. *Continuity* ("with repeated experiences an animal becomes a familiar individual").

These qualities apply whether the animal is a squirrel or bird viewed outside the classroom window or is a pet.

Traditionally, developmental theories examine a child's comprehension of other people, rather than nature and/or animals (Kellert, 1996). But the stages through which a child grows seems naturally to include other beings (Cole & Stewart, 2014). An overview of this literature is provided in the following section.

Developmental Theory

Infancy research reveals that, prior to the egocentric infant, babies are open, sensorial oriented, with "a sense of 'I' in relation to the other" (Myers, 2007, p. 9). "Beginning during the first year of life, children distinguish animate objects (human and nonhuman animals) from inanimate objects" and make distinctions about the behavior of each (Herrmann, Waxman, & Medin, 2010, p. 9982). As the child moves toward recognition of being human, he or she develops a sense of continuity as a member of the *Homo sapien sapien* (modern human) community with other beings. As identity develops, young children recognize a difference between themselves and animals but not yet in the hierarchical or binary sense that comes later as culture writes its developmental script. "Indeed, animals appear to be optimally discrepant social others by the time of early childhood—offering just the right amount of similarity to and difference from the human pattern (and from other animal patterns) to engage the child" (Myers, 2007, p. 10).

The stages (physical, psychological, and moral) through which children go as they grow have occupied developmental theorists for decades. Those that form the foundation for much contemporary thinking about child development have come from the work of theorists such as Piaget (1960), Erikson (1950, 1959), and others. While a full description of the contributions of each of these theories is beyond the scope of this book, a brief discussion of the primary findings is useful in constructing the platform upon which a child's identity and sociability emerge.

The Developing Child

Child development, can be defined as a combination of social-emotional and cognitive development and includes self-esteem, social skills and orientation, learning abilities or challenges, as well as parenting and other influences. Belsky (1984) proposed three variables or spheres that interact and influence this process: (1) individual characteristics and differences, (2) parent's psychological means, and (3) the context of both support and stressors in a child's life. Belskey's process

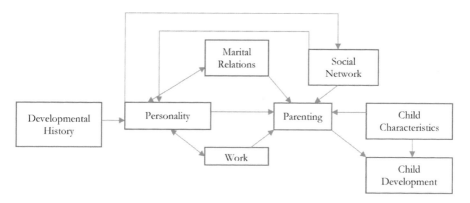

Figure 3.1: Belsky's Process Model.
Source: Adapted from Belsky, J. (1984). The determinants of parenting: A process model. *Child Development*, 55(1), p. 84.

model is useful here, as it loops place, role, and experience of companion species in to a child's network of emotional bonds, security, and the dynamics of relationships (see Figure 3.1).

Children's special relationship with animals is documented by Myers (2007) who spent a year at a mid-western university affiliated pre-school with twenty-three boys and girls, ranging in age from three and a half to six years old. In his reflection on the presence of animals (real and represented) in a nursery school, Myers (2007, p. 1) observed

> This nursery school, probably like many in North America, is in habited by protean animal figures. There are storybook animals of several sorts. Others are animated by pretend—be they stuffed, plastic, or the transformed bodies of the children themselves. Curricular animals enhance preschool-level biology. And there are living animals, outdoors and inside, constituting the locally available slice of the vast diversity of the animal kingdom. ... In the previous list of kinds of 'animals,' some seem to spring solely from literary convention or children's television or toys.

The development of children's values in regard to nature and animals seems to come later, perhaps as a reflection of parents and other adult's prioritizing it as less important than other relationships (Kellert, 1996). But not all children are the same. What influences individual differences?

In the first case, a child's individual temperament and personality influence the pace and depth of development. Many children enjoy listing

Figure 3.2: Five-Month-Old Juliana Interacts With Animal Toys and Real Her Friend, Cora.

things, organizing them, and knowing all about someone or something. For example, some like, and are proud of knowing, all the different types of dinosaurs or dogs or what foods a particular animal likes to eat. The ready apprehension of facts about animals, their habitats, their lifeways, and other information is a very effective way for children to develop basic scientific thinking and even mathematical skills.

Animals also play a special and important role in self-esteem development. Emotions are feelings and more, they include basics such as "joy, anger, disgust, surprise, sadness, fear, and possibly sexual ardor, affection" and others (Campos & Barre, 1988, p. 229). One is affected as well as effects. Emotions are related to motivation, regulate the flow of information, behavior, some of which is based on learned experiences while others seem more innate, more hardwired in to our being, as adaptive functions based on "states elicited by awards or punishers," i.e. "what we will work to attain or work to avoid or escape" (Rolls, 2005, p. 1). Others view emotions in less instrumental, scientific form and consider them

For children, when a dog responds with a tale wag or a cat purrs, this communicates a kind of caring and affection. Through this exchange, both can share in a kind of communication based on feelings. Children speak to animals in ways they would their peers or adults, explaining activities and choices in a shared world. An example is a boy who was helping unload groceries from his parent's car. He called to his dog, "We're just unloading groceries from the car, Cart" (Selly, 2014, p. 18). Using a nickname, "Cart," suggests he saw the dog more as a friend or a peer and that the dog was interested and understood what the boy was doing. Thus, this sense of the interaction being all about the child, fits developmentally with self-focus of early development. Some experiences with animals are so profound they later influence choice of career. Biologist E. O. Wilson said, "Every kid has a bug period. I never grew out of mine, and thank heavens I didn't" (qtd. in Flatow, 2013).

Tipper (2011, p. 161) proposes a relational aspect of children's interactions with animals based on the ways they are "intertwined" with other inter-generational relationships. For children

1. Animals "offer particular types of interaction which relationships with adults may not" (p. 160)
2. When they reflect on relationships with animals their knowledge comes from how they understand their worlds and "and their position within it"
3. How adults talk about the child/animal relationship influences not only how the child experiences it (i.e. if trivialized) but also how they express the relationship(s).

An important developmental characteristic that portends future relationships is empathy. Empathy, "involves sharing the perceived emotion of another" (Eisenberg & Strayer, 1990, p. 6). It differs from sympathy in terms of the dynamic of the relationship. Whereas

Figure 3.3: Friendship.
Source: Used by permission iStock (Getty Images).

empathy is "feeling with another," sympathy is "feeling for" (p. 6). In the later there is concern for another but more so as an outcome, rather than being with another in a shared experience.

Experience shows us that empathetic people react to signs of emotional distress or pain in other species and care with and for another without regard for species differences. Many of us cry at our computers at a sad Youtube video of a mother elephant whose offspring has died; of a dog drowning or in pain, or a kitten rescued by a fireman. By doing so, we are sharing in empathetic responses to pain, both emotional and physical. The environment in which a child is raised makes a difference in this empathetic development.

Up until about age five, for example, children in urban environments (the most studied who receive most of their animal-related information vicariously) do not have an anthropocentric view of the world. Instead, a view that favors humans over other animals (anthropocentrism) is not seen in urban children until and after about age five, "which is the most intense acculturation and socialization period of their lives" (Fawcett, 2002, p. 127). Thus "anthropocentrism is not a universal first step in children's construal of the biological world," (Herrmann et al., 2010, p. 9979) rather, it is learned. "It is an acquired perspective, one that emerges … . And likely reflects young children's keen sensitivity to the perspectives presented to them" (Anyaso, 2010). Children who grow up with direct experience with animals, or at least direct experience that goes beyond interaction with household pets, therefore tend to be more empathetic.

A study of 49 children ages 7–12 (Tipper, 2011) asked them "who mattered?" Qualitative interviews as well as a concentric circles map activity asked the children to respond to questions such as who is part of their family, they were also asked, prior to the interviews, to take photographs of those who matter to them. This way, the children had a say in the nature of the interview based on the photo presented. While animals were not the focus of the study, who mattered to the children clearly included them. The children spoke about past and present pets, animals belonging to other family members and friends, magical creatures, and included everyone from rats, birds, guinea pigs, monkeys, horses and others. These relationships are physical/tactile, embodied, and intimate. Of the 49 children interviewed, 90% of them (44 children) spoke about an animal or animals, and most as family members. "These research findings add powerfully to the idea that the animal is a friendly co-participant in learning and an ally to the young child" (Bone, 2013, p. 58). Furthermore, "the comforting presence of the animal as a supporter of learning underlines why animals are so effective in their pedagogical role" (p. 58). On a common sense level, it is easy to see how contact with animals helps children learn about relationships, about the process of birth and death, about love, about responsibility.

Psychological studies show the role interactions with animals play in psychological development, the facilitation of interpersonal skills, and also, as discussed later, as a predictor of potential adult psychopathy and violence (Arluke & Sanders, 1996). For animals "challenge children to temper the role of master with kindness, to blend domination with solicitude" (Melson, 2001, p. 17). Does it make a difference whether the animal is experienced in person or the same activities are witnessed in a film, on a poster, at a zoo, or in a book? It seems so.

Sources of Learning

Children learn about the natural world from three primary sources: direct, indirect, and symbolic (Corbett, 2006; Kellert, 1996). Each is valuable and yields different levels of attachments, activation of mirror neurons, and, finally, empathetic outcomes.

Direct Experience

The ideal way to develop an empathetic connection with nature and other animals is through direct experience. This is "physical contact with natural settings and nonhuman species" (Kahn & Keller, 2002, p. 118). Contact can range from hiking in fields and forests, building forts outdoors, caring for companion animals, and observing animals in the wilderness. Furthermore, evidence clear that higher quality learning comes from direct experience (Anderson & Pempek, 2005).

Indirect Experience

Indirect experience with the natural world is more restricted than is direct experience. For example, the natural setting might be a garden, a park, a zoo, aquarium, or some other adult-controlled experience. While many people believe seeing animals in zoos evokes greater care for species, research shows that attendees leave with bad feelings about captivity, with little to no greater knowledge of animal biology, behavior, or conservation needs and "rarely emerge wondering what the animal sees, feels or needs" (Fawcett, 2002, p. 126). Instead, paradoxically, despite the fun, entertainment, and exposure to animals zoos offer, the signage discourse emphasizes a "dominant mastery-othering-exploitation them[e]" by both materially and symbolically (Milstein, 2009, p. 42). Today's parents are increasingly fearful about letting their children explore the natural world without adult supervision. Thus pet-keeping becomes one of the only in person experiences many children have with animals. Pets are "the primary mode of intense, sustained involvement with most animals" (Melson, 2001, p. 28).

While the numbers of animals kept as pets is at an all-time high (see Chapter 1), if our only direct experience with another species is as pets this limited, controlled exposure "sentimentalizes our view of animals and thus impedes our appreciation and stewardship of the natural world" (Cooley, 2015). These are relationships in which the animals are often bred to be highly interactive, and even dependent upon us, a far cry from animals in the wild or who are undomesticated.

Symbolic/Vicarious Experience

The third way of learning about nature and animals is through representations, or re-presentations. There is no first person experience in this form of learning, rather this is the fantasy, re-presented, disembodied experience of learning about nature and animals by way of books, television, movies, games, and toys, which can be "metaphorical, stylized, and symbolic" (Corbett, 2006, p. 16). Learning about animals from books, movies, and television programs has come to substitute for learning with or among animals. "The television age has brought children images of animals filtered through the syntax of nature shows complete with narrator, background music, slow motion, and commercial breaks" (p. 28). These packaged productions keep animals and empathy at a safe distance, wrapping them up in commercial packages far removed from real world experiences of many species. They thus occupy "a shadow world," one which we imagine, but do not enter except technologically (p. 29).

While direct connection is the ideal way of engaging with animals and others, all too often, particularly in the modernized, industrialized world, children have mostly symbolic experiences with places and beings unfamiliar to them. "What concerns child development specialists is the explosion of vicarious experiences and the dramatic decline of available, authentic, and unprogrammed direct experiences" (Corbett, 2006, p. 16).

As is the case with the development or perpetuation of stereotypes about human beings if the only place someone different than oneself is see is on television, children often believe they have "seen" an animal if it was encountered on television or in a movie (Fawcett, 2002). Relational knowing is qualitatively different than symbolic relating and even indirect experiences. Fawcett (2002, p. 126) argues, "I believe animals are increasingly endangered in our minds and in our direct experiences, long before they actually become physically, ecologically endangered."

Children's lives are increasingly indoor, occupied by mediated screen time and this has impacted their health, development, and well being (Mayo Clinic, 2016). How he or she develops is thereby "shaped by the input that learners receive," which includes the media:

> That in urban technologically saturated communities, where direct contact with nonhuman animals is relatively limited and where images of nonhuman animals in children's books, discourse, and media often take an anthropocentric cast, young children encounter considerable support (intended or not) for an anthropocentric perspective as they seek to understand the relation between human and nonhuman animals. (Herrmann et al., 2010, p. 9982)

We know that children are influenced by what they hear and see around them as well as what they see and hear "in the media ... (e.g., stories and films in which animals talk, sing and act like humans)" (Anyaso, 2010; Inagaki, 1990; Rosengren, Gelman, Kalish, & McCormick, 1991). In a study of Canadian children's ideas and stories about three common wild animals (bats, frogs, and raccoons), the researcher found strong inter-species bonds and thinking about animals as friends with humans and with each other. Stories revealed misconceptions about species behaviors, which fueled fears about the animals (despite lack of direct experience with them). The younger the children with direct experiences with animals were, the more likely to tell stories filled with friendship narratives "no matter which animal they discussed, friendship between the animals and the humans and the attribution of subjectivity to the animal were prevalent themes" (p. 131). One child (a six-year-old) told the following story:

> I think bats are awake at night so the person would have to meeted (sic) it at nighttime. Maybe the bat wanted to know if the person flew like bats do. Maybe the person wanted to know what bats eat. The bat told the person what he eats. The bat is happy because he has a new friend now. The person also feels happy because she has a friend. They were playing in the park. (p. 132)

The researcher found that older children, around 10 or 11, despite having more factual knowledge by virtue of having had more schooling, were more likely to believe folktales and stereotypes of animals and more held fearful, negative ideas about familiar species. A child even mentioned in his story that "the boy ran away because he was scared of bats because he watches TV" (p. 133). As children get older there is evidence of a reification of dis-identification with animals and a securing and normalizing of the cultural construct of difference, a "reification of 'human' and 'animal'" that children are taught (Myers, 2007, p. 16). This represents an important cultural training moment in dualistic thinking in terms of what children are born thinking and feeling versus what they are taught about animals, as was discussed in Chapter 2. Boundaries are secured between self/other, human/animal, tame/wild that carry hierarchical valuing and thus influence adult views on the place (or lack thereof) of animals in our lives. As children learn language they are further instructed on species bias.

Much of this chapter has focused on the positive aspects of children's interactions with animals and the development of empathy. There are, however, powerful connections between a child's treatment of animals and the way he or she will treat animals and other humans as an adult. Does mistreatment of animals during childhood predict treatment others as an adult? Does witnessing domestic violence in the home contribute to lack of empathy later on? The research says yes.

Links Between Violence to Animals and Violence to Humans

To deliberately inflict pain on another living being is amongst the greatest perversions, yet what is cruel to one person might not appear to be to another. In some cultures, bullfighting, dog fighting, hunting, and trapping are viewed as natural and normal events. In others, they are considered acts of cruelty. Some individuals vary their definitions of cruel treatment by species. For example, how one treats their pet dog and a dairy or beef cow might be quite different. Insects and reptiles, particularly spiders and snakes, are often quite cruelly treated because of their lack of status. But there is evidence that abuse of animals predicts brutality toward human others during adulthood (Ascione, 1992; Ascione & Weber, 1996). For example, infamous murderers such as the Boston Strangler, Son of Sam, Jeffrey Dahmer, and others had childhoods and histories of repeated animal abuse. "Cruelty to animals in childhood was one of the significant differences in behavioral indicators between sexual murders who were themselves abused before they became abusers and murderers without such a history" (Adams, 1994, p. 69; see also Ressler, Brugess, Hartman, Douglas, & McCormack, 1986). Violence tends to beget violence and abuse of animals, often learned by example from adults, can take many forms such as the desire to control a smaller, weaker being; to intimidate another person, displaced hostility, sadism, and retaliation. Violence also includes "acts of omission (e.g. the batterer prohibit[tsp.] the feeding of a starving animal or would not allow veterinary care for an injured or ill pet) (Ascione et al., 2007, p. 356).

Having animals around, particularly pets, is no guarantee of an empathetic individual, however children who have positive relationships with their companion species, and experience emotional closeness with them, "show better developed empathy toward animals" (Beetz, 2009, p. 64). Rather, abuse of animals and other humans is often linked to lack of emotional competency, the ability to access emotional self-regulation strategies, and the ability to affectively and cognitively understand the experiences of others. According to Ascione et al. (2007, p. 365) "unfortunately it is clear that children have opportunities to learn either cruelty or kindness to animals in the context of the family." The lack of empathetic ability to perspective-take is one of the diagnostic criteria for psychiatric disorders such as antisocial personality disorder and conduct disorder (Beetz, 2009). The lack of healthy development of attachment and empathetic systems are central to this. Thus it seems clear that fostering empathy toward *both* humans and other animals helps in the development of positive psychological health. Empathy, "paves the way for the development of moral reasoning and motivates prosocial altruistic behavior" (Decety, 2011, p. 35). Encouraging children to develop close relationships with animals, as well as other children, particularly during the earliest years of life, will have a positive correlation with an attachment figure. For example, a parent who encourages a child to develop an attachment with an animal provides the possibility for the development of health emotional capabilities.

In situations of domestic violence, animals are often also victims. The perpetrator sees the threat of harming a beloved animal as an avenue to power over those he or she is abusing. Adams refers to this as "the woman-animal abuse connection" but it also includes children. Witnessing this abuse can have a significant impact on them (Williams, Dale, Clarke, & Garrett, 2008). With knowledge of the connections between childhood witnessing and experience of the interrelationships, this could be modified to be the "woman-animal-child-animal" abuse connection. This dynamic has a significant impact on animals, and living in an abusive setting is anthropocentric. For "it is women's close relationships with their animal companions that can shape their reactions to their battering, their pet's abuse and their views of themselves" (Flynn, 2009, p. 116).

But animals are more than peripheral to the violence and more than tools of the power dynamic. Since so many of us view animals as part of the family, Flynn (2009) argues that abuse of animals should be seen as its own form of family violence. Witnessing their humans be abused on top of what might be physical and psychological abuse of to themselves is also stressful to a pet. Women who are abused have reported evidence of stress in their pet's behaviors such as those witnessed among abused humans such as "shivering or shaking, cowering, hiding, and urinating" (p. 118). Adams (1994, p. 65), drawing on Warren (1987, 1990) articulates three configurations "in which sexually violent men harm women, children, and animals":

1. "A threat or actual killing of an animal, usually a pet, as a way of establishing or maintaining control over women and children who are being sexually victimized."
2. "Use of animals in sexually violating women or children, or using the animals to gain some sort of sexual gratification."
3. Research evidence reveals that "Child victims of sexual abuse injure animals." This can be foreshadowed when children injure stuffed animal toys. (p. 68)

As the previous sections have demonstrated, how a child is raised, what experiences he or she has, whether direct, indirect, or symbolic, with media content, and the nature of relational dynamics in the home, have a profound influence on the likelihood of becoming an empathetic individual. What is a useful perspective, with practical tools, for parents, educators, and concerned others to use to help children develop a positive image of themselves and a caring attitude toward others? One possibility is by receiving a humane education.

Value of Humane Education

I want to end this chapter on a positive, hopeful note. Yes, there is a connection between violence against animals and violence against humans. Yes, children learn early to privilege their own species above others, or rather to believe in a hierarchy of species that can result in, at the least, disregard and quite often tremendous suffering of those who come to be viewed as lesser than humans. At the same time, there is much reason for hope and something we can do about the way children are raised. If messages reach them early enough, about the value of being a kind, compassionate person who sees herself in relation with other beings, the world will no doubt be a gentler, more sustainable place.

The concept of a humane education was first introduced in to schools in 1915. Perhaps the best known advocate of a humane education curriculum is Zoe Weil. Weil (2004, p. 6) compiled of list of what she believes constitutes being humane:

- Kindness
- Compassion
- Honesty and trustworthiness
- Generosity
- Courage
- Perseverance, self-discipline, and restraint
- Humor and playfulness
- Wisdom
- Integrity
- A wiliness to choose and change

The word "humane" sounds pretty anthropocentric, containing as it does, the word "human." Yet, its origins are with the concept of civility and care, and in later usage "characterized by sympathy with and consideration for others; feeling or showing compassion towards humans or animals; benevolent, kind ("Humane," 2015). This term is finding traction as an alternative to empathy, particularly when it comes to shared compassions between humans and other animals. Empathy is closely related to the development of sociality and emotional intelligence. Emotional intelligence is defined as "the ability to perceive emotions, to access and generate emotions, as well as to understand and regulate emotions in oneself and others" (Mayer & Salovey, 1997, p. 22).

Inspiring this way of being in young people is one of the goals of a humane education and it can and should be a part of every type of class a student takes and an approach to the world parents can employ. This view incorporates animals as the "fourth educator" discussed earlier in this chapter (Bone, 2013, p. 57). For example, co-investigating with a child where a product comes from, where it is made, who made it, what the ingredients are, where it is disposed of, and the environmental implications of the consumption of the product are one way. Another is to examine how meat, dairy, eggs, leather come to us, who they start out as, and what the implications of that type of economy are. This is a form of cultural and media literacy, that is examined in more detail in the next chapter. Children eventually make their own decisions about whether or not to eat animals (Hussar & Harris, 2009). Their moral-decision making process is certainly influenced by adults and children around them. A study (Herzog, 2011) found that parents often blur moral boundaries around animals as meat, reflecting their own perspectives, upbringing, and value systems. Thus, whether an animal is considered pet/friend, food/clothing, a process of categorization is learned, and then either reinforced or challenged during an individual's lifetime. The "process of obfuscation" (concealing that real animals become food) "begins at the very beginning of life for many babies—with infant formula ('baby milk')" (Cole & Stewart, 2014, p. 76). As discussed in Chapter 2, religious customs and culture play powerful roles in whether animals are viewed as someone humans are in relationship with or superior to (environmental ideology).

In Weil's (2004, pp. 19–20) development of a humane education, she identified four elements that form its foundation:

1. Provide accurate information to students so they understand the consequences of their decisions as citizen consumers.
2. Foster the 3Cs: Curiosity, Creativity, and Critical Thinking through which young people can critically evaluate information in the interest of solving problems.
3. Instill the 3Rs: Reverence, Respect, and Responsibility so that young people will find responding from a place of integrity and kindness natural.
4. Offer positive choices that benefit self, community, other beings, and the planet as a positive response to make a difference in the world.

Together these qualities ultimately lead to a more informed person who won't be overwhelmed by pressing racial, economic, political, and environmental problems facing him or her because they offer a way in to and through to make changes and a difference.

Awareness of the ever increasing disconnect between the real and the re-presented is crucial if we as educators, parents, legislators, teachers, and media makers are to help children become empathetic adults. For example, although the highly popular movie *Chicken Run* was subversive, in which chickens imprisoned at an egg farm were threatened with death for not laying eggs, how was it that

> Burger King offered promotional tie-ins at the time of the film's release, allowing children to take home a toy representation of the characters with why they had been invited to identify, while simultaneously consuming actual animals who had been subjected to the very fate the film's heroes had fought again, which the audience had been encourage to support. (Cole & Stewart, 2014, p. 4)

There is dissonance between screen, toy, and flesh wherein young humans are taught that is normal to think of animals as toys and food.

Rather than use these interactions to emphasize difference, and promote human distinctions, content creators instead might show how similar we are, how kinship matters. As advocated in Myer's (1998/2007) study "we should reconsider our self-image as a species, as a separate 'humanity'" (p. 181).

Note

1. Of course the costs of pet keeping are not insignificant.

References

Adams, C. J. (1994). Bringing peace home: A feminist philosophical perspective on the abuse of women, children, and pet animals. *Hypatia, 9*(2), 63–84.

Anderson, D. R., & Pempek, T. A. (2005). Television and very young children. *American Behavioral Scientist, 48*, 505–522.

Anyaso, H. H. (2010, May 17). Kids understand the relationship between humans and other animals. *Northwestern News*. Retrieved from http://www.northwestern.edu/newscenter/stories/2010/05/waxman2.html

Arluke, A., & Sanders, C. R. (1996). *Regarding animals*. Philadelphia: Temple.

Ascione, F. R. (1992). Enhancing children's attitudes about the humane treatment of animals: Generalization to human-directed empathy. *Anthrozoös, 5*(3), 176–191.

Ascione, F. R., & Weber, C. V. (1996). Children's attitudes about the humane treatment of animals and empathy: One-year follow up of a school-based intervention. *Anthrozoös, 9*(4), 188–195.

Ascione, F. R., Weber, C. V., Thompson, T. M., Heath, J., Maruyama, M., & Hayashi, K. (2007). Experiencing intimate violence and by nonabused women. *Violence Against Women, 13*(4), 354–373.

Bataille, G. (1976/1992). *The accursed share: An essay on general economy*. R. Hurley (trans.). New York: Zone Books.

Beck, A. M., & Katcher, A. H. (2003). Future directions in human-animal bond research. *American Behavioral Scientist, 47*, 79–93.

Beetz, A. M. (2009). Empathy as an indicator of emotional development. In A. Linzey (Ed.), *The link between animal abuse and human violence* (pp. 63–74). Brighton: Sussex Academic Press.

Belsky, J. (1984). The determinants of parenting: A process model. *Child Development, 55*(1), 83–96.

Benoit, D. (2004). Infant-parent attachment: Definition, types, antecedents, measurements, and outcome. *Paediatrics & Child Health, 9*(8), 541–545.

Bone, J. (2013). The animal as fourth educator: A literature review of young children in pedagogical relationships. *Australasian Journal of Early Childhood, 38*(2). Retrieved from http://www.earlychildhoodaustralia.org.au/our-publications/australasian-journal-early-childhood/index-abstracts/ajec-vol-38-2-2013/

animal-fourth-educator-literature-review-animals-young-children-pedagogical-relationships-free-full-text-available/

Bowlby, J. (1953). Transitional objects and transitional phenomena. *International Journal of Psycho-Analysis, 34*, 89–97.

Bowlby, J. (1960). Grief and mourning in infancy and early childhood. *Psychoanalytic Study of the Child, 15*, 19–52.

Bowlby, J. (1969). *Attachment and loss, Vol. 1: Attachment*. London: Pimlico.

Bowlby, J. (1988). *A secure base: Parent-child attachment and healthy human development*. London: Routledge.

Campos, J. J., & Barre, K. C. (1988). Toward a new understanding of emotions and their development. In C. Izard, J. Kagan, & R. B. Zajonc (Eds.), *Emotions, cognition, and behavior* (pp. 229–263). New York, NY: Cambridge University Press.

Cole, M., & Stewart, K. (2014). *Our children and other animals: The cultural construction of human-animal relations in childhood*. New York, NY: Taylor & Francis.

Cooley, M. (2015, March 25). In. B. Wilcox. History of the human-animal relationship is key to nature preservation, Stanford scholar says. https://news.stanford.edu/pr/2015/pr-beasts-and-books-032515.html

Corbett, J. B. (2006). *Communicating nature: How we create and understand environmental messages*. Washington, DC: Island Press.

Dancy, R. B. (2011). *You are your child's first teacher: What parents can do with and for their children from birth to age six*. New York, NY: Potter/TenSpeed/Harmony.

Decety, J. (2011). The neuroevolution of empathy. *Annals of the New York Academy of Science, 1231*, 35–45.

DeSchriver, M. M., & Riddick, C. C. (1990). Effects of watching aquariums on elders' stress. *Anthrozoos, 4*, 44–48.

Dodman, N. (2016). *Pets on the couch*. New York, NY: Simon & Schuster.

Durkheim, E. (1897/1951). *Suicide: A study in sociology* (J. Spaulding & G. Simpson, Trans.). New York, NY: The Free Press.

Eisenberg, N., & Strayer, J. (1990). Introduction. In N. Eisenberg & J. Stayer (Eds.), *Empathy and its development* (pp. 1–14). CUP.

Eliot, G. (1857/2015). *Mr. Gilfil's love story*. New York, NY: Penguin.

Endenburg, N., & van Lilith, H. A. (2011). The influence of animals on the development of children. *The Veterinary Journal, 190*(2), 208–214.

Erikson, E. H. (1950). *Childhood and society*. New York, NY: Norton.

Erikson, E. H. (1959). *Identity and the life cycle*. New York, NY: International Universities Press.

Fawcett, L. (2002). Children's wild animal stories: Questioning inter-species bonds. *Canadian Journal of Environmental Education, 7*(2), 125–139.

Flatow, I. (2013, June 21). E. O. Wilson's advice for future scientists. *National Public Radio*. Retrieved from http://www.npr.org/2013/06/21/194230822/e-o-wilsons-advice-for-future-scientists

Flynn, C. (2009). Why family professionals can no longer ignore violence toward animals. *Family Dialog: A Journal of Theology 48*, 147–57.

Freud, S. (1913/1950). *Totem and taboo* (J. Strachey, Trans.). New York, NY: Norton.
Freud, S. (1930). *Civilization and its discontents*. New York, NY: Dover.
Friedmann, E. (1995). The role of pets in enhancing human well-being: Physiological effects. In: I. Robinson (Ed.), *The Waltham book of human-animal interaction: Benefits and responsibilities of pet Ownership* (pp. 33–53). Pergamon Press, Oxford, UK.
Friedman, E., Katcher, A. H., Lynch, J. J., & Messent, P. R. (1983). Social interaction and blood pressure: Influence of animal companions. *Journal of Nervous and Mental Disease, 171*(8), 461–465.
Gandini, L. (1998). Educational and caring spaces. In In C. Edwards, L. Gandini, & G. Forman (Eds.). *Hundred languages of children: The Reggio Emilia approach* (2nd ed., pp. 161–178). Westport, CT: Ablex.
Friesen, L. (2010). Exploring animal-assisted programmes with children in school and therapeutic contexts. *Early Childhood Education, 37*, 261–267.
Gardner, H. (1998). Foreword: Complementary perspectives on Reggio Emilia. In C. Edwards, L. Gandini, & G. Forman (Eds.). *Hundred languages of children: The Reggio Emilia approach* (2nd ed., pp. xv–xviii). Westport, CT: Ablex.
Harlow, H. F., & Zimmermann, R. R. (1995). Affectional responses in the infant monkey. *Science, 130*, 421–431.
Headey, B. (1999). Health benefits and health cost savings due to pets: Preliminary estimates from an Australian national survey. *Social Indicators Research, 47*, 233–243.
Herrmann, P., Waxman, S. R., & Medin, D. L. (2010). Anthropocentrism is not the first step in children's reasoning about the natural world. *PNAS* 9979–9984.
Herzog, H. (2011). *Some we love, some we hate, some we eat*. New York, NY: Harper Perennial.
"humane, adj." *OED Online*. Oxford University Press, December 2015. Retrieved February 10, 2016.
Hussar, K. M., & Harris, P. L. (2009). Children who choose not to eat meat: A study of early moral decision-making. *Social Development, 19*(3), 627–641.
Inagaki, K. (1990). The effects of raising animals on children's biological knowledge. *British Journal of Developmental Psychology, 8*, 119–129.
James, A., Jenks, C., & Prout, A. (1998). *Theorizing childhood*. Cambridge: Polity.
Kahn, P. H. (1997). Developmental psychology and the biophilia hypothesis: Children's affiliations with nature. *Developmental Review, 17*, 1–61.
Kahn, P. H., & Keller, S. R. (2002). *Children and nature: Psychological, sociocultural, and evolutionary investigations*. Boston, MA: MIT Press.
Kellert, S. R. (1996). *The value of life*. Washington, DC: Island Press.
Kellert, S. R., & Westervelt, M. O. (1983). Historical trends in American animal use and perception. *International Journal for the Study of Animal Problems, 4*(8), 133–146.
Ko, H. J., Youn, C. H., Kim, S. H., & Kim, S. Y. (2016). Effect of pet insects on psychological health of community-dwelling elderly people: A single-blinded, randomized, controlled trial. *Gerontology, 62*(2), 200–209.
Kohlberg, L. (1958). *The development of modes and choices in years 10 to 16* (PhD dissertation). University of Chicago.

Langford, D. J., Crager, S. E., Shehzad, Z., Smith, S. B., Sotocinal, S. G., Levenstadt, J. S., ... Mogil, J. S. (2006). Social modulation of pain as evidence for empathy in mice. *Science, 312,* 1967–1970.

Langford, D. J., Tuttleb, A. H., Brown, K., Deschenes, S., Fischer, D. B., Mutso, A., & Sternberg, W. F. (2010). Social approach to pain in laboratory mice. *Society for Neuroscience, 5,* 163–170.

Linzey, A. (2009). *The link between animal abuse and human violence.* Sussex: Sussex Academic Press.

MacKinnon, C. A. (2004). Of mice and men: A feminist fragment on animal rights. In C. R. Sunstein & M. C. Nussbaum (Eds.), *Animal rights.* New York, NY: Oxford.

Malaguzzi, L. (1984). Personal communication. In L. Gandini (1998). Educational and caring spaces. In C. P. Edwards, L. Gandini, & G. E. Forman (Eds.), *The hundred languages of children* (2nd ed., pp. 161–178). London: Ablex.

Marino, L., Reiss, D., & Gallup, G. G. (2009). Mirror self-recognition in bottlenose dolphins: Implications for comparative investigations of highly dissimilar species. In S. T. Parker, R. W. Mitchell, & M. L. Boccaia (Eds.), *Self-awareness in animals and humans* (pp. 380–391). New York, NY: Cambridge.

Mayer, J. D., & Salovey, P. (1997). What is emotional intelligence? In P. Salovey & D. J. Sluyter (Eds.), *Emotional development and emotional intelligence: Educational implications* (pp. 3–34). New York: Basic.

Mayo Clinic. (2016). *Screen time and children: How to guide your child.* Retrieved from http://www.mayoclinic.org/healthy-lifestyle/childrens-health/in-depth/screen-time/art-20047952

Melson, G. (2001). *Why the wild things are: Animals in the lives of children.* Cambridge, MA: Harvard University Press.

Milstein, T. (2009). 'Somethin' tells me it's all happening at the zoo': Discourse, power, and conservationism. *Environmental Communication, 3*(1), 24–48.

Morrow, V. (1998). My animals and other family: Children's perspective on their relationships with companion animals. *Anthrozoos, 11*(4), 218–226.

Murray, H. A. (1943). *Thematic apperception test.* Boston, MA: Harvard.

Myers, O. G. (1998/2007). *The significance of children and animals: Social development and our connections to other species.* West Lafayette, IN: Purdue University Press.

Oaklander, M. (2017, April 5). Science says your pet is good for your mental health. *Time.* Retrieved from http://time.com/4728315/science-says-pet-good-for-mental-health/

O'Haire, M. (2010). Companion animals and human health: Benefits, challenges, and the road ahead. *Journal of Veterinary Behavior, 5,* 226–234.

Piaget, J. (1932). *The moral judgment of the child.* London: Kegan Paul, Trench, Trubner, & Co.

Piaget, J. (1960). *The Psychology of Intelligence.* Totowa, NJ: Littlefield Adams & Co.

Ressler, R. K., Brugess, A. W., Hartman, C. R., Douglas, J. E., & McCormack, A. (1986). Murderers who rape and mutilate. *Journal of Interpersonal Violence, 1*(3), 273–287.

Rolls, E. T. (2005). *Emotion explained.* New York, NY: Oxford University Press.

Rosengren, K. S., Gelman, S. A., Kalish, C. W., & McCormick, M. (1991). As time goes by: Children's early understanding of growth in animals. *Child Development, 62,* 1302–1320.

Searles, H. (1960). *The nonhuman environment: In normal development and schizophrenia.* New York, NY: International Universities Press.

Selly, P. B. (2014). *Connecting animals and children in early childhood.* St. Paul, MN: Redleaf Press.

Snyder, G. (1990). *The practice of the wild.* San Francisco, CA: North Point Press.

Sullivan, R., Perry, R., Sloan, A., Kleinhaus, K., & Burtchen, N. (2011). Infant bonding and attachment to the caregiver: Insights from basic and clinical science. *Clinical Perinatology, 38*(4), 643–655.

Swartz, K. B., & Evans, S. (1994). Social and cognitive factors in chimpanzee and gorilla mirror behavior and self-recognition. In S. T. Parker, R. W. Mitchell, & M. L. Boccaia (Eds.), *Self-awareness in animals and humans* (pp. 189–206). New York, NY: Cambridge.

Taylor, F. (2003). Content analysis and gender stereotypes. *Teaching Sociology, 31*(3), 300–311.

Tipper, B. (2011). "A dog who I know quite well": Everyday relationships between children and animals. *Children's Geographies, 9*(2), 145–165.

Ulrich, R. S. (1993). Biophilia, biophilia, and natural landscapes. In S. R. Kellert & E. O. Wilson (Eds.), *The Biophilia hypothesis.* Washington, DC: Island Press.

von Heydebrand, C. (1946). *Childhood: A study of the growing soul.* London: Anthroposophic Publishing Company.

Warren, K. J. (1987). Feminism and ecology: Making connections. *Environmental Ethics, 9*(1), 3–20.

Warren, K. J. (1990). The power and the promise of ecological feminism. *Environmental Ethics, 12*(3), 125–146.

Waxman, S. R., Herrmann, P., Woodring, J., & Medin, D. L. (2014). Humans (really) are animals: Picture-book reading influences 5-year-old urban children's construal of the relation between humans and non-human animals. *Frontiers in Psychology, 5,* 172.

Weil, Z. (2004). *The power and promise of humane education.* Gabriola Island, BC: New Society.

Williams, V.M, Dale, A. R., Clarke, N., & Garrett, N. K. (2008). Animal ab7use and family violence: Survey on the recognition of animal abuse by veterinarians in New Zealand and their understanding of the correlation between animal abuse and human violence. *New Zealand Veterinary Journal, 56*(1), 21–28.

Wilson, C. C. (1991). The pet as an anxiolytic intervention. *Journal of Nervous and Mental Disorders, 179,* 482–489.

Wilson, E. O. (1984). *Biophilia.* Cambridge, MA: Harvard University Press.

Wilson, E. O. (1993). Biophilia and the conservation ethic. In D. J. Penn & I. Mysterud (Eds.), *Evolutionary perspectives on environmental problems* (pp. 249–258). Washington, DC: Island Press.

Chapter Four

Re-presenting[1] Animals in Popular Culture

I think we love animals as images because we miss them in the flesh, and I think we love them as images because they matter to us spiritually in we ways we cannot hope to articulate.

—Doyle (2014)

Film has changed both how we see animals and how we think them.

—Brower (2003)

Film and television are some of the best tools society possesses to protect the environment and encourage conservation.

—Palmer (2015, p. xiii)

Geiko uses a Gecko to sell insurance. Coca-Cola? Polar bears. Lazy-Boy advertisements feature raccoons checking out recliners. Families of yellow labs "drive" Subarus and deal with the same family challenges and relationship issues as humans do. What Eddie Bauer or Lands' End catalog would be complete without golden retrievers in front of the fireplace? But dogs don't wear sweaters or buy adventure gear. These critterly casts of characters populate contemporary advertising for products that have nothing to do with animals. In an Orangina commercial a scantily clad animated doe/woman hybrid dances suggestively with a bear (who wears a fig leaf). In an advertisement for Yves Saint Laurent's Opium fragrance, Emily Blunt slinks through an opulent apartment. She enters a room in which a lounging leopard rises—they meet, eye to eye (see Chapter 8 for more on this). Chimpanzees are so common in commercials that people think they are less endangered than they really are (Schroepfer, Rosati, Chartrand, & Hare, 2011). And it's not just advertising that uses animals to say something about us, to sell products and services.

Television programs feature animals, particularly dogs, in programs such as the Jack Russell terrier who played Eddy in the comedy *Fraser*. Animals fill out a setting, provide comedic relief, and contribute a cuteness quotient that simply makes viewers feel good. In other words, animals complete the scene. Furthermore, animate and live animals who speak in human voices, wear clothing, and otherwise act like us, create the casts of movies. Disney films such as *101 Dalmatians* triggered the production and adoptions of hundreds of puppies who were later abandoned because they didn't behave the same ways as their on-screen peers. Other media effects include demand (and resultant over breeding of) collies after the *Lassie* movies and TV shows became popular, Old English Sheepdogs after the release of *The Shaggy Dog* (Ghirlanda, Acerbi, & Herzog, 2014), Chihuahuas by the hundreds pursuant to the popularity of the Taco Bell dog, media coverage of Paris Hilton's $8,000 accessory dog Miss London, and films such as *Beverly Hills Chihuahua* (Lewis, 2009). The fantastical dire wolves featured in HBO's megahit "Game of Thrones," resulted in fans buying and later abandoning huskies (Rozsa, 2017). Many of the dogs are purposefully bred in response to consumer demand and find long term loving homes, but thousands of others are bred in puppy mills, adopted, and abandoned once the fad fades and people are left with a being who requires many years of care. "Animal Shelters Brace for Unwanted Effects of New Ninja Turtles Movie," was the headline when ill-informed viewers rushed to adopt pet turtles and tortoises (Smith, 2014). The result is lack of knowledge about how to properly care for the animals who can live more than 50 years. This is a media effect that's rarely spoken of or written about. Nevertheless, there is no doubt that animals

> have ... provided us with more abstract riches; they are the seeds of inspiration, the terms of comparison or differentiation, the symbols in which we attempt to capture our aspirations and fears and which help us to construct meaning from the harsh and unfathomable worlds around us. (Miles & Ibrahim, 2013, p. 1862)

Yet, the fact that they are simultaneously visible and invisible is curious. Sociologist Erving Goffman (1979) asked of advertisements in which women are typically represented in subordinated, child-like positions, "Why do most ads not look strange to us?" Logically they should. Just as having human beings doing all kinds of odd behaviors should strike us as unusual, they often don't, perhaps because we pay very little direct attention to these cultural texts. Similarly, the use of animals in ads, as accessories in television programs and movies, as talking, singing, and clothed characters in films should also cause us to pause and question what we are seeing. This is particularly so if only to wonder what this disconnect, knowing animals only symbolically, might be doing in terms of our compassion, understanding, and connections with real beings.

This chapter is an overview of re-presentations of animals in media and popular culture. It examines the history of human beings and animals in terms of when, where, and why we first began and continue to re-present them. We may re-present them so often because something deep was once shared between us, something we miss. After a journey in to the history of our re-presenting them, the chapter continues with an exploration of methods scholars use to interpret images and words.

The Earliest Animals

For as long as humans have been representing anyone or anything we've re-presented animals (Berger, 1980). Our relationship with them has been intimate. Whether thought of as food, as threats, as co-inhabitants of the forest, jungle, savanna, or plains, or as companions, animals have and do play a prominent role in our lives. The earliest re-presentations of animals are tens of thousands of years old. In Europe, for example the earliest cave paintings (parietal art), such as those in the El Castillo cave in Cantabria, Spain, are at least 40,000 years old, which coincides with rise of homo sapiens and are remarkably sophisticated. The images are believed to be of deer, bison, dogs, and mammoths. There are, for example, over 300 caves in Spain and France that contain re-presentations of animals. The images in France's Chauvet Caves are roughly 35,000 years old. The Arnhem Land Plateau in Australia contains similarly ancient drawings. In the ancient period of 38,000 to 21,000 BCE, "sculpted figurines of humans and animals made of mammoth ivory are well known from many sites right across Europe, as far as Siberia" (Cook, 2014, p. 14). The major cold period known as "the Last Glacial Maximum" marks a sharp decline in both the number and style of representations of animals on tools, in caves, and on weapons and tools (until about 15,000 years ago). The famous Swimming Deer is an example of art from that period.

In the American West, images pecked or painted on rocks are collectively known as rock art and date back at least 8,000 years.

One of the most re-presented animals in Southwestern rock art in the United States are big horn sheep (Marston, 2005; van Hoek, 2015) (see Figures 4.1a & b).

Shown alone, in pairs, and in groups there's no doubt that whether they were made for spiritual or practical purposes, they were important to indigenous people living in ancient times. What art means to the creator or the viewer is highly subjective. This is particularly the case when we look back in time to images created in places and under circumstances foreign to the interpreter. This is particularly the case with prehistoric expressions.

Petroglyphs are simply "picture[s] carved in to rocks" and "the name comes from the Greek words *Petros* (stone) and *Glypho* (I carve)" (Hill, 2015, p. 5). They are found on bones, stones, antlers, pottery, cave walls, and rock outcroppings. Discovered virtually everywhere in the world, petroglyphs are clearly forms of communication. In cave

Figure 4.1a: Petroglyph on Basalt 1. Lake County, Oregon.
Source: Photograph used by permission Douglas Beauchamp.

Figure 4.1b: Petroglyph on Basalt 2. Lake County, Oregon.
Source: Photograph used by permission Douglas Beauchamp.

art, the term geoglyph refers to "sunken features produced by removing areas of material the artisan is working with; *petroglyphs*," are "any carving, scratching or pecking," while *pictographs* are paintings (p. 13).

Sometimes images were carved or painted of an animal on parts of deceased animals, also known as "portable art" (Hays-Gilpin, 2004, p. 57) or mobiliary art. For example, a mammoth engraved on a mammoth tusk, a reindeer on antlers, or small portable objects. In other cases, images were either pecked or chipped in to rock surfaces (petroglyphs) or painted on to rocks using pigments (pictographs). Both of these portrayals fall in to the category of rock art. These re-presentations of animals, plants, and humans are a special category of imaging the world. Yet, it is a world not entirely apart from that of today. In fact, researchers have identified definite gendering of rock art re-presentations of both humans and animals (Hays-Gilpin, 2004).

In the Pacific Northwest, for example, some believe petroglyphs were associated with the annual return of Salmon (Hill, 2015, p. 26). Tlingit legends tell a story of another animal, the Raven, who sometimes took human and other times took bird form. Interpretations vary as to what these images mean, and any "meanings" are speculative as those who originally created the art are long gone. Furthermore, most scholars who interpret meanings are outside the living cultures who made the art. The words "possibly ... probably. ... Perhaps ... frequently occur when we talk about the meaning of the petroglyphs" (Davidson, 2017). Some of the theories range from a kind of doodling, storytelling, purely artistic efforts, conveyance of information about nearby hunting and fishing, directions, territory markers, or possibly religious and spiritual insignia. However, we do know that most of the re-presentations are related to the world in which early people lived which included a close connection with animals.

For many indigenous people, past and present, animals and humans are constantly and eternally in relationship in the world (see Chapter 1). One is not superior to the other. Animals have needs and humans have needs and the best world is one in which both are met and the balance is kept. These amazing reproductions are not just some primitive peckings, but sophisticated re-presentations with a point of view. Unlike our present era where the view is anthropocentric, situating humans as superior to all other beings, earlier humans "in all probability, identif[ied] with other animals, perceiv[ed] their kinship with them, and develop[ed] a belief system around them" (Smith, 1992, p. 128).

Shamanism, one possible explanation for the purpose of these images, is grounded in belief "that all things in the world are alive and whatever happens in the world is due to the behavior of life forces" (Smith, 1992, p. 34). According to this perspective, some individuals are endowed with special abilities in this regard, a gift, a blessing, and become guardians and seers. They serve as conduits between the known and invisible worlds, often taking animal forms or have animal helpers, particularly in the forms of wolves, crows/ravens, birds, and bears.

It is not uncommon for modern people to think of the ancients as intellectually simple and physically rough and uncoordinated (modern advertising does nothing to challenge this view). However, in a study of 1,000 quadruped walking illustrations obtained on the Internet, in books of fine art, photographs of reliefs and sculptures, scholars found that prehistoric re-presentations of animals are in fact more accurate than many found after that time (Hovarth, Farkas, Boncz, Blaho, & Kriska, 2012). While the photographer Eduard Muybridge provided the first photographic evidence of animal locomotion, it appears early people also observed their movements. In fact, representing them more accurately than later images:

> When the researchers looked at 272 paintings and statues of four-legged animals made during modern times but before Muybridge's findings in the 1880s, such as a famous horse sketch by Leonardo da Vinci, it turned out that these more recent artists were much worse: They only got the sequence right 16.5% of the time. Remarkably, even the 686 paintings and statues studied that were made more recently than 1887, after scientists knew for sure how four-legged animals walked, still got it right just 42.1% of the time. ... of 307 renditions analyzed, just 58.9% of depictions in natural history museums were correct, along with 56.9% of those in taxidermy catalogues, 50% of animal toy models and 36.4% of illustrations in animal anatomy textbooks. (Stromberg, 2012)

For early peoples, observations of animals were not merely a pastime, but a matter of survival. Therefore, we can suppose that, compared to artists of later eras, early peoples were more directly connected to nature. The creators of cave paintings and carvings were likely to have observed their subjects closely and thus depicted the walk of the animals, for example, in a more life-like manner. An example is one of the most frequently represented animals in north Mexican rock art—deer (Murray, 2014). The images of them are so specific, including characteristic poses that there is "often ... sufficien[t] naturalistic detail to permit species identification" (p. 197). Most are of the full bodies but sometimes they are simply hoof prints or antlers but with enough variation that it is easy to identify whether it is a white tail or a mule deer.

Rock art scholar Noel W. Smith (1992) notes, initially we can regard these markings as "merely representations of animal life that the hunters lived with and as indications of their sophisticated artistic achievements" (p. xi). But they are more complex than that, there is something deeply psychological in whatever they might mean that is fundamental to human psychology. But "the human-animal theme appears so prominent in such a variety of ways that it almost shouts from the caves" (p. 125), particularly, as he argues, with shamanism, but for whatever reason there is no doubt these marks and drawings were made by people who were closely connected with other species and in a lived, every day, manner.

An important related topic is the *meaning* to which people give objects and images. That those of us living many thousands of years after these images were created can, in any way, translate what individuals of a different culture, time, and place. And, "something which is true of 99% of modern humans is not necessarily true of prehistoric people" (Bahn, in Smith, 1992, p. ix). Yet we strive to understand them. The psychological process of embedding meaning is one early anthropologists and psychologists attributed to the concept of totem.

The word "totem" originates in from the North American Algonkian Ojibwa word *Ototeman*, meaning *"his brother-sister kin"* (Tiwari, 2002, p. 21; ital. orig.). In his conversation of the origins and sources of totem names, Lang (1912/2017, p. 373) states totemism is "an intimate relationship which is said to exist between a group of kindred people on one side and a species of natural or artificial objects on the other side, which objects are called the totems of the human group." There is a deep relationship (real or imagined) between human beings and their totem figure(s). These "objects" might in fact be living beings when they are in animal form. A totem is not meant to refer to the actual animal associated with it, but rather renders the essence of the being into a, "the symbol, device, or work of art, representing the animal" (Lang, 1912/2017, in Hubbard, p. 96). Thus the totem or crest animal is ancestor, protector, oracle, and kin.

According to Freud (1918/1998, p. 3) a totem is "an animal, either edible and harmless, or dangerous and feared; more rarely the totem is a plant or force of nature (rain, water), which stands in a peculiar relation to the whole clan" (p. 3) of which there are three kinds: (1) clan (usually an animal viewed as a common ancestor and guardian spirit thus not to be harmed), (2) sex (men and women each had their own), and (3) individual (not passed on to offspring). While Frazer (1910/2011), Freud (1918/1998), Durkheim (1912/1961) and others wrote of totems and indigenous people in a rather patronizing voice, referring to them as uncivilized and savages, this languaging is more of a reflection of the times than any overt racism. Their ideas about the deep connection between a people and what they value nevertheless comes through limitations of the era. For example, Durkheim recognized the deep moral and cognitive nature beliefs and symbols play in a society and how systems of knowing and perceived truths flow from them. As such, the totem is a visible marker of the belief or idea which, when emblazoned on objects such as rocks, walls, trees, utensils, or other forms of representation this totem "becomes part of them, and this world of representations is even by far the more important" (Durkheim, 1912/1961, p. 137). This emblamematism (*'emlématisme'*) is central to the life of a culture. He noted the difference between the real being and its representation as also important:

> Of course they do not come from the specific thing to which we connect them, but nevertheless, it is true that their origin is outside us. If the moral force sustaining the believer does not come from the idol he adores or the emblem he venerates, still it is from outside of him as he is well aware. The objectivity of its symbol only translates its eternalness. (1912/1961, p. 264)

Animals in Art

While a complete history of the re-presentation of animals in art (broadly defined to include jewelry, ceramics, sculpture, as well as painting) is beyond the scope of this book, a brief discussion is warranted. Whether as portraiture or imitation of real or imagined animals, everyone from puppies to monkeys (Frida Kahlo, *Self Portrait with Monkey*, 1938) populate art over the ages.

Early art, such as that of ancient Greece, Rome, and Egypt show animals used to represent deities, as companions for the elite. Pottery, tombs, jewelry, and interiors were decorated with images of animals. The goddess Baste was show in cat form in ancient Egypt and guarded the gateway to the underworld. The jackal god Anubis is considered the patron of lost souls, oversees the mummification process, and is a guide for the dead.

Animal re-presentations in art become less prevalent throughout the world until the 19th century when their real life presence in the home began to change. From animals who lived primarily outside, doing work herding, pulling plows, giving rides, or functioning more as tools than as loved ones, animals began to come inside in Europe and the North America as each became increasingly industrialized. This change was reflected in art as it became increasingly common to show how animals and people interacted in their everyday lives, particularly in leisure. Examples include Edouard Manet's *The Races at Longchamp* (1864) and *Woman with Parrot* (1866). Dogs were particularly important features in art, either as purely decorative additions indicate the wealth and leisure of the artworks' subjects. They were also used to invoke empathy for animals as well as humans, as in Edward Landseer's famous calendar dog. This painting: *A Distinguished Member of the Humane Society* (1838) is said to have been of a rescued dog "Bob," found off the coast of Newfoundland, who was reputed to have saved 23 humans from drowning. The image was used by the British Union for the Abolition of Vivisection (today known as Cruelty Free International) to suggest how selfless animals are compared with human beings.

How is it then that a real animal, or the idea of a real animal, gets rendered in to symbolic form? What function might this serve for human beings and other animals?

Figure 4.2: A Distinguished Member of the Humane Society.
Oil on canvas. Source: Used by permission, Tate.

Reading the Re-presented

In *Picturing the Beast*, Baker (1993/2001) asks two questions that reflect central queries of Animal Media Studies (AMS):

1. Why should it be that the animal, frequently conceived as the archetypal cultural 'other' plays such a potent and vital role in the symbolic construction of human identity in such a variety of contemporary instances? [why the go-to resource for saying things about ourselves?]
2. What is the relation of these kinds of cultural representations to the circumstances of actual living animals in the same culture, and what can the animal rights movement learn from this evidence?

To begin answering these questions, let's consider what has been discussed so far: our very first symbols, re-presentations, were of nonhuman animals (Berger, 1980). What might have started out as more relational, about the animal in the world, re-presented in caves, rock art, petroglyphs or other forms, became at some point almost, if not entirely, about us. Picturing other animals served, in some ways that persist today, to honor them, but does this imaging bring us closer to or push us further apart from real animals? If the only way we know another is by the way media re-presents him or her, what do we believe to be truth?

Whether as national symbols, sports team names, mascots, and logos, or as trade characters for products, nonhuman animals become necessary and needed only as long as their metaphorical value as stands-ins-for us remains. In a study of natural history books read by children, for example, the most important thing they learn is "about the proper structure of human society" (Ritvo, 1985, p. 80). As such, "the turn to animals, in art as in theory, is an attempt to envision a different understanding of what we humans are and consequently to enlarge or change the possibilities for what we can think and what we can do in the world" (Weil, 2013, p. 10). But what about them?

As discussed later, nonhuman animals are used in children's books (Ritvo, 1985; Williams et al., 2010), in comic strips (Rifas, 2010), on greeting cards (Brabant & Mooney, 1989; Henry, 1947), in advertisements (Freeman & Merskin, 2008; Lerner & Kalof, 1999; Magdoff & Barnett, 1989; Spears, 1996), and in news stories (Freeman, 2014). They are there to say something about us, not about them. Particularly in visual re-presentations they do metaphorical work relaying or revealing our motivations and/or emotions. An example is a greeting card with the image of cute puppy or kitten on the front and the words "I'm sorry." This picture, with inevitably large eyes, ears, and compelling qualities (neoteny), functions to soften the words that follow. Anthropomorphism, attributing human thoughts, feelings, behaviors to other beings, can be helpful or problematic, depending on how and how much. At one extreme, avoiding anthropomorphism results in seeing animals purely as objects, "as lacking emotions, intelligence, and interests" (McKenna, 2013, p. 9). But too much, "results in humans ignoring the needs, interests, and intelligences of animals" in their own rights, leading to treatment as "a kind of defective human," or at least as child-like, "doted on but dependent" (p. 9), and "as people in disguise" (p. 14). But without that felt sense of similarities, we would be unable to successfully interact with animal others, and we do have a lot in common!

"The mind," state Lakoff and Johnson (1999), "is inherently embodied. Thought is mostly unconscious. Abstract concepts are largely metaphorical." Reason has been the determinative criteria, as discussed in earlier chapters, for determining, for example, who is an animal, who deserves consideration, who matters. Reason "includes not only our capacity for logical inference, but also our ability to conduct inquiry, to solve problems, to evaluate, to criticize, to deliberate about how we should act, and to reach an understanding of ourselves, other people, and the world" (pp. 3–4). Today we know these qualities not to be solely human. Language, another determinant of difference, we now know, comes from fundamental basic neural systems present in other animals.

In *The Order of Things*, French philosopher Michele Foucault (1966/2005) uses the term "heterotopia" to refer to a place where multiple meanings and identities exist (p. xix). Heterotopia builds on, but exceeds the concept of utopia as an ideal space, and instead heterotopia is confrontation with the exteriorization of idealizations with the sameness of the familiar. On the one hand, this type of re-presentation illuminates the sameness of animals and human animals. On the other, as human creations, they keep the real animal in a tightly knit tapestry of Otherness, as apart from or only valuable in those attributes that can be seen as being "like us." Otherwise incongruent, unrelated, or even contradictory items or beings might, in the space of a re-presentation, are shown together. Taken together the ensemble comes to seem unremarkable, at least on the surface. Yet there is, upon analysis, something disturbing about the juxtapositions. Referencing Magritte (qtd. in Foucault, 1983, p. 38) once again, Foucault wrote

> Between words and objects one can create new relations and specify characteristics of language and objects generally ignored in everyday life ... Sometimes the name of an object takes the place of an image. A word can take the place of an object in reality. An image can take the place of a word in a proposition.

As such, the word "Cat" (or gato or chat) is not the real animal. The word C-A-T references feline-ness, which is not the same as the actual animal. In fact, the attachment is arbitrary, any word might do. But in its accepted use it evokes an idea that differentiates the small four-footed being from dog, bear, horse, or wasp. This type of analysis is not meant to unnecessarily complicate the everyday. Rather, the intent is to reveal the taken-for-grantedness of language and images. Animals have been linguistically degraded and are discursively inscribed. For example, pigs, figure in expressions such as

> Porker, hogwash, male chauvinist pig, gas hog, road hog, living high on the hog, happy as a pig in muck, going hog wild, piggish, and crying like a stuck pig. There are fascist pigs and Nazi pigs; prostitutes and policemen are called pigs. (Lawrence, 1993, p. 325)

There are dozens more, and not only for pigs. Other generalized expressions include "'Don't touch me, you animal!' 'He's a wolf,' 'stop pawing me,' 'Hello, my little chickadee'" (Lakoff, 1987, pp. 409–411). Furthermore, in language, humans are the only species with "being" added after the name. A nonhuman animal is an "it" rather than a "he" or "she." To test this as an exercise in the hegemony of species, try writing about animals in Microsoft Word. Spell check will try to force you to negate the gender and deindividualize the animal should you use the personal pronoun "he" or "she." Another example is calling meat "beef" not "cow"; "pork" not "pig." Animals are also identified according to function, i.e. farm (versus farmed), or, in scientific research, data points, rather than individuals (Durham & Merskin, 2009). Some animals fulfill more than a single function and there is thinking and language to support these different ways of being. Take the Rabbit, for example. There is the house bunny, the Energizer bunny, the Easter bunny, laboratory experiment, dinner jacket, Bugs Bunny, *Hop the Bunny* children's book, and rabbit flesh served for dinner.

Because nonhuman animals in media are largely compliant, obedient, trust us, often we find discursive practices such as re-presentation "ideologically invested in so far as they incorporate significations which contribute to sustaining or restructuring power relations" (Fairclough, 2002, p. 91). This projection has parallels in, for example, the concept of slavery as a positive good—that white slaveholders rationalized the keeping of other humans believed that slaves were incapable of surviving without them and, in fact, enjoyed and appreciated their "masters." Milstein (2012) notes this same dynamic in zookeeper's discursive reframing pertaining to zoo'd gorillas: "Why would they want to leave? We're nice to them, give them a nice space, feed them, etc." (p. 178).

Language is similarly saturated with zoological references/idioms. In English, for example we can be "busy as a beaver," "sly as a fox," "wise as an owl," and "slippery as an eel." Reveal a secret? You've "let the cat out of the bag" (see Table 4.1).

Women are referred to as foxes, chicks, cougars, and kittens and references to female genitalia are among the worst insults men can hurl at one another. A sexually aggressive man? An animal, a stud, a buck. Animal metaphors are used to construct enemies, for example as was used by President George W. Bush after 9–11 (Merskin, 2004), as anti-immigrant discourse (Santa Ana, 1999), and when "European colonists dehumanized Native Americans or Nazis dehumanized Jews, what remained? In their eyes, what was left was a creature that seemed human-had a human-looking form, walked on two legs, spoke human language, and acted in more-or-less human ways—but which was nonetheless not human" (Smith, 2011, p. 4). "Because some humans assign other humans the status of 'animals' it needs to be noted that being human is, in itself, a subjective status either self-appointed or granted by others favorably inclined toward their object of designation, while alienating other" (Mavhunga, 2011, p. 17). Thus, who is vermin, a pest, an animal, a beast, is in the eye and heart of the beholder.

Kafka's (1917/2015) short story "A Report to an Academy" is often explained as a parallel allegory of German Jews in Prague. It is the story of an ape who has "become" human by learning to speak human, he understands he is different from his human captors, but by gaining the ability to speak he also loses knowledge of his own culture. "It illustrates the significance of a fundamental problematic of 'the animal question': how does one have access to 'the animal'—whether the animal who has been 'civilized' to exist in human society or the animals with whom we share the world?" (Weil, 2013, p. 4). Another example is the book *Ishmael*, by Daniel Quinn (1992). This work of fiction uses

Table 4.1. Zoological References in Language.

A bird in the hand is worth two in the bush	Monkey see, monkey do
Alley cat	Nest egg
All bark and no bite	Open a can of worms
Ants in one's pants	Pet peeve
At a snail's pace	Pick of the litter
Awkward as a cow on rollerskates	Pig out
Birds and the bees	Poor as a church mouse
Black sheep (of the family)	Puppy love
Blind as a bat	Raining cats and dogs
Bull in a china shop	Rat race
Butterflies in one's stomach	Scared as a rabbit
Cash cow	Sick as a dog
Cat nap	Sly as a fox
Cat got your tongue?	Smell a rat
Chicken out	Straight from the horse's mouth
Clam up	Strong as a horse/ox
Copy cat	Swimming with sharks
Dog days	Until the cows come home
Dropping like flies	Watch like a hawk
Ducks in a row (get your)	Weak as a kitten
Eagle eyed	Which came first, the chicken or the egg?
Eager beaver	Wild as a tiger
Fishy	Wild goose chase
Gentle as a lamb	(the) world is your oyster
Get the lion's share	Wolf in sheep's clothing
Guinea pig	You can't teach an old dog new tricks
Have a cow	
Hold your horses	
Holy cow!	
Horse around	
I'll be a monkey's uncle!	
In the dog house	
Kill two birds with one stone	
Kitty corner	
Let sleeping dogs lie	
Like shooting fish in a barrel	
(A) little bird told me	
Mad as a hornet	
Make a beeline	

a gorilla as primary teacher about how the planet has become one of Takers and Leavers, the Takers being human beings who believe they are the top of the developmental hierarchy, have completed all evolutionary processes, and that all other beings exist to serve them (i.e. the industrialized West). Leavers include indigenous people, animals, and those with closer connections to the planet who have found sustainable, ethical ways of relating to one another.

Baker's (1993/2001) second question, about the impact of re-presentations on real animal's lives, will be answered in a variety of ways in the remaining chapters of this book. However, that nonhuman animals communicate, particularly with each other, is no longer debated. That they in fact experience psychological as well as physical trauma when transported, experimented upon, and confined is also well documented (Ferdowsian & Merskin, 2012). Whereas trauma and disability studies work to give testimony to those who might be physically or psychologically unable to speak, or find the words to describe their experiences, we can draw upon this knowledge to understand why a re-presentation could be similarly problematic, re-traumatizing, for animals. Dog-shaming videos, for example, make a point of using the animals as objects of ridicule, humiliation, and bullying that seem, at first glance, harmless, yet reveal deep-seated objectification on our part (Merskin, 2014) and, at the same time, connect us to how these communication tools function and affect real animals.

Vital to understanding of media is identifying the power of images and words to either reveal or conceal. Thus ideologies that support hegemonic order support everyday groupthink. The "logic" of the ideas is one that sustains the economic, political, and social structure of things as they have always been and are presumed to always be. Thus, those who hold power will advocate a worldview that supports the status quo. Not mere mental events or spectacles, representations become ways of seeing the world. Nonhuman animals have long been used as assists in this process. For example, national animal symbols wield power and have long been used to generate sense of community, national identity, to reinforce political actions and positions, deeply entrenched in culture. It is a direct representation of us in them. Kalof and Amthor (2010, p. 165) point out the multilayered meanings of animals are tethered to the historically-specific norms and values of the society in which they occur, and it is widely acknowledged that the shaping of the social world is accomplished in large part by cultural representations-those depictions, illustrations, likenesses, icons, and pictures that are produced by a culture.

The intention is not to say anything in particular about a species, but rather use common understandings of them; even stereotypical re-presentations, to stand in for something about us. For example, the eagle in the United States and the bulldog in Great Britain are symbols of a national self. Comic strips often present animals as the source of stress or as destroyers of property (Carmack, 1997). Wild animals on British television were often portrayed as "bad" (Paul, 1996). In another study they were the "bad guys," villains, and threats (Church, 1996). In commercials they are often presented as problems, creating problems for humans such as allergies, or disrupting human activities or events (Lerner & Kalof, 1999).

This process not only usurps the real animal but renders him or her invisible. "What is betrayed in the effort (and skill) with which the propagandists concentrate our attention the physical bodies of the depicted rival animals is the extent of their need to distract us from the very *animality* of the self's symbol" (Baker, 1993/2001, p. 43).

Does Media Re-presentation Matter?

To be represented in mass media, particularly in the United States, is to be validated. Absence equals erasure. As a social institution whose influence is barely rivaled by family, religion, or education, the mass media provide a curriculum, a way of learning about ourselves and the world around us. In fact, in 1979, media scholar Neil Postman predicted television would be "the second curriculum" outpacing schools as source of learning particularly because, "Television is newer and more powerful but because its effects are continuously reinforced by other media of communication, including records, tapes, radio, photography, and film" (p. 163). This prediction came to pass in ways nearly unimaginable when we add the influence of the Internet on learning, if we accept Postman's definition of curriculum as "a course of study whose purpose is to train or cultivate both mind and character" (p. 163).

As was described in Chapter 2, in a hegemonic system of social control such as the one employed in the United States and other industrialized nations, influencing thoughts, and beliefs is central to organizing citizens into people who accept and support the status quo. The anthroparchal system of domination of the environment and animals, privileges humans (Cudworth, 2011). Anthroparchy thus "involves different forms and practices of oppression, exploitation, and marginalization" of varying extents and levels (Cudworth, 2011, p. 157). As discussed in Chapter 1, *anthro* (human) centered ways of being sees everything as about the human. Rather than seeing ourselves in relation to others, this perspective sees others as lesser than or at least in service to us. The mass media, as ideological tools for the re-presentation of mainstream, dominant ideas and values, thereby tend to present animals in ways that are consistent with an anthropocentric view consistent with a utilitarian environmental ideology.

Symbolic annihilation (erasure through lack of representation) as well as stereotyping both serve to confine a being to particular categories thus become closer or further from Us. This varies by categories into which we consider the animal (pet, food, farmed, wild, threat) and by species. While animals might appear "visible," since we see them everywhere from Internet memes to talk shows, animals' real nature is often erased or obscured. They are "at the same time the center of visual attention, and wholly absent" (Malamud, 2012, p. 39).

What do we learn from the media? As is the case with people we are unlikely to meet or have not yet met in person, knowledge of members of other species that comes almost entirely from television, movies, the Internet, or other symbolic means, is likely to be stereotypical (Merskin, 2010). Stereotypes "get hold of the few simple, vivid, memorable, easily grasped, and widely recognized characteristics about a person, reduce everything about the person to those traits, exaggerate and simplify them, and fix them without change or development to eternity" (Hall, 1997, p. 258). It is not only people who are stereotyped, animals are as well. For example, what people believe about wolves, based on media portrayals is that they are animals who are always a threat to humans, are always and only ferocious, who kill livestock and pets regularly and for no reason, premediatively target and attack humans and our interests. Or, as discussed in Chapter 6, media can also create falsely positive stereotypes, as is the case with the polar bear. Advertising, news, cinema, television programs, and the Web as carriers of deliberately constructed messages, use animals and their images in ways that directly and indirectly impact both animal and human lives.

As discussed in Chapter 3, children learn from the stories they read and are told, the images they see, the experiences they have, and in particular what media show them. In some cases, it is the only source available from which they learn about aspects or individuals in the world who are unlike them. This chapter focuses on learning about animals vicariously through media and popular culture portrayals. While movies, advertisements, television programs, and other forms of communication are highly entertaining and can, in their own way, bring animals nearer to us, research is clear that, in the absence of direct experiences with animals, the more likely a child (and as an eventual adult) will have a distorted view of them. Thus, the kinds of re-presentations, the language used to describe animals, all matter in not creating overly positive or overly negative apprehension. When animals are rendered symbolically (such as in animation), the circumstances and conditions of their real lives are made invisible. As a result, they are even more vulnerable, particularly when they are laughed at, presented as fools, or used as symbolic stand-ins for human emotions (in greeting cards, comic strips, commercials, and multi-media content). Re-presentation is a tool of power and a dynamic that needs to be unpacked in order to reveal how it reifies the human/non-human dichotomy and operates as ideological screening. For example, American news coverage of farmed animals typically reinforces the status quo agribusiness view of them as bodies not beings, tending to objectify them discursively through: (1) commodification, (2) failure to acknowledge their emotional perspectives, and (3) failure to describe them as inherently valuable individuals; while the news sometimes addresses farmed animal welfare, discussions of whether it is right for us to breed, use, kill, and eat them are rare (Freeman, 2009, 2014).

That humans have been re-presenting other animals since early days is a given, but the development of technologies that reached masses of people practically simultaneously is a relatively new development. The dawning of the 20th century yielded new media forms that have been introduced at an astonishing speed ever since. As a form of social control, media mainstream acceptable ways of thinking and behaving through re-presentations of idealized forms of everyday life. "Acknowledge the extent to which human understanding of animals is shaped by representations rather than by direct experience" (Baker, 1993/2001, p. 1) is crucial. Capitalist systems of economics require wide scale engineering of communication systems that present consistent, persistent, and consistent messages (DeFleur & Dennis, 1978/1998). Meanings thereby accumulate through forms of media that present some groups and individuals as superior to others (including species), thus buttressing the existing system. Under capitalism, the primary source of revenue generation for privately held media corporations is through advertising. Since the early days of magazines, newspapers, and later electronic media such as radio and television, giant food production companies, for example such as the Swift Company, Tyson Foods, and others, produced messages that emphasized the importance of use and consumption of animals far removed from the actual conditions of production (Marchand, 1985), workers, and the animals. During the 1920s, public relations pioneer Edward L. Bernays created print and radio advertising campaigns for companies such as Beechnut "Packing" Company to increase the consumption of eggs and bacon for breakfast (Tye, 2002).

Multi-media campaigns for products such as SPAM as well as product placement in television and radio programs and movies further reinforced the naturalness of consumption. Trade characters such as Elsie the Cow for Borden Ice Cream, present animals as willingly giving themselves to the production process, in fact they are happy to do so. In a print advertisement marketing Borden's milk, Elsie the Cow writes home "Dear Mamma: I'm so excited I can hardly chew! We girls are sending our milk to Borden's now. Love, Elsie" (Bunnish, 2003, p. 193). These type of happy cow advertisements are not a thing of the past. A series of commercials presents happy singing cows for the Real California Cheese brand whose tagline reads "Great cheese comes from Happy Cows. Happy Cows come from California." The campaign, introduced in 2000, is intended to promote the state's dairy products and displace assuage any cognitive dissonance associated with decline in milk production as consumers become more aware of where their milk comes from. The campaign created by Deutsch Los Angeles, built on the brand's original "Real California Cheese" brand which started in 1982. Happy Cow merchandise such as a happy cows calendar or hand puppets, are available for purchase on their website (www.realcaliforniacheese.com).

Signage outside butcher shops regularly present caricatures of happy cows designed to make the consumer feel good about his or her purchase(s). Animal activist organization People for the Ethical Treatment of Animals (PETA) took the board to task for misrepresenting the circumstances under which more than 29 million cows suffer and die in the dairy and meat industries annually ("Cows Used for Food.")

In summary, rather than bringing us closer in understanding them, which is what healthy levels of anthropomorphism can do, these re-presentations further distance them from us. One of the consequences is that, in the case of endangered species, repeated exposure in media tends to result in viewers believing animals such as chimps are less endangered than they actually are (Schroepfer et al., 2011). Re-presentations of predatory animals such as sharks, bears, cougars, and wolves can make people more fearful and distrustful than is necessary (Peschak, 2014; Røskaft, Bjerkec, Kaltenbornc, Linnellb, & Andersen, 2003). Furthermore, to re-present animals as only bad or only good not only belies their true nature, but also represents real risk to them and to us. Pragmatist John Dewey (1954, pp. 3–4), wrote that *animals* "do not float unsupported; they do not even just rest upon the earth. They *are* the earth in one of its manifest operations. It is the business of those who are concerned" with animals "to make this fact evident in its various implications" (ital orig). Thus, animal re-presentations in all forms of media matter because this imagery "has real effects on human-animal relations" and by extension, on their and our lived experiences (Brower, 2003). Thus, it is important to think how real animals and animated animals are used in media.

Note

1. In this book, the term representation is modified to re-presentation given that whenever we move from the real to the re-presented it is no longer an

actual being or object but rather what it looks like. The artist René Magritte (1898–1967) illustrated this process in his famous painting *The Treachery of images (La Trahison des images) (Ceci n'est pas une pipe)* (1929). Also known as "This is Not a Pipe," the painting confronts the issue of real versus re-presented. What we see in the painting is a pipe, it has all the qualities of pipe-ness, but is in fact purely a representation of one.

References

Bahn, P. G. (1992). Foreword. In N. W. Smith (Ed.), *An analysis of Ice Age art: Its psychology and belief system*. New York, NY: Peter Lang.

Baker, S. (1993/2001). *Picturing the beast: Animals, identity, and representation*. Manchester: Manchester Books.

Berger, J. (1980). *Why look at animals? From About looking*. New York, NY: Vintage.

Brabant, S., & Mooney, L. A. (1989). When "critters" act like people: Anthropomorphism in greeting cards. *Sociological Spectrum, 9*(4), 477–494.

Brower, M. (2003). Review of animals in film by Jonathan Burt. *Society & Animals, 11*(3), 299–301.

Bunnish, C. (2003). Borden incorporated. In J. McDonough & K. Egolf (Eds.), *Encyclopedia of advertising* (Vol. 1, p. 193). New York, NY: Taylor & Francis.

Carmack, Betty J. (1997). Realistic representations of companion animals in comic art in the USA. *Anthrozoos, 10*(2/3), 108–120.

Church, J. H. (1996). How the media portray animals. *Animals' Agenda, 16*(1), 24–28.

Cook J. (2014). *The swimming reindeer*. London: British Museum Press.

Corbett, J. (2006). *Communicating nature: How we create and understand environmental messages*. Washington, DC: Island Press.

Cudworth, E. (2011). *Social lives with other animals: Tales of sex, death, and love*. New York, NY: Springer.

Davidson, I. (2017). Images of animals in rock art: Not just "good to think." In B. David & I. J. McNiven (Eds.), *Oxford handbook of the archaeology and anthropology of rock art*. Oxford: Oxford University Press.

DeFleur, M. L., & Dennis, E. (1978/1998). *Understanding mass communication: A liberal arts perspective*. New York, NY: Houghton Mifflin.

Dewey, J. (1954). *Art as experience* (pp. 3–4). New York, NY: Putnam.

Doyle, B. (2014). *Children & other wild animals*. Corvallis, OR: Oregon State University Press.

Durham, D., & Merskin, D. (2009). Animals, agency, and absence: A discourse analysis of institutional animal care and use committee meetings. In S. McFarland & R. Hediger (Eds.), *Animals, agency, and authority* (pp. 229–250). Boston, MA: Brill.

Durkheim, E. (1912/1961). *The elementary forms of religious life* (C. Cosman, Trans.). New York, NY: Oxford.

Fairclough, N. (2002). Language in new capitalism. *Discourse & Society, 13*(2), 163–166.

Ferdowsian, H., & Merskin, D. (2012). Parallels in sources of trauma, pain, distress, and suffering in humans and nonhuman animals. *Journal of Trauma & Dissociation, 13*(4), 448–468.

Foucault, M. (1966/2005). *The order of things*. New York, NY: Taylor & Francis.

Foucault, M. (1983). *This is not a pipe*. Berkeley, CA: University of California Press.

Frazer, J. G. (1910/2011). *Totemism and exogamy: A treatise on certain early forms, of superstition and society* (Vol. 3). New York, NY: Macmillan.

Freeman, C. P. (2009). This little piggy went to press: The American news media's construction of animals in agriculture. *The Communication Review, 12*(1), 78–103.

Freeman, C. P. (2014). *Framing farming: Communication strategies for animal rights*. New York, NY: Rodopi.

Freeman, C. P., & Merskin, D. (2008). "Having it his way": The construction of masculinity in fast food TV advertising. In L. C. Rubin (Ed.), *Food for thought: Essays on eating and culture* (pp. 277–293). New York, NY: McFarland.

Freud, S. (1918/1998). *Totem & taboo*. New York, NY: Moffat, Yard, & Co.

Ghirlanda S., Acerbi, A., Herzog, H. (2014). Dog movie stars and dog breed popularity: A case study in media influence on choice. *PLOS ONE 9*(9).

Goffman, E. (1979). *Gender advertisements*. New York, NY: Harper & Row.

Hall, S. (1997). *Representation: Cultural representations and signifying practices*. Thousand Oaks, CA: Sage.

Hays-Gilpin, K. A. (2004). *Ambiguous images: Gender and rock art*. Walnut Creek, CA: Altamira.

Henry, W. E. (1947). Art and cultural symbolism: A psychological study of greeting cards. *The Journal of Aesthetics and Art Criticism, 6*(1), 36–44.

Hill, B. (2015). *Native rock carvings of the Northwest Coast*. Surrey, BC: Hancock House Publishers Ltd.

Hovarth, G., Farkas, E., Boncz, I., Blaho, M., & Kriska, G. (2012). Cavemen were better at depicting quadrupeds than modern artists: Erroneous walking illustrations in the fine arts from prehistory to today. *PLOS One, 7*(12), 1–10. Retrieved from http://journals.plos.org/plosone/article?id=10.1371/journal.pone.0049786

Kafka, F. (1917/2015). A report to the academy. In N. N. Glatzer (trans.). *Franz Kafka: The complete stories*. New York, NY: Schocken Books.

Kalof, L., & Amthor, R. F. (2010). Cultural representations of problem animals in *National Geographic*, Études Rurales, 185, 165–180.

Lakoff, G. (1987). *Women, fire, and dangerous things*. Chicago, IL: University of Chicago Press.

Lakoff, G., & Johnson, M. (1999). *Philosophy in the flesh*. New York, NY: Basic Books.

Lang, A. (1912/2017). Method in the study of totemism. *American Anthropologist, 14*(2), 368–382.

Lawrence, E. A. (1993). The sacred bee, the filthy pig, and the bat out of hell: Animal symbolism as cognitive Biophilia. In S. R. Kellert & E. O. Wilson (Eds.), *The Biophilia hypothesis* (pp. 301–341). Washington, DC: Island Press.

Lerner, J. E., & Kalof, L. (1999). The animal text: Message and meaning in television advertisements. *Sociological Quarterly, 40*(4), 565–586.

Lewis, G. (2009, December 10). Chihuahuas crowding California shelters. NBC News. Retrieved January 10, 2015, from: http://www.nbcnews.com/id/34352750/ns/healthpet_health/t/chihuahuas-

Magdoff, J., & Barnett, S. (1989). Self-imaging and animals in TV ads. In R. J. Hoage (Ed.), *Perceptions of animals in American culture* (pp. 93–100). Washington, DC: Smithsonian Institution Press.

Malamud, R. (2012). *An introduction to animals and visual culture*. Basingstoke: Palgrave Macmillan.

Marchand, R. (1985). *Advertising the American dream*. Los Angeles, CA: University of California Press.

Marston, E. (2005). *Songs of ancient journeys: Animals in rock art*. New York, NY: George Braziller Publishers.

Mavhunga, C. C. (2011). Vermin beings: On pestiferous animals and human game. *Social Text, 29*(1), 151–176.

McKenna, E. (2013). *Pets, people, and pragmatism*. New York: Fordham.Merskin, D. (2004). The construction of Arabas as enemies: Post-September 11 discourse of George W. Bush. *Mass Communication & Society, 7*(2), 157–175.

Merskin, D. (2010). *Media, minorities, and meaning: A critical introduction*. New York, NY: Peter Lang.

Merskin, D. (2014, June 6–7). *The need not to suffer: Animals, humiliation, and the media*. Presentation. Animal Vulnerabilities Conference, University of Oregon.

Miles, C., & Ibrahim, Y. (2013). Deconstructing the meerkat: Fabular anthropomorphism, popular culture, and the market. *Journal of Marketing Management, 29*(15/16), 1862–1880.

Milstein, T. (2012). Banging on the divide: Cultural reflection and refraction at the zoo. In E. Plec (Ed.), *Perspectives on human-animal interaction: Internatural communication* (pp. 162–181). London: Routledge.

Murray, W. B. (2014). Deer: Sacred and profane. In D. L. Gillette, M. Greer, M. I. Hayward, & W. B. Murray (Eds.), *Rock art and sacred landscapes* (pp. 195–206). New York, NY: Springer.

Palmer, C. (2015). *Confessions of a wildlife filmmaker*. Philadelphia, PA: Bluefield.

Paul, E. S. (1996). The representation of animals on children's television. *Anthrozoös, 9*(4), 169–181.

Peschak, T. P. (2014). *Sharks and people: Exploring our relationship with the most feared fish in the sea*. Chicago, IL: University of Chicago Press.

Quinn, D. (1992). *Ishmael*. New York, NY: Bantam.

Rifas, L. (2010). Funny animal comics. In M. K. Booker (Ed.), *Encyclopedia of comic and graphic novels* (Vol. 1, pp. 234–242). Santa Barbara, CA: ABC-CLIO.

Ritvo, H. (1985). Learning from animals: Natural history for children in the eighteenth and nineteenth centuries. *Children's Literature, 13*, 72–93.

Røskaft, E., Bjerke, T., Kaltenborn, B., Linnell, J. D. C., & Andersen, R. (2003). Patterns of self-reported fear towards large carnivores among the Norwegian public. *Evolution and Human Behavior, 24*, 184–198.

Rozsa, M. (2017, August 3). "Game of Thrones" fans are buying, and abandoning, huskies in droves. *Salon.* http://www.salon.com/2017/08/03/game-of-thrones-direwolves-huskies/

Santa Ana, O. (1999). "Like an animal I was treated": Anti-immigrant metaphor in U.S. public discourse. *Discourse & Society, 10*(2), 191–224.

Schroepfer, K. K., Rosati, A. G., Chartrand, T., & Hare, B. (2011). Use of "entertainment" chimpanzees in commercials distorts public perception regarding conservation status. *PLOS One.* http://www.plosone.org/article/info%3Adoi%2F10.1371%2Fjournal.pone.0026048

Smith, C. (2014, August 10). Animal shelters brace for unwanted effects of new Ninja Turtles movie. *NBC Bay Area, Bay City News.* Retrieved January 10, 2015 from http://www.nbcbayarea.com/news/local/Animal-Shelters-Brace-for-Unwanted-Effects-of-New-Ninja-Turtles-Movie-270672501.html

Smith, N. W. (1992). *An analysis of Ice Age art: Its psychology and belief system.* New York, NY: Peter Lang.

Smith, T. L. (2011). *Less than human: Why we demean, enslave, and exterminate others.* New York, NY: Macmillan.

Spears, N. E. (1996). Symbolic role of animals in print advertising: Content analysis and conceptual development. *Journal of Business Research, 37*(2), 87–95.

Stromberg, J. (2012, December 5). Cavemen were much better at illustrating animals than artists today. *Smithsonian.* Retrieved from http://www.smithsonianmag.com/science-nature/cavemen-were-much-better-at-illustrating-animals-than-artists-today-153292919/?no-ist

Tiwari, S. K. (2002). *Tribal roots of Hinduism.* New Delhi: Sarup & Sons.

Tye, L. (2002). *The father of spin: Edward L. Bernays and the birth of public relations.* New York, NY: Henry Holt.

Van Hoek, M. (2015). Andean Petroglyphs and Yanantin. The Case of El Olivar, Ancash, Peru. *Rupestreweb.* http://www.rupestreweb.info/yanantin.html

Weil, K. (2013). *Thinking animals: Why animal studies now?* New York, NY: Columbia University Press.

Williams, J. A., Podeschi, C., Palmer, N., Schwadel, P., & Meyler, D. (2011). The human-environment dialog in award-winning children's picture books. *Sociological Inquiry, 82*(1), 145–159.

Section Two

Case Studies

Chapter Five

Knuffle Bunnies and Devoted Ducklings

The Formation of Gender Identity in Picture Books

> Children are the living messages we send to a time we will not see.
> —Postman (1982/1994, p. xi)

> Until one has loved an animal, a part of one's soul remains unawakened.
> —(Anatole France)

> The intuitive connection children feel with animals can be a tremendous source of joy. The unconditional love received from pets, and the lack of artifice in the relationship, contrast sharply with the much trickier dealings with members of their own species.
> —de Waal (2001)

Childhood is replete with special friendships. Some are imaginary; others are with peers, while others are with animals, both real and imagined. The relationships children form with animals are on par in terms of significance with those made with other children and are key sites for the development of individual differences related to "language; nonverbal communication; theory of mind; biological concepts; categories; social understanding' and, above all, the self" (Myers, 2007, p. xv). As discussed in Chapter 2, scholars have long debated and poets opined about the rather mysterious connection children have with other animals in terms of whether it is natural (Wilson, 1984), culturally cultivated (Shepard, 1996), or both (Melson, 2001). Yet anyone who has witnessed a child interact with animals can see that something special is going on. For anyone who has spent time with other species, or watched the interactions between little humans and little animals, an almost magical something happens: they touch, kiss, talk to, and hold them. There is a pattern to this relating:

> Young children demonstrate finely attuned sensitivities to certain basic and somewhat variable qualities of animals as interactants, even as the children also show certain biases as intersubjective and linguistic young humans. We repeatedly find a small set of core traits of animals (including humans) uniting a whole range of animal-related activities of children. (Myers, 2007, p. 4)

Ironically, the importance of animals in the lives of children is one of the least studied aspects of child development (Melson, 2001; Tipper, 2011). Even famous child researchers such as Piaget and Bowlby failed to address the bonds children have with animals. Melson (2001, p. 11) points out, "Nowhere can animals be found in the voluminous literature on children's play and peer relationships." Yet when asked about who matters to children most in their lives, many will identify an animal (Tipper, 2011). Furthermore, animals are important symbolic carriers of meaning in one of the first forms of mass communication children encounter: picture books. Not only are picture books significant carriers of cultural messages about gender, social class, and race, but also animals. The animals within these stories are also gendered, both in appearance and mannerisms and also through the interpretations of those who read the books out loud to children, explaining interactions, scenes, and answering questions the child might have. This chapter examines gender and species in children's picture books. More specifically, it is an examination of children's symbolic relationships with animals (real and imagined). This study is in part a response to the lack of discussion of children's relationships with animals in general as well as an analysis of re-presentations of animals in picture books in particular.

A selection of picture books from the *School Library Journal's* (*SLJ*) "Top 100 Picture Books for the 21st century" (2012) list for Pre-Kindergarten to age two were textually analyzed in order to ascertain how many of the stories are about animals, how many of those include girls, and if animals in the stories are coded according to gender. Using the theory of intersectionality as a lens, a textual analysis reveals what these award winning books say about gender and species. In *LJ*'s "Top 100 Picture Books for the 21st century," for Pre-Kindergarten to age two, readers voted on individual Top Ten picture books from which the list of 100 was compiled. *SLJ* is the "official organ of the library associations of America and of the United Kingdom" (1878). This analysis is important to parents and other adults interested in the well being of children. Not only do early books and stories influence whether children grow up to be readers, and how well they read, but also predict their likelihood to succeed in school and contribute to the development of identity, as well as education in societal values (Arbuthot, 1984; Duursma, Augustyn, & Zuckerman, 2008). Interactions between parent and child also correlate to higher reading levels in children. *SLJ* notes the importance of these early books, "the first books a child encounters will influence how they read for the rest of their lives." Few studies have considered the importance of the representations of animals in these books. Those that have largely regard them in the context of gender roles supported or challenged. The present study takes the animal analysis deeper by not only examining whether or not stereotypical gender roles are present in the books, but also which species of animals are re-presented and asks whether these are positive or negative.[1] I argue that certain species of animals other than humans are stereotyped in ways similar to how human beings are, based on a binary system of good/bad, safe/threat, and so forth.

The following sections present a brief discussion of children, identity, and gender development, followed by an examination of the relationship between children and animals. This is followed by the results of a textual analysis of the representation of gender, race, and species in a selection of picture books. Research questions include: What gender roles are presented in picture books? Which animals are featured? What species are re-presented? And are the species presentations positive or negative?

Early Animals

"Three Little Kittens," "Three Blind Mice," and other animal-rich rhymes and stories such as of those Aesop have for centuries given children access to the lives of animals, at least symbolic ones, and "delineated the characters and passions of men [sic] under the semblance of Lions, Tigers, Wolves, and Foxes" (Bewick, 1885, p. iv). "Three Little Pigs," "Little Bo Peep," and "The Three Bears" teach children not only about themselves as seen in the adventures and experiences of anthropomorphized animals, but also (accurately or inaccurately) about qualities and characteristics of different species. Through games, songs, and activities children learn the names of different animals, often acquiring the alphabet through associations such as A is for Aardvark or W is for Whales. In particular, many of the stories teach gender roles, either through the re-presentation or by way of a parent or other reader's interpretation of the goings-on of the story.

As early as age five children already have absorbed many gender stereotypes into their understandings of themselves and the world (Martin & Ruble, 2004; Turner-Bowker, 1996). Storybooks play important roles in teaching children about morals (Ashton, 1983; Green, Bigler, & Catherwood, 2004; Jennings, 1975; Trepanier-Street & Kropp, 1990) and can reinforce dominant ideologies. While they can also challenge stereotypes, more often than not, most storybooks are consistent with mainstream views of what is feminine and masculine in a society. Some of this early education includes animals who are gendered in books. Patt and McBride (1992), for example, found that children used masculine pronouns significantly more than feminine or neutral pronouns to refer to animals or people when gender is unknown. Furthermore, when teachers (and parents) read aloud to children they often gender the characters in their interpretations of the stories.

Growing Books and Reading

The development of books designed to educate and entertain children parallel the changing roles of children in everyday family life. Prior to the invention of moveable type in Europe[2] around 1450, most books for children were instructive, written by monastic teachers, were educational in nature, and intended for the offspring of the wealthy (Sutherland & Arbuthnot, 1986). During the middle of the 15th century a major technological change developed in Europe that would, among other things, mark a difference between childhood and adulthood— the printing press with moveable type (Postman, 1982/1994, p. 27). By creating "a new symbolic world" which included and excluded those who were literate from those who were not, the mass printing of materials also created audiences. "Prior to printing, all human communication occurred in a social context" (p. 27). However, once printed stories were available, a psychological space and time emerged in which individual interpretation, isolation, and privacy were created. This highly individual act could also be social when involving children who were read to, entertained, and educated through books.

In the 17th and in to the early 18th centuries, few children (or adults for that matter) were literate. News, stories, and other communications were spread by word-of-mouth and bedtime stories were told to children, not read. Tales were passed on as part of oral traditions and many, such as *Grimm's Fairy Tales*, were not originally designed for children (Zipes, 2003).

The first zoological book published for children was *A Description of Three Hundred Animals* (1730) (Ritvo, 1985, p. 72). There was the rare entertaining book in the late 17th century, such as *Contes de ma Mère l'Oye* (a.k.a. *Mother Goose*), but books of this time intended for children were primarily of two types: (1) "the useful, didactic books ... written to instruct them in manners and morals," whose illustrations bore a resemblance to medieval bestiaries, and (2) adult books they read for entertainment, such as *Robinson Crusoe* (1719) or *Gulliver's Travels* (1726) (p. 6). The earliest children's picture book is thought to be *Orbis Pictus* (*The World in Pictures* or *The World Illustrated*) (1657) by Moravian bishop and educator Johannes Amos Comenius (Sutherland & Arbuthnot, 1986). The book's preface suggests Comenius recognized children's desire for engaging and interesting material: "See then here a new help for Schooles, a Picture and Nomenclature of all the chief things in the World, and of mens Actions in their way of Living! To entice Witty Children to it ... to stir up the Attention ... by sport, a merry pastime" (Ritvo, 1985, p. 61).

The ability of the printing press to produce in color aided the development of picture books. By 1880 there were, according to one account, "at least fifty children's books about animals, vegetables, and minerals" (Ritvo, 1985, p. 72). Many books emphasized "the order of creation" as taught by religion, thus emphasizing studious habits, scientific knowledge, and religious values. At the same time, many of the religious values meant treating animals kindly and well, intertwining natural history with interesting stories that contained moral lessons. For example, Elisabeth F. Bonsall's (1903), *The Book of the Cat* (see Figure 5.1).

Anthropologist Claude Lévi-Strauss (1966) pointed out, "animals are good to think." Many times, this thinking *about* (as opposed to with) has to do with a social norms and values. Thus, "the most important lesson taught by animal books ... was about the proper structure of human society" (p. 80) (i.e. humans at the top), and that animals were created for human use (and within that, that some species sought "or at least accept[ed] without protest, human companionship and exploitation" (p. 81). Thus lessons of early animal books that targeted children included: biology is destiny, some human beings are inferior to others, all animals are inferior to humans, that animals they are meant (and in fact want) to be used, and understand this as an obligation. As such animals "may function as a meaning system through which children make sense of both themselves and their surrounding environments" (Melson, 2001, p. 15).

Books of the 19th century viewed children as "innocent little creatures easily led astray," containing material that was "heavily didactic as well as moralistic" (Sutherland & Arbuthnot, 1986, p. 9). Family structure emphasized the supremacy of the father and the message was that children who ignored adult guidance would be "in grave danger" (p. 9). The children portrayed were prim, proper, and primarily white and middle class.

In the early years of the 20th century, children's curiosity figured in books, and they were shown as mischievous and with more agency than in the past. At this time the children's book sector of publishing grew rapidly and over time began to include more realism, had global reach, and embraced a new consciousness of children's worlds being something apart from that of adults. For example, books of the 1960s

Figure 5.1: *The Book of the Cat: With Facsimiles of Drawings in Colour* (1903).
Source: Used by permission of the Library of Congress.

and 1970s included challenges to authority and power of peers. Multi-ethnic and multi-racial faces were included more often and new forms of family life appeared. The Civil Rights Movement, Women's movement, LGBTQ movements, as well as increased consciousness about the human impact on the planet. These topics influenced and continue to find their way in to children's books—some books were entirely devoted to these issues while others reflect this progression more in tone. Despite on-the-ground social changes, studies conducted in the 1970s (Weitzman, Eifler, Hokada, & Ross, 1972), 1980s (Collins, Ingoldsby, & Dellman, 1984), and 1990s (Albers, 1996; Narahara, 1998) found that women continued to be re-presented in children's books as passive and less active than are male characters who tend to be the leaders, active, and independent. Male characters were most often the lead or primary character in the story, whereas females supported the stories. "The message in these primers is rather clear: Boys live exciting and independent lives, whereas girls are primarily auxiliaries to boys. To put it more bluntly: It's a man's world, kids!" (Bender & Leone, 1989, p. 36). The findings of these studies suggest that despite social changes, stereotyping is still present in these important sources of learning. This includes gender stereotypes in aspects of these books that might not be taken as seriously, i.e. the animal re-presentations. Thus, what are they learning? "Most children's books are about boys, men, and male animals, and most deal exclusively with male adventures. ... when women can be found in the books, they ... [remain] inconspicuous and nameless" (Weitzman et al., 1972, p. 11238).

In the 2000s, American and European culture began acknowledging individual differences in children, the influence of place on identity (urban versus rural), those who seem to be naturally drawn to reading and those who are not. Sutherland and Arbuthnot (1986) argue that, in many ways, children's books produced in the last and current century are better than their predecessors as children's exposure to mass media, in particular television, and knowledge of the world and world events in general, has resulted in the coverage of a greater number of subjects, more accuracy in informational books, higher quality of writing, and a greater level of candor today versus the past.

Picturing Books

Children's literature is a vast category of forms of communication that includes books, magazines, and poetry. While greatly reduced, given the amount of time and attention children spend with screens, printed materials still figure prominently in children's reading repertoire. This might include reading a cereal box, asking what a word is on television, in a newspaper or magazine story, in a comic strip, as well as in school in terms of what is written on flyers, blackboards, electronic presentations, and text books. Children's literature is something a bit different.

Books that target young children, particularly in their earliest development, tend to emphasize images over words. They are fiction and the complex dynamic between usually limited amounts of text and mostly pictures operate to tell a story. The assumption is that young, prelingual, children better understand stories told mostly through images than through words, and "yet there is no irrefutable psychological or pedagogical reason young children should be told the vast majority of their stories through combinations of words and pictures" (Nodelman, 1988, pp. 1–2). In fact, there is some evidence that pictures distract young readers (Samuels, 1977). Adults reading books to children typically provide explanation and interpretation of the images. Research demonstrates that young children who are read to have increased literacy (Armbruster, Lehr, & Osborn, 2002; Wells, 1985) and experience emotional and social gains (Kuo, Franke, Regalado, & Halfon, 2004). Those who read to children or interpret pictures in books exert tremendous influence on the read-to child's understanding of the material. In addition, children also spend time simply looking at the pictures on their own. The tales appeal to children, much in the same way fairy stories do, because the point of view is often similar to that of a child's animistic thinking, even if the peer happens to be of another species.

Picture books, defined as "books intended for young children which contain information or tell stories through a series of many pictures combined with relatively slight texts or no texts at all" (Nodelman, 1988, p. vii) are a unique form of visual art in that, while they have many of the same aesthetically pleasing qualities of other expressions, their purpose is primarily to help tell stories. The images are not intended to encourage readers to imagine a story around them, rather they have a specific purpose in the narrative structure of a story: they exist to illustrate, to clarify, and occupy most of the space on a given page. What text there is dependends upon the image to bring the story to life. There is a simultaneous amplification and limitation in the books as they alternate between engagement with the words and engagement with the text. "As a result of these unusual features, picture books have unique rhythms, unique conventions of shape and structure, a unique body of narrative techniques" (p. viii). The images serve, among other things, "as elements of mood," or as representations of the setting in which the story takes place (Sutherland & Arbuthnot, 1986). There needs to be a relationship, however, between the representation and the image for them to be mutually reinforcing. As children grow, it is psychologically important for them to identify with others and books often provide an opportunity to feel connected to the worlds of others, whether on the basis of social class, race, gender, or species. "Picture books offer young children a resource that expands their world, connects them to the values of society, and helps define who they are" (Narahara, 1998, p. 16).

Today there are pop-up books, picture books (some with text, some without), easy-to-read books, reading-level targeted books, adventure and science books, vocabulary focused, natural history, fantasy, poetry, fables, legends, and how-to guides that feature animals. "There is rarely any need to urge children to read stories about animals. Pet stories bring out children's desire to nurture and protect, and as they mature, they learn about the piteous vulnerability of animals at the hands of cruel owners or hunters and trappers. Such stories encourage a compassionate sense of kinship with animals" (Sutherland & Arbuthnot, 1986, p. 372).

Children seem particularly interested in animal stories, "whether they creatures that behave like human beings, animals that behave like animals but can talk, or animals that behave like animals, whether there are people in the story or not" (Sutherland & Arbuthnot, 1986, p. 112). The animals might be clothed, communicate in words, or by gestures. Because of the parallels with human lives, the "perceptiveness about human foibles and emotions" is at the heart of the importance of these stories (p. 112). These stories often "parody the lives of human beings" (p. 112), particularly adults who, from the child's perspective are often presented as overly ambitious, self-centered, jealous, and narcissistic. Furthermore, these books often contain the message that adults aren't always right, there's no need to be perfect, there are consequences for our actions, and being different is okay. Stories in which animals don't behave so much as people but more like members of their own species, other than they speak, often target younger children. Typically, they are stories of one individual trying to keep up with others, for example, a little duckling who is smaller and tries to keep pace with his larger siblings.

Learning About Gender

Little attention has been paid, however, to the role of animal characters and gender assignment. "Most children's books are about boys, men, and male animals, and most deal exclusively with male adventures. ... When women can be found in the books, they ... [remain] inconspicuous and nameless" (Weitzman et al., 1972, p. 11238). Gender, as used in this chapter, is defined as cultural or social binaries that narrowly categorize individuals according to socially agreed upon characteristics that are either feminine or masculine. Gender, the noun, is not synonymous with sex, which is a biological distinction. Rather gender is the socially agreed upon mental constructions of what is feminine or masculine and the nature of those characteristics. For example, ascribing certain colors to masculine (blue) or feminine (pink), as well activities that are viewed as "natural" for men (work; success) and women (caretaking; beauty). The media children consume, are provided with, and that parents interpret for them, are replete with information about gender roles. "Gender development is a critical part of the earliest and most important learning experiences of the young child" (Peterson & Lach, 1990, p. 188). Stereotypes that exist in the mind of the reader who is helping the child interpret the pictures can result in the passing on of these assumptions. For example, in picture books, when mother's described the characters and pictures to toddlers (DeLoache, Cassidy, & Carpenter, 1987), they used pronouns such as "his," "he," and "him" when in fact there was nothing to indicate whether the character was male, female, masculine or feminine. This kind of interaction with parents and other adults who interpret books impart not only gendered, but also speciesist, stereotypes. While reading and describing, adults impart their understandings and preconceptions to children, often unintentionally due to what is obvious and visible and what is below the surface of re-presentations. There is both manifest (denotative) and latent (connotative) content in media texts. Manifest content is that which is visible and countable. For example, the number of boys or girls in a particular story or the types of roles they play in the book. Latent content requires interpretation, and is that part of deep structural meaning associated with cultural assumptions, givens, and those aspects that go without saying if one is a part of such a culture. Examples include using particular colors to signify boys or masculine characteristic such as blue and pink for feminine girl-associated items. As such "illustrated books, in particular, tend to significantly affect gender development" (Gooden & Gooden, 2001, p. 91). Thus, if gender is assigned it can be assumed to draw on already learned stereotypes.

> Children are not passive observers. As they develop, children look for structure in their lives and are driven by an internal need to fit into this structure. They observe the world and try to develop sets of rules that they can apply to a wide variety of situations. A child's knowledge of his own gender and its implications is known as gender identity. As children acquire gender identities they also acquire stereotypical ideas about what it means to be a boy or girl. (Shaw, 1998, p. 24)

A study of 60 preschool and elementary children (evenly divided groups of boys and girls) in ages ranging from 4 to 5, 7 to 8, and 10 to 11 years of age presented them with cards that contained drawings of a bear (Arthur & White, 1996). Researchers found gender-neutral bear characters were assigned age and gender based on size (larger bears presumed to be adults), and the assumed-to-be-male child bears were most often in the company of adults in the books. In the pictures some were involved in stereotypical gendered activities such as showing affection between large and small bears, watching television, and some were neutral. Children were asked to make up stories about the bears and to name them. The researchers found the biggest differences in gender assignment were between the youngest children (in the 4–5 year age range) and the older groups. The younger children typically assigned their own gender to the bear, which is consistent with theories of development that say younger children seen the world primarily in terms of themselves. The two older age groups reflected stereotypes. Bears who were shown alone were more likely to be labeled as males than those engaged in showing affection who were labeled female. Boys stereotyped animals more often than girls. This result suggests the importance of recognizing how early stereotyping can take place and the importance of creating children's books and activities that counter cultural training. Thus, we know children learn gender-based stereotypes early and these limiting representations be reinforced depending on the representations in books and other media and in the ways those helping them understand a stories describe them.

Method

A selection of picture books from the *School Library Journal's* (*SLJ*) "Top 100 Picture Books for the 21st century" (2012) list for Pre-Kindergarten to age two were studied in order to ascertain how many of the stories are about animals, how many of those include girls, and if animals in the stories are coded according to gender. *SLJ* is a trade publication for librarians, founded in 1876 by Dewey decimal system founder Melvil Dewey. The publication, now on line, presents news about the library world, articles on professional practice, and other related issues. Readers of the journal "include library professionals from school and public libraries, as well as educators from preschool to high school, and publishers and vendors with an interest in serving children and young adults" (http://www.slj.com/about-us/#_). For this chapter, the top ten books in the list were textually analyzed as well as a 10% random sample of the remaining 90 winners. To ascertain whether these top picture books contain gender stereotyping of humans and other species, the top 10 from the list of 100 were evaluated, followed by a 10% sample of the remaining 90. Hard copies of the books were obtained from the local public library (see Table 5.1).

Employing LaDow's (1976) content analytic method, each book was read and analyzed for the following: Main character, Female illustrations, Male illustrations, Female and Male illustrations combined, Male animal illustrations, Female animal illustrations, or Neutral illustrations. In addition, front and back covers were analyzed.

Whereas earlier studies use content analysis, the present study uses textual analysis to ascertain not only how many of a category is present but also why and what the impact might be on those who are re-presented. The semiotics of picture books focuses on the codes and contexts upon which meaning making depends and is a useful tool for analyzing them. There is then a kind of grammar underlying how these forms of communication work. Research questions guiding this study are:

(1) What gender roles are presented?
(2) Which animals are featured?
(3) What species are re-presented?
(4) Are the species presentations positive or negative?

Table 5.1. Titles Analyzed.

Where the Wild Things Are (1963)
Don't let the Pigeon Drive the Bus (2003)
Good Night Moon (1947)
The Snowy Day (1962)
Make Way for Ducklings (1941)
Bark, George (1999)
The Monster at the End of this Book (1971)
Green Eggs and Ham (1960)
The Little House (1942)
Madeline (1939)
Sylvester and the Magic Pebble (1969)
The Grinch who Stole Christmas (1957)
May I bring a friend? (1964)
Bread and Jam for Frances (1964)
Gardener (1995)
Stella Luna (1993)
Knuffle Bunny (2004)
Alexander and the Terrible, Horrible, No Good, Very Bad Day (1972)
The Very Hungry Caterpillar (1969)
May I bring a Friend? (1964)

Findings

Of the 20 books examined, many were Caldecott Medal winners. Research on Caldecott winners found main characters tend to be white and male whose lives are full of adventure and excitement (Engel, 1981). The same can be said of the books in this study, whose publication dates range from as far back as 1939 (*Madeline*) to as recent as 2004 (*The Monster at the End of This Book*).

Gender Roles (Human)

Consistent with other studies, humans outnumber animals in these popular picture books. As shown in Table 5.2, adult male human roles were professional/occupational with characters presented as police officers, postal workers, and train conductors. When human fathers were presented, in all cases but one, even if they were not at work, they wore a suit and tie or similar professional type clothing. *Knuffle Bunny* (2004) was the exception in terms of the father shown as care giving and taking on the household task of doing laundry. As one of the most progressive books, *Knuffle Bunny* had the only re-presentation of a father who is also a caretaker. In the story, little Trixie's favorite stuffed toy, Knuffle Bunny, ends up in the washing machine. It is her father who takes the laundry to the laundromat, Trixie in tow. While other men in the story are shown in more traditional re-presentations, her father, as one of the main characters, is actively involved with her life.

Table 5.2. Human Roles.

Role	Total	Dominant
Male Human	26	16
Professional	18	8
Nurturing	1	1
Female Human	28	1
Professional	2	0
Nurturing	26	0
Humans of Color	6	1

Only two of the books had girls as the main character (and one animal book, *Frances*). In terms of race, all of the characters that were human were white, with the exception of *The Snowy Day* (1962), in which the main character, Peter, is a boy of color as are the other three secondary characters in the story. Diversity is present in *Bark, George!* (1999) in terms of some of the human beings in the background.

Gender Roles (Animal)

The gender roles of animals paralleled those of human portrayals, as shown in Table 5.3. Typical family structures persisted of the "professional" father and homemaking mother. *Where the Wild Things Are* (1963) is the Number 1 book on this *ALS* list. The lead character is human who encounters wild beasts on an island. This, along with the Dr. Seuss books, had animal-like characters such as Grover in *The Monster at the End of the Book* (1971). These characters either by name or appearance cues, code as male.

While animals figured often as background characters, in several of the books they were the main characters. For example, in *Don't Let the Pigeon Drive the Bus!* (2003). This character, who could be read as gender neutral, presents as male. In *Make Room for Ducklings* (1941)

Table 5.3. Animal Roles.

Role	Total	Dominant
Male Animal	55	12*
Professional	2	2
Nurturing	1	1
Female Animal	21	4
Professional	0	0
Nurturing	21	4

* These characters were not specific animal species but were also not humans. Not included in the totals are the creatures (5) in *Where the Wild Things Are*, Grover in *The Monster at the End of This Book*, Sam in *Green Eggs & Ham*, and the Grinch, in *How the Grinch Stole Christmas*. In this last book, Cindy Lou, is also not identifiable as a human or animal, but codes as female because of name and pink pajamas.

this nuclear family of mom, dad, and babies is led by a father figure who determines much of what the family will do and who, while the hatchlings are young, leaves for a "trip." The names of the ducklings (Jack, Kack, Lack, Mack, Nack, Ouack, Pack, and Quack) read as male as well. In *Bark! George*, the young pup, George, is male and his mother attends to him and eventually takes him to a human male veterinarian.

Table 5.4. Species Representations.

Species	Primary Character	Secondary Character	Background Character
Wolf (costume)	X		
Pigeon	X		
Ducklings	X		
Dog	X	X	X
Cat			X
Fox			X
Mouse			X
Goat			X
Tiger (Fierce)			X
Lion (mean & hungry)			X
Lions (at a party)			X
Giraffe			X
Pigs			X
Hippo			X
Elephant			X
Chickens (hens & roosters)			X
Mules	X	X	
Monkeys			X

Which Animal Species?

Amongst the books analyzed, species varied widely. In some cases, there seemed to be more in terms of numbers, such as ducklings, because the story focused on a family (*Make Room for Ducklings*). In other, the tale was about a single animal.

Positive or Negative?

Main characters who were animals in the books were largely positive (see Table 5.4). Ambiguous characters such as Grover or the Grinch redeem themselves by the end of the books. In two cases, lions were presented as fierce and scary, as was a tiger, supporting stereotypes of big cats as being only and always fearsome and dangerous. However, in *May I Bring a Friend?* (1964), animals such as hippos, lions, pigs, and an elephant are presented as feminine (wearing pink bows and/or clothing) and are not threatening. Animals one sees less often in many books found their ways in to two of these on the list: donkeys and badgers. Badgers, who are rather fearsome when encountering humans in real life, are softened in the book *Bread and Jam for Frances* (1964) which tells the story of a badger family and the little girl, Frances, who finds many foods make good eating. Donkeys, the main characters in *Sylvester and the Magic Pebble* (1969), are shown as thoughtful, contemplative, and devoted to family when Sylvester learns how much he loves home. *Stella Luna* (1993) is the story of a little bat who is raised first among birds, learning their ways, then returns to the bat world with a greater knowledge of how others do things. This positive portrayal of bats is one that competes with many of the fearsome associations of bats in other forms of popular culture. The book also includes scientific information about bats, their needs, and the threats they face in the real world.

Conclusion

The intention of this chapter was to add not only to research on what children's picture books teach about gender, but also about animals and gender. Revisiting the research questions: What gender roles are presented? Which animals are featured? What species are re-presented? Are the species presentations positive or negative? The findings suggest many preexisting gender stereotypes about "proper" human roles are also applied to animal characters.

By learning about species hierarchy, children are taught which animals fit into which categories based on obedience, trainability, and uses, particularly when it comes to domestic species (Ritvo, 1985). Children's relationships with animals are different from those of adults and they figure in self-reports of children as very important family members and friends, despite the neglect of their significance in research.

Along with the vitally important role representations play in children's constructions of self in terms of gender, race, sex, class and so forth, mediated portrayals of animals, perhaps their closest first friends significantly impact the lives of real animals. The more distanced children are from understanding the real behind the represented the less likely they are to be empathetic. Research evidence shows that lack of care for animals and abuse of animals while young relates to violence committed against other human beings and animals when we are adults. Furthermore, the quality of interaction between parent-readers, children's literature, and children's reception of book contents (particularly as it concerns gender roles and species), is important. Children's book authors could play an important role in considering not only how the book's message reaches children, and work to better both the gendered and species lessons of the books, but also consider how parents might interpret what is written.

These suggestions speak to the important role of picture books, animals, and interactions in children's development. The consequences for animals and humans are significant. There are real animals in the world whose lives are impacted by what we humans think of them. Therefore, parents and other interested adults can make a big difference in children's empathetic development by interpreting picture books in ways that offer an inclusive, complex, and more accurate view of animals and people.

Notes

1. Species re-presented in these books were mainly mammals and birds. While there are no doubt children's books that include amphibians, insects, and fish, none were present in the sample.
2. Books were mass-produced in China by the 9th century, using blocks with carved words and images to which ink was applied and pressed in to paper (http://afe.easia.columbia.edu/song/tech/printing.htm). Movable type reached Europe in the 15th century and is attributed to Johannes Gutenberg, who, around 1450, invented a mechanical metal moveable-type press. See Eisenstein (1983).

References

Albers, P. (1996). Issues of representation: Caldecott gold medal winners 1984–1995. *New Advocate, 9*(4), 267–228.

Arbuthot, M. H. (1984). *Children and books.* Chicago, IL: Scott Foresman & Company.

Armbruster, B., Lehr, F., & Osborn, J. (2002). *Teaching our youngest: A guide for preschool teachers and childcare and family providers.* Early Childhood Task Force. US Department of Education and the U.S. Department of Health and Human Services. Retrieved from http://www.ed.gov/teachers/how/early/teachingouryoungest/index.html

Arthur, A. G., & White, H. (1996). Children's assignment of gender to animal characters in pictures. *Journal of Genetic Psychology Research, Theory, & Human Development, 157*, 297–301.

Ashton, E. (1983). Measures of play behavior: The influence of sex-role stereotyped children's books. *Sex Roles, 9*, 43–47.

Bender, D. L., & Leone, B. (1989). *Human sexuality: 1989 annual.* San Diego, CA: Greenhaven.

Bewick, T. (1885). *The fables of Aesop: And others, with designs on wood.* London: B. Quaritch.

Collins, L. J., Ingoldsby, B. B., & Dellman, M. M. (1984). Sex-role stereotyping in children's literature: A change from the past. *Childhood Education, 90*, 278–285.

DeLoache, J. S., Cassidy, D. J., & Carpenter, C. (1987). The three bears are all boys: Mothers' gender labeling of neutral picture book characters. *Sex Roles, 17*(3/4), 163–178.

de Waal, F. (2001). *The ape and the sushi master.* New York, NY: Basic Books.

Duursma, E., Augustyn, M., & Zuckerman, B. (2008). Reading aloud to children: The evidence. *Archives of Disease in Childhood, 93*(7), 554–557.

Eisenstein, E. L. (1983). *The printing revolution in early modern Europe.* New York, NY: Cambridge University Press.

Engel R. (1981). Is unequal treatment of females diminishing in children's picture books? *The Reading Teacher, 34*, 647–652.

Gooden, A. M., & Gooden, M. A. (2001). Gender representation in Notable Children's picture books: 1995–1999. *Sex Roles, 45*(1/2), 89–101.

Green, V. A., Bigler, R., & Catherwood, D. (2004). The variability and flexibility of gender-typed toy play: A close look at children's behavioral responses to counterstereotypic models. *Sex Roles, 51*, 371–386.

Jennings, S. (1975). Effects of sex typing in children's stories on preferences and recall. *Child Development, 46*, 220–223.

Kuo, A. A., Franke, T. M., Regalado, M., & Halfon, N. (2004). Parent report of reading to young children. *Pediatrics, 113*(6), 1944–1951.

LaDow, S. (1976). *A content-analysis of selected picture books examining the portrayal of sex roles and representation of males and females.* East Lansing, MI: National Center for Research on Teacher Learning. (ERIC Document Reproduction Service No. ED123165).

Lévi-Strauss, C. (1966). *The savage mind*. London: Weidenfeld and Nicholson.
Martin C. L., & Ruble D. (2004). Children's search for gender cues: cognitive perspectives on gender development. *Current Directions in Psychological Science, 13*, 67–67.
Melson, G. (2001). *Why the wild things are: Animals in the lives of children*. Cambridge, MA: Harvard University Press.
Myers, O. G. (2007). *The significance of children and animals: Social development and our connections to other species*. West Lafayette, IN: Purdue University Press.
Narahara, M. (1998). *Gender stereotypes in children's picture books*. East Lansing, MI: National Center for Research on Teacher Learning National Council of Teachers of English (NCTE). NCTE Orbis Pictus award for outstanding nonfiction for children. Retrieved from http://www.ncte.org/awards/orbispictus
Nodelman, P. (1988). *Words about pictures: The narrative art of children's picture books*. Athens, GA: University of Georgia Press.
Patt, M. B., & McBride, B. A. (1992). *Gender equity in picture books in preschool classrooms: An exploratory study*. Paper presented at the Annual Meeting of the American Educational Research Association, Atlanta, GA.
Peterson, S. B., & Lach, M. A. (1990). Gender stereotypes in children's books: Their prevalence and influence on cognitive and affective development. *Gender and Education, 2*, 185–196.
Postman, N. (1982/1994). *The disappearance of childhood*. New York, NY: Vintage.
Ritvo, H. (1985). Learning from animals: Natural history for children in the eighteenth and nineteenth centuries. *Children's Literature, 13*, 72–93.
Samuels, S. J. (1977). Can pictures distract students from the printed word: A rebuttal. *Journal of Literacy Research, 9*(4), 361–364.
Shaw, V. (1998). *Sexual harassment and gender bias*. New York, NY: The Rosen Publishing Group.
Shepard, P. (1996). *The others: How animals made us human*. Washington, DC: Island Press.
Sutherland, Z., & Arbuthnot, M. H. (1986). *Children and books* (7th ed.). Glenview, IL: Scott, Foresman, & Company.
Tipper, B. (2011). "A dog who I know quite well": Everyday relationships between children and animals. *Children's Geographies, 9*(2), 145–165.
Trepanier-Street, M., & Kropp, J. J. (1990). Children's recall and recognition of sex-role stereotyped and discrepant information. *Sex Roles, 16*, 237–249.
Turner-Bowker, D. M. (1996). Gender stereotyped descriptors in children's picture books: Does "curious Jane" exist in literature? *Sex Roles, 35*, 461–488.
Weitzman, L. J., Eifler, D., Hokada, E., & Ross, C. (1972). Sex-role socialization in picture books for preschool children. *American Journal of Sociology, 77*, 1125–1150.
Wells, C. G. (1985). Preschool literacy-related activities and success in school. In D. Olson, N. Torrance, & A. Hildyard. (Eds.), *Literacy, language, and learning: The nature and consequences of literacy* (pp. 229–255). Cambridge: Cambridge University Press.
Wilson, E. O. (1984). *Biophilia*. Cambridge, MA: Harvard University Press.
Zipes, J. (2003). *The complete fairy tales of the brothers Grimm* (3rd ed.). New York, NY: Bantam.

Chapter Six

Polarizing Bears

The Semiotic Disconnect

Chew Polar Bear or it will chew you.
—"captious slogan for Polar Bear Chewing Tobacco" (1914)

For humans, the Arctic is a harshly inhospitable place, but the conditions there are precisely what polar bears require to survive—and thrive. "Harsh" to us is "home" for them. Take away the ice and snow, increase the temperature by even a little, and the realm that makes their lives possible literally melts away.
—Sylvia Earle (2012)

Stories ... can separate us from animals as easily as they can connect us, that the elevation of one animal to the sphere of particular human concern is likely to come at the expense of another. And the best stories are likely to complicate our relationships, not simplify them.
—Beha (2011)

In early December 2007, a polar bear cub was born at the Berlin zoo. This was the second pregnancy for the mother, Tosca, a former circus bear. As after the first birth, she again left her cubs to die. This time, zoo officials intervened and put both babies in incubators. Only one survived: a tiny, white, cuddly, cute cub they named Knut. Berlin zoo officials tried to keep word of his birth, rejection, and survival a secret, but it wasn't long before the global public learned his story. On March 27, 2007, excitement was palpable as crowds at the zoo awaited the appearance of the four-month old media sensation and chanted *"Wir wollen Knut!"* (trans. "We want Knut!"). Should the zoo have saved him? That question preoccupied global media and audiences. Some said "no," that the cub was meant to die, according to natural order, and should not have been artificially sustained. But most Berliners, and eventually much of the world, cried out on his behalf, responding to emotionally laden headlines throughout media such as "Rejected by Mom" and "Berlin Rallies Behind Baby Bear" (BBC 2007). The *New York Times* posed the question: "Impossible Not to Love the Little Guy? Not Quite" (*New York Times* in 2007).

Knut was such a cause célèbre that Berlin's coat of arms, a brown bear, was changed in press photos to white. What was it about Knut's struggle that set his story apart from those of the many other zoo animal tales heard and seen in media every day? According to one source, "He was a cute polar bear baby, who was rescued by people at a time when the polar bear had become a symbol of man's [sic] destruction of nature. Knut's personal history intervened in and themed the major international discourse on climate change" (2013).

The survival of the little cub, and the fact that humans could play a role in it, became metaphoric for the struggle of all polar bears, in fact the entire planet, in the face of global warming. But also, "long before Knut became a facsimile of himself" (he was taxidermied and displayed after death) "he had become first an asset and then an industry" (Engelhard, 2017, p. 23). The merchandising of Knut toys, pajamas, "Knut ringtones … commemorative coins and candies, pop music hits … DVDs, magazine stories, children's books, posters, T-shirts, and several films," illustrate the slippery nature of animal re-presentations (p. 23). Drawing on critical race theory, and employing Carol Adam's semiotic concept of the absent referent, this chapter interrogates the disconnect between the symbolic polar bear, representations of the bears in media and popular culture, and the potential effects of human cultural mediation on our understanding of other species.

The following sections discuss polar bears as real animals, as mythological, charismatic, and condensation symbols, how they are used in media and communications as for conservation causes, and how an unrealistically positive portrayal might impact their lives and ours. Research questions include: (1) how do real animals become concretized in to symbols? and (2) how do powerful animals in reality become cuddly beings when fictionalized?

Figure 6.1: Polar Bear.
Source: Used by permission iStock/Getty Images.

Real Polar Bears

Polar bears (also known as Sea Bear, Ice Bear *(Isbjorn)*, *Nanuq* (Inuit), White bear, *beliy medved* (Russian), Lord of the Arctic, Old man in the Fur Cloak, and White sea deer) belong to the scientific category *Ursus*

Maritimus and are the only bears classified as a marine mammal (polarbearinternational).[1] Males weigh from 775 to 1300 pounds and females range from 330 to 650 pounds (see Table 6.1 for more Bear Facts). Among the largest of all land predators the "sea bear" lives in five countries (United States, Canada, Greenland, Norway, and Greenland) and feeds primarily on seals who they reach from ice platforms. They were described as a commodity in Japanese writings as early as the 7th century CE (nearly 350 years before they were mentioned in Icelandic Norse documents) when, for example "the governor of Koshi Province presented two live white bears to Empress Kogyoku" (Engelhard, 2017, p. 30). Western fascination with polar bears and all things Arctic is rooted in first contact circumstances where the bears were coveted and given as rare gifts, and even functioned as a form of "live currency" in

Table 6.1. Polar Bear Facts.

Scientific name:	Ursus Maritimus
Conservation Status:	Vulnerable
Speed:	25 MPH max (adult in sprint)
Weight:	Male: 990 lbs. Female 330–550
Height:	Females 5'11"-7'10"; Males 7'10"-9'10"
Diet:	Ringed and bearded seals; occasionally walrus, beluga and bowhead whale carcasses, bird's eggs
Population:	Between 20,000–25,000 in world
Habitat:	Arctic; edge of pack ice. 9 Canada, Alaska (US), Greenland, Russia and Norway)
Live:	Solitary except during breeding and cub rearing. Denning only during maternity, March-April. Young born November-January.
Fun fact:	The largest and most carnivorous bear in the world; females only have five litters during
	Life, which is one of lowest reproductive rates of mammals.

Sources: http://www.defenders.org/polar-bear/basic-facts; https://www.natgeokids.com/uk/discover/animals/general-animals/polar-bear-facts/

the trading cultures of the medieval Norse (p. 31). Throughout Icelandic, Danish, and English culture, live bears became parts of menageries (such as that of King Henry III).

In today's world, real bears, this "sentinel species," faces devastating environmental conditions such as habitat loss due to oil drilling and global warming (Engelhard, 2017, p. 3). The impacts of the noise of drilling and climate change are resulting in abortions of cubs, earlier and longer fasts, low birth weight babies from mothers who are weakened from extended fasts, poaching, and the effects of toxic wastes that accumulate in seal blubber, their main food. Organizations such as Polar Bears International predict that, without action on climate change and stopping sea ice loss, the bears could be gone by 2,100, with 2/3 gone by 2,050 (Polar Bear FAQS).

A real polar bear walks the line between who we perceive him or her to be and the realities of his/her lived experience. In particular, the appropriation of positive qualities of bear-ness (the ability to walk on two legs, and a white[2] furry, cuddly appearance) into concepts related to the Arctic mystique ("whiteness, its relative rareness, and the remoteness of its home") reduces the bear to a type that has little relationship to the actual conditions faced by real animals (Engelhard, 2017, p. 13).

The Imagined Bear

The "special drawing power" of polar bears has historic origins that are consistent with public fascination with all things Arctic, including the people who live there (David, 2000, p. 171). The Arctic, to Britons "was as much ideological as physical terrain" in terms of identity and justification of nation and empire (Hill, 2009, p. 3). It was during the early part of the 20th century that the Arctic became a colonization hot spot when the *imagined* Arctic, and its inhabitants, entered the public imagination most strongly through re-presentations of it.

Objectifying the Arctic and the interchangeability of animals and humans began with the human exhibits of Polar Eskimos[3] ("one woman (Atangana), three men (Qisuk, Nuktaq, and Uisaakassak), and two children (Minik and Aviaq)" brought to New York City by explorer Robert Peary in 1897 (Huhndorf, 2001, p. 79). This was done at the request of anthropologist Franz Boas and others who were encouraged by the popularity of other live human exhibits at the World's Columbian Exposition in Chicago in 1893 (see Chapter 1 for more on Human Zoos). Thus, Boas collected live "specimen[s] for scientific study" who became objects of public fascination, made to dress, despite the heat, in furs (p. 79). As a result of exposure to non-endemic illness, stress, and other factors, many of these individuals became ill, as do most people who are held captive. In short order, four of the six died, but were watched in this condition as well. Brains and bones of the dead were removed for study. The surviving male adult was returned to his community and the child, an eight-year-old, was placed with a white family. Many more expeditions ventured to the Arctic and returned with cultural objects, animals, and human beings.

Public fascination peaked with Robert Flaherty's 1922 "documentary" *Nanook of the North*. Later revealed to be staged and manipulated, the film generated "nanookmania," leading to branding of products with interchangeable "Eskimo"/polar bear/penguin characters, such as Eskimo Pies ice cream.[4] Much like Edward Curtis's re-presentations of Plains indians,[5] Flaherty created a film designed to appeal to the "Southern [white] imagination" and the indigenous people were dressed in polar bear skins even though, "people didn't wear polar bear skin pants around here ... " (qtd. in Huhndorf, 2001, p. 123).

These re-presentations fueled a sense of the Arctic as the last frontier, where rarities still existed such as gold, species seen nowhere else, a foreboding exotic environment, stark, and harsh weather which relied "on the conventional tropes of discovery, conquest, and appropriation" along with "complementary paradigms of natural history" (Huhndorf, 2001, p. 84) that worked to naturalize colonialism and "mask[ed] ... motivations and hid[e] ... violence" (p. 84). Furthermore, this framing "provide[ed] a rationale for colonial expansion" (p. 16) with strongly gendered (masculine) and paternalistic associations that presented the Animal and the Other and Animal Other as seamless substitutes for one another. Similarities between ("the Eskimo and the polar bear") to an extent … are alike, the lines of their successful adaptation to the Arctic being parallel. The pretty of both, though not the principal prey of some Eskimo groups, is the ringed seal. Their hunting methods—waiting patiently at the aglu, various kinds of stalking—are strikingly similar. (Polar bears arrived in the Arctic ahead of the Eskimo, and it is likely Eskimos learned, or at least refined, some of their techniques by watching bears hunt). … Both make their living at the edge of the ice and along the shore. And both live with the threat of starvation if the seals disappear. (Lopez, 1986/2013, p. 94)

Thus, most animal collections at museums and zoos include polar bears. For example, Figure 6.2 is the taxidermied body of a polar bear killed in 1878 to serve as an exhibit in the zoological collection for the Stavanger Museum.

Trophy hunting in Alaska began in the 1950s when hunters could safely shoot from planes, snowmobiles, and helicopters. The killings were so great that not long after policies were needed to insure the

Figure 6.2: Isbjorn (Polar Bear).
Source: Svalbard, 1878. Stavanger Museum, Stavanger, Norway.

bear's survival. "These stories, of course, are from another era; but the craven taunting, the witless insensitivity, and the phony sense of adventure that propelled them are not from another age. They still afflict us" (Lopez, 1968/2013, p. 113) as they do them. Animals often go from admired to demonized and back again, as is also the case with the wolf. In the case of polar bears, "whatever remorse they [Europeans] suffered over their harsh treatment of the polar bear eventually became admiration, but for a bear that was a really curious image of themselves" (p. 113). The bear was viewed, as "an impediment to Western progress and then an amusement, a nuisance, finally became a vaguely noble creature, wandering in a desolate landscape, saddled with melancholy thoughts a romantic, estranged, self-absorbed creature" (p. 113).

"Only one Arctic mammal could rival the popularity of the big game of Africa and Asia, and of perennial favourites such as the elephant, and that was the polar bear" (David, 2000, p. 171). Polar bear rugs as trophies on to which naked babies and women are posed is a relatively recent phenomenon. Hunting for trophy purposes is not part of traditional Inuit practice because, prior to the introduction of guns, it was simply too dangerous and thereafter, the rare killings were for sustenance. Using the skins for decorative purposes was not popular until the 1960s when global demand went in to overdrive. Unregulated sport and commercial hunting in the 1960s and 1970s resulted in such a real threat to polar bears that, in 1973 the five polar bear countries signed a landmark document, The Agreement on the Conservation of Polar Bears, to begin regulating these killings in order to conserve the bears.

The 1972 passage of the Marine Mammal Protection Action (MMPA) in the United States ended trophy hunting in Alaska. This did not include Canada where the bear is not regarded as a marine mammal and hunting is allowed if led by Inuit guides using traditional transportation. The Inuit rarely participate, but Canada seemed to want to leave this open as a possible revenue stream. In the 1980s, The Department of Economic Development and Tourism created programs to train Inuit members as guides and outfitters including a return to using dog teams from the previously popular use of snowmobiles.

Yet who is the polar bear? Very few of us have likely met one in person. Even then, our idea of the bears is, like with most wild animals, first influenced by what we have seen or heard in the media about them. Occasional news stories about human/bear encounters slip out of places where locals deal everyday with the great white beings, but mostly, particularly for Europeans and Americans, advertising is the place most bears can be found. In advertising and in films a person "constructs an image while not in direct sensory contact with the object or objects from which the imagery of the imagining is constructed." The re-presentation likely draws from the image creator's understandings of what audiences believe to be true, and are produced "within the parameters of accepted canons of taste" (David, 2000, p. 11). Polar bears fit not only in to the concept of white wild animal but more so grew out of the larger Arctic stereotype.

Imaging the Bear

Whaling, missionary activity, and fascination with Inuit life ways intensified with exploration of and attempts to map the North West Passage well in to the mid to late 19th century. The region itself, as well as its inhabitants, only recently emerged from stereotypical fascinations of the collective unconscious that is "no less significant ... than the exoticism of the Orient or the darkness at the heart of Africa," evident during the 19th and 20th centuries (David, 2000, p. 6; see also Said, 1985; Adas, 1989; Smith, 1992). Even today, if the only way a person knows a place or a people or a species, is through second hand re-presentations such as media, the re-presentation is vulnerable to the agenda of its producer.

Smith's (1992, p. ix) "image to imagination" process of deconstructing re-presentations is a useful framework for thinking about these dynamics. As such, a person "constructs an image while not in direct sensory contact with the object or objects from which the imagery of the imagining is constructed" (p. ix). Re-presentations are thereby created and symbols used that not only reflect the unconsciousness of the creator but his or her sense of producing a final image "within the parameters of accepted canons of taste" (David, 2000, p. 11). Polar bears fit in to the construction of an Arctic stereotype which draws on Edward

Said's concept of "latent orientalism" .... For Europeans the bear has operated as "a symbol of the implacable indifference of an inhospitable landscape" (Lopez, 1986/2013, p. 113). Furthermore, Brody's (1987, p. 19) description of the Inuit person in popular culture as an outsider is consistent with the "image to imagination" concept:

> The Eskimo makes his and her appearance with a smile. Imposed on the stereotypical background of impossible terrain and intolerable weather is an eternally happy, optimistic little figure; a round furry and cuddly human with a pet name ... Gorge themselves as they binge on raw meat and blubber, a stereotypical Eskimo of the impossible north wages his battle against environment in astonishingly good humour.

Thus the polar bear is similarly situated as an entanglement of both real and re-presented, as displayed in this 1951 advertisement for Maidenform Bras:

This is the same psychological dynamic that occurs with animals who one knows only symbolically or in the artificial setting of a zoo or aquarium. Thus "in the absence of primary representations, the public [must] rely on hearsay and half-truths, some of which date[e) back to the classical world" (Smith, qtd. in David, 2000, p. 11). It is parallel to the way racial re-presentations are created, typically not by people within the group, but more often from those outside of it based on a narrow range of secondary and tertiary experiences mostly with media. Stereotypes, generalizations of persons, places, or things, also include animals. These concretized, reductive re-presentations or understandings of someone or something are one-dimensional, and treat all members of a group as the same. While most stereotypes associated with racial difference tend to be negative (such as African Americans are lazy, Native Americans are alcoholics, Latinos are dangerous), some paint an unrealistically positive view- or rather take a trait and act as if it applies to all members of the group (such as the Model Minority stereotype applied to Asian Americans). It is not representative of true individual differences and should an individual behave in a way that is inconsistent with that stereotype, he or she is often met with criticism.

In the case of animals,[6] many are also the target of limiting and limited portrayals, particularly in the case of predator species such as

Figure 6.3: Maidenform Bra Advertisement (1951).
Source: Used with permission, Hanes Brands, Inc.

wolves, tigers, leopards, coyotes, and bears. The polar bear, however, while equally as powerful, fierce, and complex as are his or her brown and black brothers and sisters, has been portrayed in ways that suggest polar bears are purely cuddly, approachable, and gentle animals.

Media coverage of Knut did little to more completely paint a picture of the bears. Similarly, the concept of charisma erases any single animal's nature, personality, and behaviors, but is a term, described in the following section, that advertisers and conservation groups use to communicate.

Charisma

Polar bears are considered charismatic mega fauna, i.e., those species who have popular appeal because of their size, inviting appearance, large ears and eyes are "cute, cuddly, majestic or furry," with otherwise positive qualities known as neoteny (Hund, 2008, p. 240). Drawing on the work of Konrad Lorenz in the 1940s, neoteny is "a shortened nose, big eyes, a disproportionately large head, and round and soft body features paired with playfulness or curiosity turn us all gooey inside" (Engelhard, 2017, p. 27). This cuteness triggers the release of hormones that stimulate pleasure centers in the brain in humans that encourage nurturing and protection (think about puppies, kittens, baby polar bears, and the popularity of toy animals). Charismatic mega fauna distinguishes species who, "serve as symbols and rallying points to stimulate conservation awareness and action" (Heywood, 1995, p. 491) and includes animals such as pandas, bald eagles, lions, wolves, tigers, cougars, koala bears, whales, dolphin, gorillas, penguins, elephants, eagles, harp seals, and bears.

Charisma is a term typically employed to describe humans with "a grace, a talent" and "the capacity to inspire devotion or enthusiasm" (*Oxford English Dictionary*). Etymologically the term comes from the Greek word *Kharis* (favor or grace freely given) and is that something special, a quality, that is hard to name, yet attracts admirers and followers. Sociologist Max Weber (1968) used this term to describe a form of authority, as

> [A] certain quality of an individual personality by virtue of which he is set apart from ordinary men and treated as endowed with supernatural,

superhuman, or at least specifically exceptional powers or qualities. These are such as are not accessible to the ordinary person, but are regarded as of divine origin or as exemplary, and on the basis of them the individual concerned is treated as a leader. (p. 48)

Expanding on this concept, it is not only who this person is, but also what he or she does—what this charismatic quality leads to or what it says about the society. The power lies not only in qualities the charismatic individual possess but more so, what others believe he or she has, the acceptance of them, that forms "a complex set of social relations" (Christensen, 2005, p. 227). Weber also noted there is often a magical quality to charisma. I argue that some animals are also charismatic. The relational aspect of charisma is evident amongst zoo animals who stand as species exemplars, but also for the public's beliefs about them. When applied to animals other than humans, charisma has semiotic significance and functions as admiration, awe, and respect when incorporated in to forms of communication.

Charismatic species are used by advertisers, media makers, and conservationists because they have mass appeal, traits (even if they are dangerous) that are admired, and who gain psychic traction when employed as advertising brands, public relations tools, and fundraising emblems. They are used in marketing and merchandising for zoos, as stuffed toys for products related to movies, television shows, and comic strips, to promote causes, and for ecotourism. Thus, images of large animals are often used to sell travel and vacation destinations, ecotourism trips, and in advertising as brand images for products manufactured and mostly sold in the West. For example, tourists traveling to Africa mostly want to see the "big five" charismatic mega fauna: rhinoceros, lions, leopards, elephants, and Cape buffalo (Mawdsley & Surridge, 2012, p. 5).

The term "charismatic mega fauna" is primarily applied to large animals in the developed world where engagement with large living mammals is very different from that in other parts of the world where experience is more often direct than purely symbolic. Whereas lions, tigers, and bears are more often viewed as dangerous or imminently nuisances or threatening to life and limb in places where real animals are encountered on a daily basis, those whose experiences are more often vicarious tend to view large animals quiet differently.

A recent example is the July 2015 killing of the beloved lion Cecil in Zimbabwe by American dentist Walter Palmer. To many, Cecil was thought of as a beautiful animal, with charismatic qualities such as honor, bravery, strength, and courage. But lions are also large, dangerous creatures whose behaviors are feared by those who live in close proximity to them. The global outcry over Cecil's murder, primarily by geographic and cultural outsiders, was not only who he was as an individual, but more so what he stood for in the collective imagination.

The same can be said of polar bears who represent not only their species as human-like in many regards[7] but also the general vanishing of species, making them attractions for "last chance tourism" (Lemelin, Dawson, & Stewart, 2013, p. 3). Furthermore, "the polar bear has become the most evocative species in the media showing the struggle to survive in a changing environment" (p. 120). Thus tourists want to see them before they disappear, which speaks as much to their vulnerability as our sense of our own.

The polar bear has been doing the symbolic work of attracting public attention to the impact of global warming. In 2009, at the Copenhagen Climate Change Conference, the International Union for the Conservation of Nature (IUCN) suggested that more "flagship" species (an alternative term for charismatic mega fauna) could be brought on board to "share the polar bear's burden" and if one is good, many (a fleet) would be great in terms of having the power to influence public opinion and be used as a public resource for selecting spokes-species. Thus "stag horn corals, the ringed seal, the leatherback turtle, the emperor penguin, the quiver tree, clownfish, the arctic fox, salmon, the koala, and the beluga whale" were added to poster-species by the IUCN.

In a world increasingly driven by advertising dollars and the power of intellectual property that is embedded in brands and trademarks, flagship species operate as conservation movement tools as well to draw attention to causes and raise public awareness of species in peril. Which one is chosen and why varies according to cultural context and purpose. For example, the whale might be an entirely appropriate animal to bring attention to international conservation issues, whereas an otter might not, for "an otter-watching tour would not necessarily establish the moral imperative of conservation" (Barua, Root-Bernstein, Ladle, & Jepson, 2011, p. 431). Furthermore, "To select flagships for desired uses requires attention to socio-cultural and biological characteristics of species" (pp. 431–432).

Polar Bears in Popular Culture

In recent years, children's books about polar bears or with polar bear characters have flooded the market. As discussed in Chapter 3, children have a natural connection with animals and are drawn to them as peers. Furthermore, they can potentially learn scientific information about the bears, information on race, and gender issues, and other topics depending on how parents interact during reading, particularly with picture books. For example, there are many children's books on the melting of ice and environmental loss that include polar bears and why it is important to be resourceful conservationists in the face of this. At the same time, these books can provide inaccurate information. For example, in Hans de Beer's *Little Polar Bear and the Whales*, beluga whales are rescued by Lars the bear, whereas in real life this would not be the case as the bears have been known to prey on the white whales.

Early children's books that included polar bears often portrayed them as frightening creatures. Today, more than any other animal, the polar bear has come to represent the Anthropocene, a "new interval in *geological* history" (ital. orig). (Hamilton, Bonneuil, & Gemenne, 2015, p. 2) that is a major turning point in the history of the planet, not only in a purely scientific sense of rock strata but also recognizes the inter connectedness of all systems and the human influence on them. With ancient mythological import, the bear has become the "poster animal" for global warming. Little known outside of their intimate relationship with Inuit culture (other than in zoos or more recently as the object of fascination of ecotourism) what most of us know about them comes almost entirely from the media. As discussed earlier in this book, animals are widely used to generate revenue for corporations and organizations. Polar bears in particular have commercial and semiotic value that is "reprocess[ed] into money-making productions such as status symbols, fighters, dancers, bicycle riders, roller skaters, musicians, zoo exhibits, trophies, teddy bears, and advertising icons" (Bieder, 2005, p. 102).

On the one hand, polar bears function as "condensation symbols," which are "words or symbols that "sti[r] vivid impressions involving the listener's most basic values" (Graber, 1976, p. 289). As such, particularly in environmental literature, polar bears stand in for and absorb fears and anxieties about ecological disaster. These beings figure largely in the collective imagination not only based on their size, but also

> In part, our fascination with it springs from the charisma all carnivores share: their quickness, intensity, and acuity, magnified by their strength. It is the idea of their unfettered existence, their calm in the crucial moments, that attract us. We see ourselves in them. (Engelhard, 2017, p. 6)

On the other hand, the symbolic polar bear is also distorted in to overly positive representations on greeting cards, in print advertising (Coca Cola, Frosted Cheerios), television commercials (Nissan LEAF), and in movies (*The Golden Compass, Arctic Tail*) that paint a falsely positive image of the bear's nature as well as likely contribute to a sense that they are less endangered than they really are (Ross, Vreeman, & Lonsdorf, 2011).

> As the bear was packaged into zoos and circuses, served as a representative figure in art, films, and photographs; was snapped up as a toy; engraved on postage stamps, portrayed on playing cards; squeezed between book covers; launched into song and dance; and manipulated in literary metaphors to stand for wilderness or rites of passage, it disappeared as a real biological animal from peoples' lives. (Bieder, 2005, p. 136)

Were a human to encounter a polar bear based on this inaccurate information, the result would be a disaster for both. For example, a 2010 television advertisement for the Nissan LEAF automobile shows a weary polar bear making his or her way from the Arctic to a driveway in suburban America, just to give the car's purchaser a big hug (and yes, they used a real bear), an 800-pound female named Agee (Reich, 2010).

No corporation has likely benefited more from the symbolic power of polar bears than Coca-Cola. What do a carbonated beverage and polar bears have to do with one another? Is Coca-Cola something the average bear consumes? The answers are "nothing" and "no."

The polar bear has become part of the visual discourse of global climate change and is featured in global advertising campaigns for Coca-Cola dating back to 1922 that was inspired by a Labrador retriever who a creative worker felt looked like a polar bear. During the following 70+ years, the bear made a strong re-appearance in the now-famous "Northern Lights" commercial which first aired during the 1994 Olympics. A company CEO said, "We want to help the polar bear ... by helping conserve its Arctic habitat. That's why we're using one of our greatest assets, our flagship brand, Coca-Cola, to raise awareness for this important cause" (cited in Engelhard, 2017, p. 211). In the ad, a humanized coke-drinking bear navigates a ski jump, and polar bear families select Christmas tree ornaments in holiday advertising for the soft drink. In 2007, director Ridley Scott created a seven-and-a-half-minute video.

In a 2013 short film version, a father bear tries rehearsing an acceptance speech about accepting difference, while troublesome young cub Kaia feels misunderstood and constantly gets in to trouble. Befriended by a dancing Puffin, she demonstrates to the whole community the value and fun of difference. None of this, of course, has anything to do with soft drinks and is quite inaccurate in terms of real polar bear behavior. In this tender tale of parental nay saying and adolescent angst, there are some gross inaccuracies (Pomeroy, 2013). For example, polar bears don't dance, drink soft drinks, or live in groups. In addition, besides the fact that male polar bears are a threat to, and even kill cubs, the mother would not have older and younger cubs living together as the ad shows older brothers Zook and Jack and then younger Kaia. Instead, by the time cubs are around age two, the mother drives them off.

Does Coke give back? Kind of. In 2011, Coca-Cola used the success of the polar bear campaigns to generate awareness of their philanthropic efforts in the "Arctic Home" campaign designed to raise $3 million for the World Wildlife Fund's polar bear conservation efforts. This use prompts the question of whether corporations who use animals and animal images and names to promote their products should be required to give some portion of their profits to the species' welfare and conservation.

In addition, as indicated earlier, research shows that using bears, or other wildlife, to advertise products can have the opposite effect than intended on their conservation: "Academic research of marketing unsurprisingly shows that the more abstract and anthropomorphized an animal character is, the less consumers think about the real animal and its natural context" (Engelhard, 2017, p. 212).

Conclusion

Fear of loss polar bears has motivated conservation programs. Mostly this is more about us than about them. What does the loss of *them* mean to *us*? *For* us? As it was for the wolves in the 19th century, the view was (and persists) that the more killed the better. In the Arctic, whalers and others "shot the animals with colonial indifference" (Lopez, 1986/2013, p. 111). Knut died at the young age of four, in 2011. He drowned after falling in to the pool in his enclosure (the result of encephalitis and a brain aneurism). So adored, his hide was taxidermied so that visitors could forever visit the famous bear. His body toured before finding a final resting place in the permanent collection of Berlin's Natural History Museum, and not without controversy ("Knut the polar bear," 2013).

Over the past eight thousand years we have regarded the Polar Bear as "food, toy, pet, trophy, status symbol, commodity, man-eating monster, spirit familiar, circus act, zoo superstar, and political cause célèbre. We have feared, venerated, locked up, coveted, butchered, sold, pitied, and emulated this large carnivore. It has left few emotions unstirred" (Engelhard, 2017, p. 7). But is this the real bear? And what do these different ways of "knowing" the bear mean for their continued life on Earth?

Notes

1. Canada is the only nation to classify them as land mammals.
2. The polar bear's "whiteness ... symbolic of their purity and that of their environment—too is an idealization" (Engelhard, 2017, p. 210). The bears begin life pure white in color but their fur darkens as they age, becoming more yellowish. The whiteness is more a refraction of light, the same one that makes ice appear white.

3. As Huhndorf notes, at the 1977 Inuit Circumpolar Conference, the term "Eskimo" was rejected due to its pejorative connotations as mostly outsiders use it. However, in this circumstance the term is used when specific designations such as "Inupiat," Native Alaskan, or "Yup'ik" are not and the term has continued use within the indigenous groups.
4. "Eskimo" is used not as a pejorative but rather as situated in literature.
5. Drawing on Klopotek, I use the the uncapitalized term "indian" "which connotes the symbolic character of the white imagination, akin to a troll or an elf," and the upper case term "Indian," to denote the people descended from the original human inhabitants of the Americas. ... "The purpose of making the distinction between indians and Native Americans in writing is to emphasize the extent to which the indian is truly a construction of the white imagination having little resemblance Native Americans. Of course the concept of any universal term or category for all the indigenous nations of the Americas is itself deeply rooted in colonialism, but such terms—for better or worse—have become more meaningful at the beginning of the 21st century" (Klopotek, 2001, p. 20).
6. Valuing animals or making comparisons with humans does not devalue humans. Having compassion for all living beings is what matters and we need not choose one over the other.
7. Many cultures draw close associations with bears. For some it is bears ability to walk upright. The polar bear nurses her babies sitting upright, "in the Arctic, only humans and bears hunt seal mammals," they have wide range of vocalizations, keen senses of hearing and smell, and "for a long time people even believed that bears have sex in the missionary position" (Engelhard, 2017, pp. 10–11).

References

(2007, March 20). Berlin rallies behind baby bear. *BBC News*. Retrieved from http://news.bbc.co.uk/1/hi/world/europe/6470509.stm

(2007, March 21). Germany: Impossible not to love the little guy? Not quite. *New York Times*. Retrieved from http://www.nytimes.com/2007/03/21/world/europe/21briefs-germancub.html

(2013, February 12). Knut the polar bear life size model to go on show in Berlin. *Guardian*. Retrieved from https://www.theguardian.com/world/2013/feb/12/knut-polar-bear-model-berlin

Adas, M. (1989). *Machines as the measure of men: Science, technology, and ideologies of Western dominance*. Ithaca, NY: Cornell.

Barua, M., Root-Bernstein, M., Ladle, R. J., & Jepson, P. (2011). Defining flagship uses is critical for flagship selection: A critique of the IUCN climate change flagship fleet. *AMBIO: A Journal of the Human Environment, 40*(4), 431–435.

Beha, C. (2011, December 22). Bears, dolphins, and the animal stories we tell. *New York Times*. Sunday Book Review. Retrieved from http://www.nytimes.com/2011/12/25/books/review/bears-dolphins-and-the-animal-stories-we-tell.html

Bieder, R. E. (2005). *Bear*. London: Reaktion.

"charisma | charisma, n." (2015, June). OED Online. Oxford University Press, Retrieved August 2015.

Brody, H. (1987). *Living Arctic: Hunters of the Canadian north*. Vancouver, BC: Douglas and McIntyre.

Christensen, D. R. (2005). Inventing L. Ron Hubbard: On the construction and maintenance of the hagiographic mythology of Scientology's founder. In J. R. Lewis & J. A. Petersen (Eds.), *Controversial new religions* (pp. 227–258). New York, NY: Oxford University Press.

David, R. G. (2000). *The Arctic in the British imagination*. Manchester: Manchester University Press.

Earle, S. (2012, April 20). Save the polar bears, save ourselves. *Huffington Post*. Retrieved from http://www.huffingtonpost.com/sylvia-earle/to-the-arctic-3d-documentary_b_1435984.html

Engelhard, M. (2017). *Ice bear: The cultural history of an arctic icon*. Seattle, WA: University of Washington Press.

Graber, D. A. (1976). *Verbal behavior and politics*. Urbana, IL: University of Illinois Press.

Hamilton, C., Bonneuil, C., & Gemenne, F. (2015). Thinking the Anthropocene. In C. Hamilton, C. Bonneuil, & F. Gemenne (Eds.), *The Anthropocene and the global environmental crisis* (pp. 1–13). New York, NY: Routledge.

Heywood, V. H. (1995). *Global biodiversity assessment*. Cambridge: Cambridge University Press.

Hill, J. (2009). *White horizon: The Arctic in the nineteenth-century British imagination*. Albany, NY: SUNY.

Huhndorf, S. M. (2001). *Going native: Indians in the American cultural imagination*. Ithaca, NY: Cornell.

Hund, A., (2008). Charismatic megafauna. In S. G. Philander (Ed.), *Encyclopedia of global warming and climate change* (2nd ed., pp. 237–242). Thousand Oaks, CA: Sage.

Klopotek, B. (2001). "I guess your warrior look doesn't work every time": Challenging Indian masculinity in the cinema. In M. Basso, L. McCall, & D. Garceau (Eds.), *Across the great divide: Cultures of manhood in the American West* (pp. 251–273). New York, NY: Routledge.

Lemelin, H., Dawson, J., & Stewart, E. J. (2013). Introduction. In R. H. Lemelin, J. Dawson, & E. J. Stewart (Eds.), *Last chance tourism: Adapting tourism opportunities in a changing world* (pp. 3–9). New York, NY: Routledge.

Lopez, B. (1986/2013). *Arctic dreams*. New York, NY: Simon & Schuster.

Mawdsley, J., & Surridge, M. (2012). *Climate-change vulnerabilities and adaptation strategies for Africa's charismatic megafauna*. Report. Washington, DC: Heinz Center for Science Economics & Environment.

Polar Bear FAQs. (2015). *Polar Bears International*. Retrieved from http://www.polarbearsinternational.org/about-polar-bears/faqs

Pomeroy, S. R. (2013, December 20). Coca-Cola's polar bear film is full of lies. *Slate*. Retrieved from http://www.slate.com/blogs/wild_things/2013/12/20/coke_s_polar_bears_film_adorable_but_the_biology_is_all_wrong.html

Reich, H. (2010, September). Yes, that's a real polar bear in Nissan's Leaf commercial. *Autotrader*. Retrieved from http://www.autotrader.com/car-news/yes-thats-a-real-polar-bear-in-nissans-leaf-commercial-71924

Ross, S. R., Vreeman, V. M., & Lonsdorf, E. V. (2011). Specific images characteristics influence attitudes about chimpanzee conversation and use as pets. *PLOS One*, 6(7). Retrieved from http://www.plosone.org/article/info%3Adoi%2F10.1371%2Fjournal.pone.0022050

Said, E. W. 1985. *Orientalism*. Harmondsworth: Penguin.

Smith, B. (1992). *Imagining the Pacific: In the wake of the Cook voyages*. New Haven, CT: Yale University Press.

Weber, M. (1968). *On charisma and institution building*. Chicago, IL: University of Chicago Press.

Chapter Seven

The Plight of the Prairie Dog

The prairie dog is, in fact, one of the curiosities of the Far West, about which travelers delight to tell marvelous tales, endowing him at times with something of the politic and social habits of a rational being, and giving him systems of civil government and domestic economy, almost equal to what they used to bestow upon the beaver.

—Irving (1835/2006, p. 252)

Prairie dogs are the eyes of the community.

—Williams (2008, p. 53)

If you kill off the prairie dogs, there will be no one to cry for the rain. Diné belief.

—Qtd in Toelken (2008, p. 391)

Figure 7.1: Two Prairie Dogs Sharing Their Food.
Source: Used by permission iStock/Getty Images.

They are called *petit chien*, pispiza, prairie marmot, barking ground squirrel, and prairie squirrel. All are names for a little 2–3 pound, approximately 12" long (plus 3–4" tail) rodent (see Figure 7.1). Colonial settlers wrote in journals and diaries about prairie dogs comparing them with puppies and squirrels, as combinations of both, using language that would typically describe human settlement behaviors to that of the animals. More deeply, these tiny monitors "embody two million years of evolving intelligence" (Williams, 2008, p. 33) as they scan the horizon for signs of kin, threat, and foe.

This chapter explores questions such as: what factors contribute to the paradox of the prairie dog being both cute friend and rural enemy? and "does Disney's nature-as-entertainment distance audiences from the plight of real animals?" In particular, Settler Colonialism is used as a theoretical framework for unpacking the complicated relationship between humans and animals of the American West, the enemification of these important little beings, and a specific case of the presentation of prairie dogs in the Disney True Nature Adventure film *The Vanishing Prairie* (1954). Adams' (1990/2015) semiotic concept of the absent referent is applied when thinking about how the media represent and distance us from animals versus the conditions of their lived experiences, in this case from a species who was nearly 98% exterminated in North America during the 20th century.

Real Prairie Dogs

Prairie dogs (Genus: *Cynomys*) have reddish-brown fur on their backs and lighter colored undersides. There are five species: Black-tailed (the most common), Gunnison's (live in 4 Corners region), Utah (threatened under the U.S. Endangered Species Act), White-tailed (Utah, Colorado, Wyoming, Montana), and Mexican (listed as endangered). They belong to the squirrel family of rodents and live in the prairie grasslands of the American west as well as in parts of Canada and Mexico (Slobodchikoff, Perla, & Verdolin, 2009). At one time, estimates held their co-existence at 30–60 million, and, prior to the 1800s, with numbers exceeding 5 billion (Fahnestock & Detling, 2002) (see Table 7.1 for more facts).

The typical prairie dog diet consists of grasses such as the Western wheatgrass, globe mallow, blue grama, and buffalo grass (Slobodchikoff et al., 2009). These burrowing mammals live in colonies known as towns or villages and in family groups called coteries. The name "Prairie Dog" comes from colonial settler observations of the little animal's barking or chirping calls when alerting others of danger. The British *Collins English Dictionary* defines prairie dogs as "gregarious sciurine rodents."

Prairie Dogs are keystone species as their activities and bodies serve important ecological roles as their burrowing aerates and fertilizes soil, and provides homes for other animals. Prairie Dogs are also food for many other animals, such as badgers, coyotes, hawks, eagles, and the critically endangered black-footed ferret.[1] It is estimated that prairie dogs impact the lives of at least 130–150 other animals and plants in their ecosystems.

The diurnal prairie dog exhibits several behaviors that are easily anthropomorphized. For example, they live collectively in large groups, stand upright on their hind legs, alert others of impending dangers

Table 7.1. Prairie Dog Facts.

Scientific Name:	Cynomys
Weight:	1.1–3.3 lbs.
Length:	12-16 in.
Phylum:	Chordata
Group names:	Coterie
Mating Season:	March
Gestation:	33-38 days; pups born April or May
Litter size:	3-4 pups average
Higher Classification:	Ground Squirrel
Lower classifications:	Black tailed, Mexican, Utah, Gunnison's, White-Tailed Live in underground burrows, in large colonies
Diet:	Grasses, sedges, forbs (flowering plants), roots, and seeds. Occasional insects.
Population:	10-20 million (95% less than once were)
Habitat:	Great Plains from southern Canada to northern Mexico.
Fun fact:	Largest recorded black-tailed prairie dog town was about 100 miles long and found in Western Texas.

Sources: http://www.defenders.org/prairie-dog/basic-facts; https://www.worldwildlife.org/stories/8-surprising-prairie-dog-facts

(accompanied by dog-like "bark" called a "jump-yip"), and "kiss" (i.e. they touch front teeth as a way of recognizing relatives). In fact, an Arizona biologist, who has been studying Prairie Dog sounds for more than three decades, argues not only that Prairie Dogs have vocalizations, but that their sounds should be considered language (Jabr, 2017):

> Beyond identifying the type of predator, prairie-dog calls also specified its size, shape, color and speed; the animals could even combine the structural elements of their calls in novel ways to describe something they had never seen before. … Prairie-dog communication is so complex, Slobodchikoff says—so expressive and rich in information—that it constitutes nothing less than language.

These characteristics make them attractive and relatable to humans. Furthermore, their small size, large eyes, and chubby bodies have a neotenized quality that further endear them to us.

However, Prairie Dogs are also known by less romantic and even derisive words. For example, those who hunt and kill them typically refer to them as desert rats, sage rats, varmints, and vermin. The slang expression "prairie-dogging" means to need to find a bathroom, or, in the American cartoon Dilbert, to "pop one's head from an office cubicle."

Where once prairie dogs numbered in the billions in the North American and Mexican West, since the 1880s their populations have been reduced by 98–99% through hunting, poisoning, fumigation, and other violent means of extermination. The black-tailed prairie dog once lived on over 100 million acres of prairie is today found on only 800,000 (Williams, 2000). Because of their small size and lack of visibility, until recently Prairie Dogs weren't considered in many government, scientific, or environmental management plans (Jones, 1999). In wasn't until the late 1970s, when a prairie dog predator, the black-footed ferret, gained notoriety as the most endangered mammal on the planet that attention turned to the status of the prairie dog.

The reality for Prairie Dogs is that 70% of their colonies have disappeared due to habitat destruction. They exist today only 1–2% of the land they once use to inhabit. There are four major sources of decline, most attributable to human actions:

1. Poisoning—due to perceived competition with cattle for food, the anticoagulant Rozol is legally used to kill black-tailed prairie dogs. Kaput-D was authorized in 2012–2013 (Jones, 2013, p. 25). These poisons result in internal bleeding that lasts up to 72 hours and causes extreme suffering and puts dangerous chemicals in to the environment.
2. Shooting—for recreation. This not only cause the suffering of individual animals but also disrupts groups, causes stress making the animals more susceptible to diseases.
3. Development—Prairie Dog colonies are typically located in flat areas that are desirable for building.
4. Disease—Sylvatic/bubonic plague (*yersina pestis*) brought in on fleas from other animals. Prairie dogs have no natural immunity to this disease, which was brought in to American in the 1800s.

Prairie Dogs have few legal protections, except for the two subspecies who are listed as threatened or endangered. The lack of protection and a view of them as harmful rather than helpful are tied to cultural prejudices. "Ranchers argue that prairie dogs compete with cattle for forage, injure livestock that step in their burrows, pose a public health threat, and cause environmental damage. They further claim that prairie dogs are abundant—even suffering from overpopulation—and deserve no legal protection" (McCain, Reading, & Miller, 2002, p. 233).

Strange as it may seem, humans and prairie dogs have quite a bit in common. Besides both being mammals, we are also closely tied to land, live in families and communities, adjust our ways of living in relation to other species, and impact other animals through our practices. However, due to human agricultural methods such as free-ranging cattle in the American west (cows allowed to roam unrestricted rather than living in fenced pastures) many farmers and ranchers believe cattle compete with the small animals for grass. What is this belief, that prairie dogs are a threat to cattle for grass, based upon? Prairie dog towns are stark—made up mostly of sparse vegetation, dirt, and rocks. Having low or little foliage is a survival strategy-the better to see predators. Thus overgrazed areas are ideal places to build dens and burrows. Science shows there are no significant differences in weight between cattle who graze in areas where there are prairie dogs and where there are not. According to a grassland ecologist, "there has been no documented evidence that prairie dogs compete with domestic livestock under densities typically encountered on the Great Plains." In fact, the little mammals burrowing turns over and aerates the soil, and as a result, the vegetation while sparse is nutritionally richer and the cattle seek out these places. They are highly social, community oriented individuals. In fact, "the prairie dog stands for community. ... The prairie dog lives because of community" (Williams, 2008, p. 39) yet they are seen as impediments to development and individualism.

Why would an animal, who science says plays such a pivotal role in maintaining the health of grasslands, be so hated and hunted? What is the basis for the anti-prairie dog attitude despite sympathetic, even lovable portrayals in media and popular culture? When, why, and how did the prairie dog become a pest in the collective imagination? One explanation is found in the mythology of the American West.

Symbolic Prairie Dog

While the prairie dog was in greater numbers than most animals in the American west, it has a somewhat less mythological heritage than do some Western animals. Perhaps this is because of its small size or other factors, but it seems not to figure as prominently in First Nations stories as do eagles, coyotes, wolves, or rabbits.

We share other similarities with prairie dogs. For example, we both mourn the passing of a family member or friend. Bekoff writes (2017)

> I just watched an adult prairie dog who I think is a female trying to retrieve the carcass of a smaller prairie dog off the road five times—she clearly was trying to remove the carcass from the road—I stopped and finally after the cars stopped she dragged the carcass off the road, walked about 10 feet away, looked at me and looked at the carcass, went back to the carcass and touched it lightly with her forepaws, and walked away emitting a very high-pitched vocalization.
>
> I waited a few minutes to see if she would go back to the carcass and she began to move toward it, looked at me, and stopped—so I left because I didn't want to disrupt her saying good-bye if that was what she was going to do—minutes later, when I finally caught up with another rider who was about 100 meters ahead of me, he told me he saw her try to remove the carcass from the road twice.

Prairie Dogs and Humans have something else in common: we both colonize. However, while they do so as a way of communal living, known as "coloniality," humans take land through occupation. Prairie dogs are as representative of the American west as are bison, but they symbolize something quite different due in part to their size, both as small bodies and with an originally large population (this same prejudice led to extermination of the passenger pigeon). The Lewis and Clark expedition, for example, sent back a multitude of plants and animals, some never seen or described before. "Many of their new discoveries remain vital symbols of the West: the prairie dog, ponderosa pine, grizzly bear, and coyote" (Slatta, 2001, p. 203). At the same time, as European settlers expanded westward, issues of enough (food, water, land) as well as who or what impeded what was viewed as a God-given right (Manifest Destiny) to take what was there, informed attitudes about nature that still exist today. Thus, the paradox of imagined plenty and experience of lack for many settlers contributed to a framing of this iconic species as pests and is a narrative that runs throughout North American history.

The framing of both humans and animals as impediments to "progress" (i.e. colonial occupation and land grabbing) includes (dis)regard of bison, coyotes, prairie dogs, and Native Americans. Each was defined, at different times and in different places as "the _____ problem." While the prairie dog has several characteristics that were viewed positively by Euro American colonial settlers, such as their resourcefulness, sociability, cuteness, and family structures, they were also viewed negatively, as interfering with the ability of humans to farm the land and as competition for resources such as grass for cattle.

Vital to understanding the dynamics between land, inhabitants, colonizers, Othering and extermination efforts is the concept of settler colonialism. Colonization is extraction and replacement of the material and the psychic world and includes, drawing on Franz Fanon, racism. It is a process "of abjection and exclusion and ... a form silencing" (Oliver, 2004, p. 88).

Both the physical and psychological conquest of space and contains within its discourse a narrative of the act being right and just, regardless of who is impacted by the move. Where a foreign government or authority imposes colonizing, the ongoing process of carrying out that agenda is known as "settler colonialism" and is practiced by those engaged in the project. This includes using those brought to the land as a colonizing workforce. "Settler colonialism destroys to replace" and insists that "invasion," in settler colonial contexts, is "a structure, not an event" (Wolfe, 2006, p. 388) or, as a Settler Colonial Studies Web site describes it

> Settler colonialism is not colonialism: settlers want Indigenous people to vanish (but can make use of their labour before they are made to disappear).

Sometimes settler colonial forms operate within colonial ones, sometimes they subvert them, and sometimes they replace them. But even if colonialism and settler colonialism interpenetrate and overlap, they remain separate as they co-define each other.

Settler colonialism is not a thing of the past but rather ongoing and global. Once populations arrive in a space, the process of inhabiting it begins and as long as the indigenous population remains, the discourse of removal and justification must be renewed. Settler colonialism is very much about land and resources. Should someone or something stand in the way of acquisition of these, he or she will be dealt with, either through efforts to integrate or, should that fail, exterminate. The organizing "irreducible element" of American settler colonialism, according to Wolfe (2006, p. 388), was the elimination of indigenous people, what became a compulsive process of dispossession, depopulation and reifying a master narrative of racial superiority.

I argue this process was also applied to the land and to the beings (plants, animals) who reside in places colonizers desire. As such, any animals who stood in the way of settler land and resource acquisition, either as real or perceived competitors for food (wolves), space, or as significant spiritual symbols for the humans (Native Americans) who were in relationship with them (wolves, bison, eagles, badgers), were similarly depopulated. Indigenous peoples were killed and/or moved to reservations and animals similarly controlled through "management" measures (culling/killing, placing in zoos or in hunting parks). Accompany these acts was and is "settler assumption of responsibility for the indigenous peoples contained within the area they exclusively claimed." This paternalism extends as well to animals and plants within those regions (Veracini, 2011, p. 172).

Many settlers sought what First Nations people did as well—the right to self-determination. However, many of the colonists viewed those who were here first as an impediment to what was believed to be natural entitlement to land. "In the quest for legitimacy, settler colonialism thereby includes appropriation of indigenous experiences, symbols, and lifeways. This occurred simultaneously with the promulgation of one or several myths about "vanishing" *indigenes, terra nullius* (barren lands), and/or assertions of manifest destiny" (Sanders, 2012, p. 29).

Settlers, unlike migrants or colonized people, move across territories and environments in ways that seem, to them, seamless, a kind of political authority to do what they believe to be the right thing, regardless of who is there and what local beliefs, values, and practices are already in place. Thus, their complicitness in attitude and participation in "isopolitical interstate associations" (Veracini, 2011, p. 172). This construct helps unpack the complex attitudes and acts that contribute to anti-species groups' (hunters, landowners, developers) beliefs that management and extermination are natural individual rights (supported by law and religion), thus keeping populations in their "proper" place. Western expansions of colonial settlers thus set up "daughter" colonies, similar in constitution and form to those the colonists came from (p. 173), reproducing power structures, belief systems, and ways of living on the land that continue to the present day.

Burrowing Under History

World War II (1939–1945) and its demands on the economy as well as feeding troops abroad, meant maximizing beef production. Thus, according to the U.S. government, this meant improving range lands (and the inaccurate thinking about prairie habitat health) which equated to killing prairie dogs. Thus "killing rodents became a patriotic act" (Williams, 2008, p. 44).

Today, many anti-Prairie Doggers think of themselves as conservationists, helping rid the west of pests, nuisances, threats to cattle and horses and to progress. Journalist Ted Williams (2000) describes his ride with a man named Rich Grable, aka "Mr. Dog," who he accompanied on a morning of 'varminting" in South Dakota:

> Mr. Dog stuck the muzzle of his Remington .222 out the truck window, resting it on a Styrofoam pad partly melted by barrel heat. Crack. He cut a prairie dog in half, sending its hindquarters cart wheeling into the air. "Dead," he announced, punching his dashboard-mounted kill counter. Two babies stood beside a burrow, one with its paws on its sibling's shoulders. Crack. Both exploded in red mist. "Can ya hear it go plop?" he cackled. Crack. A few targets dragged themselves back into their burrows, minus major body parts.

"I done somethin' to him," shouted Mr. Dog. "I done somethin' to him, too." Grable has earned his nickname; he once killed 75 straight before missing, and he's killed 452 in one day, 8,635 in a single year.

Varminting, the practice of hunting small mammals who are viewed as pests, is a common pastime of recreational shooters. There's no Prairie Dog season; they can be killed any time, and no licenses or tags are required. As a result, there are no Prairie Dogs left, for example, in Arizona where they've been completely eradicated.

Some justify varminting as simultaneously an exercise for gaining greater shooting accuracy because the targets are so small and believe they are doing a conservation service. Author Richard Conniff spent time with a group who referred to themselves as the "red mist society," otherwise known as the Varmint Hunters Association. One member said he had some bad feelings about killing the animals but he reasoned that "The killing of the prairie dogs is just a by-product of my evolving accuracy" as a shooter. Hitting prairie dogs rather than paper targets gives a more "immediate resultant effect" (Conniff, 2013).

The South Dakota Varmint Hunters Association declares, "Varminting reflects an Old West belief that there are good animals and bad animals and that nature can and should be reengineered by humans" (Williams, 2000). While the "takes" by these individuals and organizations is large, it is not as great as the eradication efforts of state, federal governments (who fund exterminations with tax payer monies) and pest-control services who, since the 1920s, have been poisoning the Great Plains. In Texas, New Mexico, Kansas, Colorado, South Dakota, North Dakota, Wyoming, and Montana prairie dogs are classified as agricultural pests and allow, and in some cases require, extermination. Enthusiasm for this was so great that a bill was introduced in 2000, in the South Dakota legislature, to change the name from prairie dog to prairie rat (Williams, 2000).

So how do these realities of the land and of the prairie dogs fit with popular culture representations of them? Are the representations consistent with prejudices or contradictory? That is the subject of the next section.

Prairie Dogs in Popular Culture

Unlike animals who, due to their size and appearance are considered charismatic megafauna, the Prairie Dog is small. Those who fancy the diminutive rodents seem to relate to them because of social ways that are consistent with American values of family, home, hard work, and diligence. Prairie dog displays/villages in zoos are popular exhibits. In the 1880s, the chief taxidermist at the Smithsonian Institution's National Museum, William T. Hornaday, described the prairie dog's appeal (despite their reputation as pests):

> Owing to his optimistic, and even joyous disposition, the Prairie-Dog has many friends, and 'happy as a Prairie-Dog' would be a far better comparison, and his absurd little tail was given him solely as a means of visible expression of good nature. But he has his enemies and detractors. The coyote loves his plump and toothsome body; the 'granger' hates him for the multitude of his holes, and puts spoonfuls of poisoned wheat into his burrow. (qtd. in Hanson, p. 47)

Prairie Dogs were even referenced as a kind of rugged masculinity in a 1963 ad for Bulova self-winding watches that read "each handsome as a dude rancher, rugged as a prairie dog" (qtd in Aquila, 1986, p. 281). A fifteen second 2010 Super Bowl commercial for Car Max featured a Prairie Dog sitting on a kitchen counter watching a CarMax.com commercial on television in which he/she learns one can get "smart vehicle history reports for every used car we sell." In the ad, dramatic music rises, the Prairie Dog turns to the camera, looks shocked, and the tag line "dramatically smart" appears on the screen (the advertiser also ran versions that included a dog and another with a chipmunk). What animals and used cars have to do one another is beyond the point, other than to attract attention. Their images can be also found on greeting cards, they are stuffed toys, function in web-based humor images as signs of conformity at the office, eager eaters (see Group Lunches at the Office), and from the popular "I Can Haz Cheezburger" site, as a pet and companion to a housecat.

A 2004 Honda Pilot commercial mixes habitats for effect but shows a couple on a weekend vacation in the forest and along a lake. The man sees prairie dogs pop their heads up out of the ground, then flashes to his office mates doing the same thing out of their cubicles and asks his female companion if they can spend a few more days in the wilderness. These happy little chubby rodent re-presentations present the Prairie Dog as happy little animals living much like humans do. That's the attraction of nature documentary and entertainment films as well.

Disnification of the Prairie Dog

To document, as a verb, is to record in some manner (photography, written, film) as evidence something occurred. The term comes from the Latin word *documentum* "lesson, proof" and in some versions, to teach (*OED*). A documentary film is designed to document and illuminate an event, a person, an animal, or an issue. It can be safely said that audiences bring to media they consume an element of trust that the documentary filmmaker is recording an event in its natural state unlike entertainment films that are highly structured, directed, edited and constructed. Documentary films, especially in the early days, were and are some of the first opportunities audiences have for seeing worlds they may or may not visit.

These films bring us closer to nature, and nature closer to us. At the same time, however, the practice of "taking photographs" and hunting with cameras, is a form of procurement, taking the real in to the realm of the re-presented where we view carefully constructed, highly edited, often anthropomorphized versions of "reality" that most likely reflect what the filmmaker intended than any real sense of the animal. Thus rarely do audiences bring critical thinking skills about technique or perspective when viewing documentaries. As research on so-called documentary photographs such as those by Edward Curtis and early filmmakers such as Robert Flaherty revealed, there can often be a high level of manipulation of which audiences are unaware. Disney cache', trust, and audience assumptions about authenticity and acceptance of truth claims are wrapped up in the Disney model of above all else selling entertainment.

There are two categories of films as they concern animals: Entertainment and Documentary. Entertainment films that use animals do so either with the animal as the focus of the story, such as *Marley and Me* (2008), or as characters, or "props" within the story. Documentary films are non-fiction forms of storytelling that have a perspective and advocate a point of view. There are two subcategories within animal oriented documentary:

1. "Contemporary blue-chip wildlife film[s]" (Porter, 2010, p. 26) which include contemporary films such as *Planet Earth* (2006), *Blue Planet* (2001), as well as historical efforts such as Disney's *Seal Island* (1948), episodes from the television series Mutual of Omaha's *Wild Kingdom* such as "King of Beasts" (1963).
2. "Vast morality play[s]" (Bousé, 2011, p. 153) that employ the classic production model include Disney's *True-Life Adventures*, The World Wildlife Fund's *Anima Mundi* (1992), *Winged Migration* (2001), *March of the Penguins* (2005), and *Grizzly Man* (2005).

Disney's *True-Life Adventure* films play in both categories, often borrowing footage from other Disney products, fictional or not, and working them in to their stories. These "information heavy films ... presented animals as anthropomorphic characters and their lives as drama, were made palatable by adding comic content, syncopating natural behavior to music, and editing the animals' actions to fit narrative needs" (Telotte, 2010, p. 72). These, as do other Disney products, use an authoritative narrator, who recites "facts" about the world being examined, drawing viewers in to animals' personal stories and uses (at that time) revolutionary filming techniques such as stop motion and time lapse photography to draw them in to what is happening. Above all, audiences are reminded of how much research was involved in preparing for this 'adventure' and thus in "making" the film, generating a sense of Disney-as-authority for audiences.

The *True-Life Adventures* "offe[r] a kind of narrative closure by placing their subjects within the cyclical patterns of nature" (Telotte, 2010, p. 78). In a 1955 *Quarterly Review of Biology* critique of the Disney-produced book based on the film *Vanishing Prairie*, the author presents an uncritical evaluation, offering no assessment on the scientific accuracy or inaccuracy of the movie, rather the taken for granted nature and acceptance of Disney, "The Disney natural history films are too well known and admired to require comment except to say that *Vanishing Prairie* is one of the best" (Swanson, 1955, p. 382).

Analysis

The Prairie Dog segment, which is part of the *VP* documentary, focuses on the social life of the little animals. As the section begins, the music rises and the narrator begins telling the story of the Prairie Dogs. They are variously described as "footloose animals" or "original" homesteaders, and their burrows are called "family residence[s]." The narration accurately describes how once these animals populated prairie lands in the millions. Notably absent is any discussion of why this is no longer the case. The voice-over discusses them as "cousins" and relatives, all the way carefully orchestrating each scene with playful, mysterious, or simply silly music as part of the scene setting. Walt Disney is credited with creating the industry standard for nature-based documentary films. "The terms of nature drama were restaged by Disney. He refocused the travel-and-safari film tradition of animals as objects to be collected to that of animals as personalities or characters in their natural habitats living out their own stories" (King, 1996).

Disney's "natural philosophy" has resulted in formulaic storytelling firmly rooted in anthropocentric attitudes about nature that include "anthropomorphism, expansionism, identification, and assignment of human motives and values" (King, 1996). This formula, long ago adopted by filmmakers such as those creating content for the National Geographic, Discovery, and Animal Planet channels has been modified but still adheres to what is known as "the Disney formula." Animal lives are described in familiar, anthropocentric terms focusing on hard work, family, steadfastness, and diligence. Music directs much of the emotion of these episodic programs, as well as providing animal biographies, family dramas, and tales of rebirth and renewal. Very little actual biological or ecological information is provided to viewers.

This is seen in early films, such as the Academy Award winning *Seal Island* (1948)

But the subsequent nature series won a total of nine awards in the 1940s and 1950s, the best-known titles being feature-length: *The Living Desert* (1953), *The Vanishing Prairie* (1954), and *White Wilderness* (1958). Other winners were *In Beaver Valley* (1950), *Nature's Half Acre* (1951), *Water Birds*(1952), and *Bear Country* (1953). Other series titles include *The Olympic Elk* (1952), and *The African Lion* (1955).

The Vanishing Prairie (1954) *(VP)* tells the disnified version of what happens on and is happening to the American prairie. The narrator (Winston Hibbler) takes viewers back to time preceding European tales of expansion when, in the narrator's racist words of the time, "The Red Man" ... "claimed this land in his primitive way." He speaks of a close relationship with buffalo, antelope, rabbits, and the little dog who barks, was "his friend and neighbor." The narrator continues the vanishing motif by describing how many of the animals of "now" still survive on nature's prairie, but they too are vanishing. Never is it said that it is human encroachment that is behind disappearance of people or other animals.

VP tells a story of many animals who live on the prairies but who are "vanishing." On a day in early spring the first stories are of birds, such as ducks, Western Grebes, Sage Grouse, and others in mating rituals. Most of the narration focuses on family life, child rearing, and gender roles in parenting. The emphasis with the Buffalo is motherhood and birth. As the camera and viewer witness the birth of a calf we are told that the "Calf must be strong, for the herd will not tolerate cripples or weaklings." The story of the Prong horn is speed; for the Big Horn Sheep, making his "last stand" above the prairie floor. The mountain lion ("he's the wanderer of the hills") is said to be "branded an outlaw" in some places but that "nature knows no good or bad." Self-preservation and protection of the young is the mother's goal. The kittens are "born nomads" and the mother must be the "family provider." In this way nature is personalized so that animals have "rights" and their "homes" become private sanctuaries to be respected and protected as an extension of civil property rights. Birth is described as "drama" and "suspense." This anthropomorphism, finding similarities and shared experiences with other beings, is something King (1996) considers instructional:

That same instinct drives us to perceive nature in human terms: how animals bond; how they "enjoy" family life and reproduce; how young animals grow up, become independent, learn their "trade," and develop survival skills. We set standards and judge—by our human template of "character"-animal intelligence, beauty and ugliness, virtue and vice, diligence and playfulness, suffering and reward, community and perdition, birth and death.

In the Prairie Dog section of *VP* the narrator focuses on family and home building. He states how constant building and repairing of one's home is at the forefront of Prairie Dog life and how danger lurks around every corner, especially for unaccompanied young animals. Their homes are described as "engineering feat[s]" where "a fellow has to use his head." The little animals are described as "permanent settlers, the original homesteaders" suggesting animals having a rightful claim on the land. The story is told about how they build their dens, protect them from rains and flooding with dikes, and go about surviving. Throughout this episode the song "Home on the Range" plays, in varying moods, from playful to sorrowful. The scene of babies in the den, "the nursery," has amplified sounds of snoring added. The narrator guides us with the 6-week old young as their mother takes them from the den and introduces them to the pleasures and perils of the world above. Viewers see the babies play, eat, and encounter rabbits, burrowing owls, a rattle snake, who is "not to be trusted," and a mother coyote who, "to protect her young [will] face anything." The Prairie Dog alarm system is illustrated when a coyote comes hunting, the challenges when buffalo wallow in the loose soil of the outer burrows, and a cat and mouse game between a Prairie Falcon and a Prairie Dog. The narrator informs us that "It is the unhappy plight of the prairie dog to be forever plagued by just about everything that walks or flies or creeps or crawls. Indeed, he's become a vanishing species because so many make a career out of pursuing him."

Conclusion

What Disney does in their so-called documentaries is what Disney does best: tell stories. They may or may not be "true," or accurate, or natural. These are highly edited productions designed to attract audiences to the Disney brand and related merchandise. The style and skill of telling animal stories by using them to say something about us is a technique adopted by many other content creators. However, what they are doing is telling their version of a story, not necessarily what the animal's story might be or about the issues facing real animals in the world. As part of Disney's focus on happiness and families and industrialized capitalist values, the stories are told that keep us happily thinking about mediated re-presentations of animals where they aren't shot or poisoned or laughed at or humiliated. Rather, they have names and families and laugh and love and go on quite well. This is not to say there's not death in Disney. The death of Bambi's mother created such an outcry. And the death of cheetah cubs to hyenas in *African Cats* was included (but not shown). Ultimately, however, the family values nature of Disney productions are those of safe distancing. That's part of what Disney teaches, that what goes on in the world of animals is much like what goes on in our lives. Moreover, Disney, with its focus on young viewers, has tremendous power in influencing what children will grow up to expect of the movies they see as adults. "Disney isn't just telling stories about animals, it's telling its audience what they can expect—and should expect—from every documentary they see" (Erbland, 2015).

To ignore settler colonialist attitudes and acts toward animals is consistent with Veracini's (2011) description of "deep colonizing" (p. 171) "where a progressive and decolonizing move for some ends up further compromising the position of others" (p. 179). An example is President elect Barak Obama's 2008 "Yes we Can" campaign speeches that recognized workers, women, African Americans, ethnic migrants, but made no mention of Native Americans who

> Are doubly absent: they are conspicuously missing from [the] list of emancipatory passages, and they are erased as an obstacle: the pioneers who "pushed westward" did not move against them (unless we are willing to consider the Indian nations that occupied the continent as part of an "unforgiving wilderness." (p. 181)

I argue that it is a similarly act of deep colonizing if we recognize the impact of westward expansion on people but ignore animals. Isopolitical relations therefore include use of animals who live in and on the lands. Public hearings, policy workshops, and conversation meetings, inevitably bring farmers, ranchers, and homeowners who speak of the small rodents "with all the usual vituperation that has been associated with rancher–prairie dog relationships of the past century or more" (Johnsgard, 2005, p. xi).

The Wild Earth Guardian report "Report from the Burrow: Forecast of the Prairie Dog 2013," was released on February 2, 2013 in honor of Ground Hog Day (aka Prairie Dog Day in some circles). The date and act of Punxsutawney Phil seeing his shadow or not is meant as a prediction for the future. In his case, will winter be longer or shorter? Similarly, the prairie dog's status can be a harbinger of things to come. Were these little rodents exterminated as many would have it, it would be a disaster for the western grassland ecosystem. Dozens of species of animals and plants depend on the little rodent's activities for their lives as well. Estimates include 150 species of animals who depend on them for food; on their burrows for shelter, and the work they do with grasses and landscapes. The federal Bureau of Land Management (BLM), part of the U.S. Department of the Interior, oversee "and manage the public lands for the use and enjoyment of present and future generations" (http://www.blm.gov/wo/st/en.html) reports that Prairie dogs are themselves food or their dens provide housing for 59 vertebrate species—29 birds, 21 mammals, 5 reptiles, and 4 amphibians. In the last 150 years, the five species have lost 93–99% of their former range (Jones, 2013, p. 3).

> The story of the Utah prairie dog is the story of the range of our compassion. If we can extend our idea of community to include the lowliest of creatures, call them "the untouchables", then we will indeed be closer to a path of peace and tolerance. If we cannot accommodate "the other", the shadow we will see on our own home ground will be the forecast of our own species' extended winter of the soul. Terry Tempest Williams (2008)

How language, media, and popular culture have re-presented these keystone beings has had a tremendous impact on their lives. If, when, and how they are portrayed in media is an important consideration in how they are viewed. Disney Studio's films, merchandising, theme parks, and other products play a pivotal role in how children learn about the natural world and their potential relationship to it. King (1996) points out: "Walt Disney did not invent popular interest in nature. But he was the first to film nature drama for commercial release according to a set of formulas that capture and cultivate later-twentieth-century attitudes."

Note

1. Protections for prairie dogs was not so much out of concern for them as it was their function as a food source for the black-footed ferret, a mammal who is considered the world's most endangered animal.

References

Adams, C. J. (1990/2015). *The sexual politics of meat*. New York, NY: Bloomsbury.

Aquila, R. (1986). *Wanted dead or alive: The American west in popular culture*. Chicago, IL: University of Illinois Press.

Bekoff, M. (2017, May 16). Grief in Prairie Dogs: Mourning a death in the family. *Psychology Today*. Retrieved from https://www.psychologytoday.com/blog/animal-emotions/201705/grief-in-prairie-dogs-mourning-death-in-the-family

Bousé, D. (2011). Wildlife films. Philadelphia: University of Pennsylvania Press.

Conniff, R. (2013, November 26). The brutal sport of prairie dog hunting. *Takepart*. Retrieved from http://www.takepart.com/article/2013/11/26/brutal-sport-prairie-dog-hunting

Erbland, K. (2015, April 20). Disneynature is creating a new generation of documentary fans. *The Dissolve*. Retrieved from https://thedissolve.com/features/exposition/996-disneynature-is-creating-a-new-generation-of-docum/

Fahnestock, J. T., & Detling, J. K. (2002). Bison-prairie dog-plant interaction in a North American mixed-grass prairie. *Oecologica, 132*, 86–95.

Hanson, E. (1986). *Animal attractions: Nature on display in American zoos*. Princeton, NJ: Princeton University Press.

Irving, W. (1835/2006). *A tour of the Prairies*. New York, NY: A. and W. Galignani and Company.

Jabr, F. (2017, May 12). Can Prairie Dogs talk? *New York Times*. Retrieved fromhttps://www.nytimes.com/2017/05/12/magazine/can-prairie-dogs-talk.html?_r=2

Johnsgard, P. A. (2005). *Prairie dog Empire: The saga of the shortgrass prairie*. Lincoln, NB: University of Nebraska Press.

Jones, S. (1999). Becoming a pest: Prairie dog ecology and the human economy in the Euromerican west. *Environmental History, 4*(4), 531–552.

Jones, T. (2013, February). Report from the burrow: Forecast of the prairie dog 2013. *Wild Earth Guardians*. Retrieved from http://www.wildearthguardians.org/site/DocServer/Report_from_the_Burrow_2013.pdf?docID=7942&AddInterest=1106

King, M. J. (1996). Audience in the wild. *Journal of Popular Film & Television, 24*(2), 60–68.

McCain, L., Reading, R. P., & Miller, B. J. (2002). Prairie dog gone: Myth, persecution, and preservation of a keystone species. In G. Wuerthnew & M. Matteson (Eds.), *Welfare ranching: The subsidized destruction of the American West* (pp. 231–236). Washington, DC: Island Press.

Oliver, K. (2004). *The colonization of psychic space: A psychoanalytic social theory of oppression*. Minneapolis, MN: University of Minnesota Press.

Porter, P. (2010). Teaching animal movies. In M. DeMello (Ed.), *Teaching the animal* (pp. 18–34). New York: Lantern Books.

prairie dog. (n.d.). *Collins English Dictionary - Complete & Unabridged 10th Edition*. Retrieved from Dictionary.com website: http://dictionary.reference.com/browse/prairie dog

Sanders, A. R. (2012, September 7). *What is settler colonialism?* Retrieved September 8, 2015 from https://colonialismthroughtheveil.wordpress.com/2012/09/07/what-is-settler-colonialism/

Slatta, R. W. (2001). *The mythical west*. Santa Barbara, CA: ABC-CLIO.

Slobodchikoff, C. N., Perla, S. B., & Verdolin, J. L. (2009). *Prairie dogs: Communication and community in an animal society*. Cambridge, MA: Harvard University Press.

Swanson, C. P. (1955). Review. *The Quarterly Review of Biology, 30*(4), 382.

Telotte, J. P. (2010). Science fiction as "True-Life Adventure": Disney and the case of *20,000 Leagues Under the Sea*. *Film & History, 40*(2), 66–79.

Toelken, B. (2008). Quoted in T. T. Williams (2008). *Finding beauty in a broken world*. New York, NY: Vintage.

Veracini, L. (2011). Isopolitics, deep colonizing, settler colonialism. *Interventions, 13*(2), 171–189.

Williams, T. (2000, January/February). The prairie dog wars. *Mother Jones*. Retrieved from http://www.motherjones.com/politics/2000/01/prairie-dog-wars

Williams, T. T. (2008). *Finding beauty in a broken world*. New York, NY: Vintage.

Wolfe, P. (2006). Settler colonialism and the elimination of the native. *Journal of Genocide Research, 8*(4), 387–409.

Chapter Eight

Catty

The Feral Feminine in Media

Where is her lurking place? In untracked wilds, in impenetrable forests of bramble, on blasted heaths, where entangled thistles suffer no foot to pass.
—Michelet (1904, p. 8)

Woman (noun). An animal usually living in the vicinity of Man, and having a rudimentary susceptibility to domestication. ... The popular name (wolfman) is incorrect, for the creature is of the cat kind. The woman is lithe and graceful in its movement, especially the American variety (*felis pugnans*), is omnivorous, and can be taught not to talk.
—Balthasar Pober (Bierce, *The Devil's Dictionary* 1906/2000, p. 239)

Unbeknownst to them, animals help us tell stories about ourselves, especially when it comes to matters of sexuality.
—Terry (2000, p. 151)

Cats and adult female sexuality are out there, in the dark future, waiting to pounce.
—Simon (2002, p. 85)

American culture is crazy for cats big and small. Cute kittens and devilish adult cats endlessly entertain us in YouTube videos. Big Cats (lions, tigers, cheetahs) with amplified ferocity are featured in Animal Planet and National Geographic specials. Furthermore, leopards and lions lithely lounge and lunge on commercials for female targeted products such as mascara and perfume because, in the psyche, they symbolize something ethereal, dangerous, and captivating connected with human women. Why are women and cats so often shown in unison? What has contributed to thinking of them as interchangeable in nature and deed?

This chapter explores the history of the representation of women as animals in general and as cats in particular exploring how both have been encoded with an erotic allure. This includes a discussion of the 1942 film *Cat People* and a textual analysis of two commercials: (1) Maybelline Colossal Cat Eyes mascara, and (2) Yves St. Laurent's Opium fragrance. The goal is to reveal the connections between femininity, felines, and ferocity by critiquing the coding that suggests sexual availability. The theory of the male gaze is used to predict and then unpack the "intense ambivalence" many men feel about female power, sensuality, and danger that can be "expressed by identifying human female love objects with cats"

> With their charm, their hidden claws, their sexual ardor, and their cool self-centeredness, cats provide a convenient metaphor for the alleged limitations of women's love; and human cruelty and duplicity can be projected on to cats. (Rogers, 2006, p. 123)

Where does this desire for women as wild originate? What makes this hybrid creature so alluring and yet so dangerous? What is it about "the chase" that entices? In the tradition of Foucault (1977), we will look first to history as "present practices can be understood only with the help of the past" (Kurzweil, 1986, p. 648).

Animal Instincts

To be feral is to exist in a natural state, both undomesticated and wild. To be feral and (human) female is an enticing blend of these traits that has a long and rich history. Tempted as we so easily are by our appetites for food and fashion, capturing something (or someone) exotic and rare is stimulating. Unpredictability is an alluring marker of female sexuality. When paired with reminders of our animality, such as representing women as half human/half animal or as possessing the ability to morph into different creatures, it is a powerful elixir. Such creatures disrupt the normal order of things, cross boundaries, and upset "normal" couplings by which otherwise distinct categories of human and animal are marked. "It is their humanity that gives them such subversive power: they inhabit the symbolically ambiguous but powerful borders between human and animal, culture and nature" (Carroll, 1988, p. 156). Furthermore, "animal alter-egos emphasize [e] their exclusion or alienation from human society" (p. 156).

Humans who become animals or animals who become human comprise the stuff of stories. Ancient tales of the transformation of humans into animals by witches and wizards are the stuff of fairy tales, horror stories, and science fiction thrillers. Whether occupying cave walls as Paleolithic paintings or defending Bella from the latest threat in the Twilight movies, shape shifting and hybridity (mixing of similar and dissimilar elements and/or identities that can reinforce and/or contradict) is the stuff of imagination. This "third space" represents a narrowing or even erasure of a clear boundary between human and animal, Us and Them, and is a dance humans have participated in throughout time (Bhabha, 1994). It is a place "where bodies and identity resist stable categories, and meaning is ambivalent, contradictory, and historically shifting" (Gúzman & Valdivia, 2004, pp. 213–214). Such shape-shifting is prevalent in many cultures where people dress up as animals and take on animal affect as part of ritual performances. For example, today, in the highlands of Mexico, Acatlan men participate in a 3,000-year-old ritual. They "dress in jaguar costumes and box each other as a kind of sacrifice to the rain god, Tlaloc" (Zorich, 2008, n.p.).

Languaging Animals

Other species symbolically substitute for human emotions and behavior in everything from greeting cards to advertising campaigns. Animals are used metaphorically in language and images as stand-ins for human emotions and behaviors. For example, someone who is sneaky might be described as "sly as a fox," or "slippery as an eel." A woman who is less than nice might be referred to with the same word used for a female dog (bitch). Colloquial language describes women as kittens (if they are sexy), catty (if they are gossipy), as cougars (if they are and like younger men), and "catting around" (if she is sexually adventuresome). A man who is dominated by a woman? "Pussy whipped," thus reflecting the "negative feline-female connotation" (Simon, 2002, p. 73). Perhaps the greatest insult one man can level at another is to call him a term used interchangeably with female genitalia—pussy—signifying someone who is weak and dominated by a woman.

During the 2016 U.S. presidential election, then candidate Donald Trump's use of the word "pussy," referring to female anatomy, came to light in a recording obtained by *The Washington Post*. In the recording Trump is speaking with *Access Hollywood* host Billy Bush, about women, while they were aboard a bus on the set of the daytime series *Days of Our Lives*. The conversation was not limited to, but included, the following:

> Trump: "I moved on her like a bitch, but I couldn't get there, and she was married. Then all of a sudden I see her, she's now got the big phony tits and everything."

and

> "I'm automatically attracted to beautiful [women]—I just start kissing them. It's like a magnet. Just kiss. I don't even wait. And when you're a star they let you do it. You can do anything ... grab them by the pussy. You can do anything." (Mathis-Lilley, 2016).

Public reaction to this gross use of power, reference, and misogyny, became symbolic fodder for the millions of men and women around the U.S. who marched, wearing pink "pussy hats" as semiotic markers in reclamation of the term. At the same time, it was a curious reappropriation of a part of female anatomy, named for an animal other than human, and stereotypically coded as pink as part of a public push back for the election of a sexist, racist, public misogynist as 45th president of the United States.

Whereas conflicts between men are described as feuds, battles, or fights competitive arguments between women are called "cat fights." In 2011, Republican presidential candidate hopefuls Sarah Palin and Michelle Bachman, for example, were said to be in "a 'catfight' rather than a 'competition'" (Bamberger, 2011, n.p.). Catfight language or meows are usually "leveled at a woman who dares to take up space, loosing anger or a controversial opinion" (Onstad, 2011, n.p.). In June 2011, Tasmanian Senator David Bushby meowed at Australian Minister of Finance Penny Wong during a debate on the floor of the Senate Economics Legislation Committee. She replied, "The blokes are allowed to yell, but if a woman stands her ground, you want to make that kind of comment. It's sort of schoolyard politics, mate. It's just extraordinary" (Onstad, 2011, n.p.).

At the same time, competition between women is also constructed as sexy. The sexual appeal of women in conflict is reflected by comedian Jerry Seinfeld's declaration: "Men think if women are grabbing and clawing at each other, there's a chance they might somehow, you know, kiss" (Berg & Schaffer, 1997). In 2007, a Miller Lite beer commercial was called "Catfight." In it, two buxom women argue over whether the beer is less filling or has great taste. They end up tearing off each other's clothing, rolling in mud, and fighting in Jello™. The commercial was eventually pulled due to protests. Covers of magazines such as *People* and *Us* as well as tabloids like *National Enquirer* portray similarly portray female rivalries as in "Meow! Rihanna, Ciara Get into Nasty Catfight." These metaphors are not neutral, rather they originate in what is believed to be common sense understandings and taken for granted cultural assumptions about people and other beings. Metaphors are powerful, they

> Offer a window on the construction of social identities. Being channels of folk beliefs, many metaphors convey biases in favor of particular social groups that are considered as the normative in detriment to those individuals who do not conform to this group. (Rodríquez, 2009, p. 77)

Through metaphoric language and images, boundaries can be tested, rules resisted, norms negotiated. The wolf, for example, has been used to symbolize wildness, appetite, sexuality, and aggression (Warner, 1994,

p. 10). These symbolic expressions exemplify how myths "carr[y] an inner truthfulness, a meaningful significance" (Krzywinska, 2006, p. 143). In the case of women, cat language, on the one hand, is dismissive, diminutive, and disempowering and on the other hand sexual, suggestive, and sultry.

Myths function as imaginary, allegorical tales but also contain essential truths. Found in all cultures at all times myths convey "a secondary, partial reference to something of collective importance" (Burkert, 1982, p. 23). The "radical Otherness" of women, children, and animals places in positions of potential "to disturb cultural authority" (O'Connor, 2015) since what matters in patriarchal societies is establishing and maintaining male superiority. This has had a significant impact on the lives of real women and animals. For example, in Irish culture "rabbits and hares were so often chosen (alongside of cats) to be associated with witchcraft" (DeMello, 2015). Tales of the milk hare, as a cause of dairy cattle going dry or the selkie, caught between two worlds as sometimes seal sometimes woman, were frightening concepts to Christian ideologies quest for supremacy over Pagan rituals and festivities. As a result, many women, rabbits, hares, and cats were slaughtered because of their perceived threat to the status quo. Thus, the "natural" order of things is defined and reified in tales and popular culture by placing man (excluding women) above women and animals.

The "problem of uncontrolled female sexuality" (Fletcher, 1995, p. 278) has consistently been at the foundation of social panics throughout history, those commonly viewed as a "threat to society's values and interests" (p. 279). Hence, under patriarchy, bestial transformations, metaphorical envisioning, and languaging of women function as a projection of (primarily) men's imaginations. Out of a deep, primitive "fear of inversion of authority between men and women," combining views about female sexuality and appetite with those of carnivorous animals makes both easy targets for control and oppression (Jardine, 1983, p. 162). "Women command," writes Jardine (1983), "and the natural hierarchy is inverted. An inversion readily translated into female sexual predatoriness" (p. 114) which is perceived as threatening.

Animal transformation in fantasy and horror is part of what French feminist theorist Julia Kristeva (1982) called "the abject." This exception to female subservience and sexual passivity is "the ... transformation brought about by the physical, emotional, and psychological effects of sex and sexual desire" (Krzywinska, 2006, p. 155). Thus, women, fertility, food, and felinity (the animal) are intimately intertwined with concepts of sex, impurity, and death. This simultaneous attraction/repulsion to the cat/woman is evident in historically and universally consistent adoration and demonization of both women and of cats.

The Meaning of Cats

The feral feminine is the comingling of characteristics of being a human female with those of a wild creature. While in some cases this offers a woman the opportunity to symbolically reconnect with her wild earth nature, it is also used in advertising, photography, and cinema to create a figure who is both alluring and dangerous because of her otherness. This idealization of both woman and animal is complex and ambivalent. It "is a most insidious agent of the inclusion of women. It is the peculiar burden and gift of the iconoclast that she will always retain a sense of spectacle: the persistent sense of feminine masquerade" (Michelet, 1904, p. 154). The *femme sauvage* is similarly illustrative of the "unruly female principle" (Williams, 1995, p. 86). In Christian mythology, she is also the fallen woman. She is shown in the form of the madness of Medusa or the strength and autonomy of Amazons. She is Kali in Hindu theology, one is both protector of children and small animals (as is Artemis/Diana in Greek & Roman mythology).

That women have a special connection with cats is an ancient, widespread belief. How both cats and women have been regarded has gone through huge swings in sentiment, from adoration to contempt. In ancient Egypt, for example, cats were respected, protected, and revered. As early as 6000 BCE the Egyptians found cats to be helpful in this rural society by keeping rodents away from the all-important grain that fed the people, the builders of pyramids, the scholars, and the Pharaohs. Killing a cat in ancient Egypt was considered a capital crime (Ruiz, 2001, p. 135) and several deities took on cat-like properties such as Bastet, the feminine counterpart to lion-headed sun god Ra. She is associated with "maternity and female sexual allure" (Rogers, 2006,

p. 114). Isis, Ra's wife, could also assume the form of a cat (Regula, 1995, p. 137).

Another early example of hybridity and the feral feline feminine is the Greek myth of the "Riddle of the Sphinx." In this story, Oedipus, King of Thebes, was ordained to kill his father and murder his mother. In order to avoid this outcome, he traveled to his home in Corinth, but decides to extend his journey to Thebes in order to visit the Oracle at Delphi. During his trip, Oedipus encounters a Sphinx at the gates of Thebes (Figure 8.1).

Figure 8.1: *Oedipus and the Sphinx*. Gustave Moreau, 1864. Oil on canvas.
Source: Used by permission: Metropolitan Museum of Art, New York.

The Sphinx, who is half woman half leopard, asks a riddle of all travelers. Those who fail to answer correctly are killed and eaten. Those who answer correctly will live to continue the journey (none had so far). The riddle? "What is that is of itself two-footed, three-footed, and four-footed?" Oedipus replies "man, for an infant man begins to move as a four-footed being, when he is grown he is two-footed and when he is an old man he is three-footed, leaning on a staff because of his weakness" (qtd. in Hendricks, 1978/2004, p. 108). Astounded by receiving the correct answer, the Sphinx kills herself.

What is significant for this chapter is that the sphinx, half woman and half cat, had the reputation for being beautiful, unpredictable, dangerous, and wily. She guarded the gateway between worlds. She was seductive in her mannerisms and bearing and yet could and did kill. So why would anyone deal with her? Because he or she could not help themselves, they were drawn to her. The Sphinx threatens Oedipus's rule (i.e. patriarchy). It is she, the feral feminine, the untamed autonomous being who stands at the gateway, in the liminal zone, between life and death. "She evokes in us a longing for something other and unknown that we have lost contact with, while she at once allures and threatens men by her mysteriousness" (Kaplan, 2002, p. 175). Furthermore, she represents the unconscious, the uncontrollable aspects of mind which threaten the rational patriarchal order. As Kaplan (2002, p. 175) notes, "The sphinx is outside the city gates, she challenges the culture of the city, with its order of kinship and its order of knowledge, a culture, and a political system which assign women a subordinate place."

Furthermore,

> sexual desire is bound up with the desire for knowledge that the Sphinx possesses, that is, the quest for truth. The desire to solve riddles is a male desire par excellence, because the female subject is herself the mystery. "Woman" is the question and can hence not ask the question nor make her desire intelligible. (Smelik, 1999, p. 73)

In addition, linkage with the "non-human, the indecipherable" further complicates her role in challenging the boundaries of culture and sex (Kaplan, 2002, p. 175). Fabulous beasts, like sphinxes, chimera, and gorgons, tend to be female or are used to symbolize male fear of female sexuality. This dynamic is probably no more evident than in the seemingly seamless conflation of femininity and felinicity.

Whereas male heroes gain the attributes of and power over cats by killing them, women become cat-like, they merge, sharing powers. Characteristics such as unpredictability, seductiveness, deceit, and lack of loyalty have and continue to be ascribed both to cats and to women. That cats, particularly female cats, are connected with sex and sin has been used to control both. During European witch hunting times, for example, women were said to take cat form (and vice versa). Middle of the night mischief, such as "luring" otherwise vulnerable innocent men into exotic sexual liaisons or attacking sleeping villagers, often resulted in injuries to the cats who, when they returned to human form in the morning, were found to have the same injuries and missing limbs (Hamel, 2003). When women were persecuted, their cats often were tortured and killed as well.

Nineteenth century artist Alophonse Toussenel (who was both anti-Semitic and Anglophobic) compared cats with prostitutes and said, "civilized society can no more dispense with cats than with prostitution ... all is not rosy in those shameful loves symbolized by the cat." Cats functioned as sexual allusion in the poems of Baudelaire (*Les Fleurs du mal*, 1857/1952): "Come, my beautiful cat, on to my loving heart;/Retract the claws from your paw, /Let me lose myself in your beautiful eyes." At the same time, poets, writers, and artists also spoke of cats as evil.

The "feline mystique" (Simon, 2002) that envelops women today includes jokes about crazy cat ladies and caricatures of lonely spinsters. Characteristics of cats and women, particularly single women, assigned by the culture include aloofness, fierce independence, and indifference. Women and cats are so closely aligned that positive characteristics such as intelligence, selectivity, and sensuality are also applied, particularly to women who are attractive, long, lithe, and move smoothly and seductively.

Women, Cats, and Popular Culture

Today "we are on the other side of the myths" (Simon, 2002, p. 52). Mediated forms of storytelling circulate meanings for us now. Yet, no matter how new they might seem, these images and allusions continue to exert considerable influence over how we apprehend and represent the world.

The feral feminine is thus a deployment of femininity with recognition of traits that are often assigned to masculinity. In Estes' (2003) view this wild woman has reconciled that within herself that is strong, perhaps unruly, exotic, and strong. At the same time, these very traits can also be used against women, reducing them to stereotypes that are seen throughout media. Cartoons such as Nicole Hollander's Sylvia, for example, poke fun at and yet provide insight to the intimate relationship (mostly) women have with cats. While politically progressive in some ways the cartoon did little to disprove the stereotype that all middle-age women end up in the arms of cats rather than men. An article in Forbes emphasizes this:

> Women who own cats have become synonymous with old spinsters or, more recently, with romance-challenged (often career-oriented) women who can't find a man. In the recent comedy The Ugly Truth, beautiful Katherine Heigl's hopeless love life is instantly conveyed by her cat ownership. (Blakeley, 2009)

Simultaneously, what is sexier than a woman in skin-tight fitting cat suit battling the forces of good? Who opposes Batman? Catwoman. This male fantasy of DC Comics' creation is sexually independent; she both purrs and hunts. "Her crimes tend to be minor: the theft of jewelry and other pretty items, or at most aiding other super villains. She never kills" (Simon,

2002, p. 80). She is classy and sleek and embodied dominatrix style by Julie Newmar, Lee Meriweather, or Eartha Kitt on the 1960s television show *Batman* and in film by Michelle Pfeiffer (*Batman Returns*, 1992), Halle Barry (*Catwoman*, 2004), Anne Hathaway (*Dark Knight Rises*, 2012). The sexy cat burglar type (also in skintight black clothing) was embodied as well by as Emma Peele (played by Diana Rigg) in the 1960s television program *The Avengers a*nd Catherine Zeta Jones in *Entrapment* (1999). That the cat character would be female went and goes without saying:

> Basically, she's very much a male fantasy creation, and epitomized the love-hate relationship men have with our power, with the stereotypical associations between women and cats. She is sexual, and therefore she must be bad.

> She is an independent woman, and therefore she must be bad. ... but she must never become so terrifying as to no longer succeed as a male fantasy of forbidden fruit ... she never gives off more than a frisson of fear ... she can be made to purr. (Simon, 2002, p. 80)

Cat Eyes

Central to this topic is the role of the gaze. Film theorist Laura Mulvey (1975) first articulated this concept as the way men look at women and the way subject positions are constructed through this way of looking. Art critic John Berger (1972) describes it in this way:

> According to usage and conventions, which are at last being questioned but have by no means been overcome—men act and women appear. Men look at women. Women watch themselves being looked at ... [Women are] aware of being seen by a [male] spectator. (ital. orig., p. 49)

According to Mulvey (1975), there are two primary modes of looking: (1) voyeuristic, which is the controlling gaze that asserts power of one being (usually male) over another (usually female), and (2) fetishistic, the substitution of an object, being, or reproduction of that object or being for the pleasure of someone else, thus transforming him, her, or it in to a fetish. With origins in anthropology, fetishes often mean items, icons, or objects imbued with, most often, religious significance. A fetish, as used in cultural studies, "simultaneously refers to commodities, to the repression and domination of nature, to alienation, and to the desire for authority that connects all of these" (Brown, 2012). A fetish is an object or being whose meaning is socially agreed upon not because of some grand universal truth but because a culture constructs it as so. Commodity fetishism is the transformation of human qualities or relationships in to that which can be bought and sold. The media re-present these characteristics in terms of agreed upon codes of representation. The scopophilic gaze thereby goes beyond simple pleasure in looking, rather is the taking of sexual pleasure in gazing upon others and commodified in to products. Examples of commodity fetishism follow in an analysis of the film *Cat People* (1942), and three advertisements, two for mascara and one for a fragrance.

Textual Analysis

Textual analysis is a method for analyzing how meaning is made in media texts. When we do such an analysis "we make an educated guess at some of the most likely interpretations that might be made of that text" (McKee, 2003, p. 1). It is an educated guess, meaning the researcher has an understanding of the historical, cultural, social, and even economic circumstances within which a media text was created.

Visual media are constructed based on systems of codes. These codes reflect certain rules of representation through which shared meanings are communicated. Understanding that media texts are polysemic (i.e. open to many interpretations), they are either accepted as is or critiqued depending on the perspective of the reader. Based on the ideas of cultural studies theorist Stuart Hall (1973/1980), meaning is both inserted in to discourse (encoded) and interpreted from it (decoded). According to Hall (1973/1980), there are three codes or positions media texts take: (1) preferred, (2) negotiated, and (3) resistant. The preferred meaning reflects the interests of dominant culture and is thus read (decoded) in the way the sender intended. A negotiated reading is when the audience fully understands how the send intended the message to be received but brings own critique and personal preferences to the experience. Finally, a resistant (opposition, counter-hegemonic) reading of a media text is when the audience member fully realizes the preferred and intended meaning of the message but intentionally resists it by interrogating and critiquing the message. Since language operates within a framework of power, meaning is articulated via institutions such as the media in ways that seem so normal and natural they are seamless. According to Evans (2001, p. 134),

> In dominant sexual codes, it is the woman's body which is taken by the man's; and more generally it is the woman who is thought of as object or complement to the male subject If she is herself the agent vis-à-vis the commodity, becoming, in this different context, a subject in relation where she's elsewhere in the objective position, there is a seeming anomaly, which provides one more indication of the conflicting places of woman and women in ideological and social practices.

The feral feminine as shown in film, advertising, clothing, and other forms of communication can thereby be read as a closed text (encourages a specific meaning) that is imbued with the interests of dominant culture. She epitomizes the wild, independent, and unattainable beingness of woman. She is desirable primarily because she is unavailable yet is also tamable/consumable as an idea/image. Dress her up in leopard print clothing (less is more of course), pose her in a forest, desert, or on the savannah, perch her in treetops, but place her just out of reach and the result is desirability. In heteronormative media discourse she alludes capture by men (other than in their gaze), but the implication is of course should the right man come along (being the spectator of the image) she can be tamed of her wily ways. The feral woman does not conform to society's image of prescriptive femininity of appropriate behavior; rather she is a spectacle of transgression. Furthermore, repressed female orality is symbolic of hunger for the flesh as a metaphor for sexual desire. Irigary (1984) wrote that "femininity' is a role an image, a value, imposed on women by male systems of representation. In this masquerade of femininity, the woman loses herself, and loses herself by playing on her femininity" (p. 84).

The relatively recent revitalization of animal print clothing and fashions for women is an example of the recurrence of the allure of this presentation. While wearing real fur has fortunately declined, the idea of it remains tied to both control and consumption of women. Originally wearing the real thing "creat[ed] an aura of unbridled sensuality, the fantasy of power tinged with the cruelty of the kill" (Arnold, 2001, p. 160). Connecting women with the wild and as well as the man who bought the fur for her ultimately results in a taming of women. Describing advertisements by the fur industry Collard (1989) says both have an interest in degrading women

> ... because they invariably fuse animals and women in the same identity as prey, an identity that appeals to the hunter in man [as it is his money that buys the coat] and the victim in women. In reality she is the prey brought down. She and the fur animal—one "alive" and the other dead—are one and the same ... Even when does not actually hunt animals, his success is still reflected in the kill. (fn, p. 55)

Simultaneously shown as victim, savage, man-eater, and maternal, the wild woman persists as zoological exotica. In a similar fashion, when women and animals are conflated, they are inspected and surveyed with the aim of controlling their actions.

This dynamic is evident in an analysis of an image of Greta Garbo in the film *Riddle of the Sphinx* (1925), Kaplan (2002, p. 175) identifies that intangible something that the feral feminine embodies. In this film, the story is not told in the usual manner, from Oedipus's perspective, but instead from that of the sphinx, giving voice to the female animal. The actor Greta Garbo was fascinating because she evoked a longing for something other, something more from her and yet "unknown that we have lost contact with, while she at once allures and threatens men by her mysteriousness" (p. 175).

Another example of feline femme fatale (seductive woman who leads men down the path of ruin) is the 1942 film *Cat People*, directed by Jacques Tourner. In the opening scene, lead character Irena (Simone Simon) is at a very busy zoo, humming what will become her mysterious theme song. She faces away from the camera toward a cage in which a black leopard is enclosed. Irena is sketching the leopard. Clearly unsatisfied with the results she rips the drawing off the pad, wads it up, and casts it aside, unconcerned. The discarded art lands at the feet of a handsome man, Oliver (Kent Smith), who catches the next toss and points to a sign about littering. Serbian born fashion designer Irena seems unaffected. She has a look that is both feline and feminine. Her eyes are drawn with the kohl type elongation. She is kitten-like in her demeanor, naïve about love and sex, yet holds within her the truth of her secret nature. She fears something within herself that legend and lore predict will come true-that when becomes aroused or angry she will become a beast.

The film is about sexual awakening, fears of empowerment, and repression of desires. Simone Simon's portrayal of Irena is that of child/kitten like. She wears a bow in her hair, toys with a pet finch until it dies, frightens a tiny Siamese kitten, and is drawn to the leopards at the zoo. She describes the sounds of leopards as being like the "screams of a woman," something she finds comforting. The film is an example of Freud's concept of repression and return of the repressed. Repression has to do with packing away, deep in the unconscious of unpleasant, disturbing, or otherwise complicated thoughts until a time that an experience or some other stimuli brings a memory, for example, or latent behavior, to the level of consciousness. The later is what is meant by "return of the repressed," when this material rises in to the conscious mind. However, it does not always reappear in the form it originally had taken. The promotional poster for the movie reads "Lovely woman ... Giant Killer Cat ... The Same Person!" The pressures for Irena to come in to herself are doubled when her psychiatrist tries to seduce her as well in part to make her face what he thinks is a fantasy that sexual desire will turn her into a murderer.

This film, as are many horror flicks, is designed to thrill and chill, even cause goose bumps, an experience called *frisson*, meaning "a 'safe' vicarious, and virtual experience of sexual transgression" (Krzywinska, 2006, p. 117). By watching what might be forbidden, rather than doing what in real life is transgressive, provides an outlet to diffuse the charge of psychic energy behind our drives. Film has been called an instrument of the male gaze that produces representations of women, the good life, and sexual fantasy from a male point of view. Considering most films are made by men, through their perspectives as writers, directors, and producers, for an audience that lives in a patriarchal culture, it should come as no surprise that women learn to see themselves as men see them.

Irena fears becoming sexually aware because of a myth that says she will turn in to a leopard should she become sexually aroused. Transformation is a common narrative device in literature, art, and cinema: "Links between women, children, animals, and various forms of magic are a constant in Western art" (p. 160). The human/animal divide is narrowed blurring the distinction between Self/Other and Civilized/Wild. Furthermore, as psychologist Carl Jung (1964, p. 137, 140) pointed out, tales of shape shifting between bestial and human illustrate "a process of awakening" which instruct women on how to relate to men, illustrating "the true function of their relatedness" and the necessity of submission to the "animal man."

All women are not created equal under the rules of objectification. "Race becomes the distinguishing feature in determining the type of objectification women will encounter" (Hill-Collins, 2000, p. 139). As such, "Black women are caricatured as over-sexualized, promiscuous, and always 'ready for sale,' while white women are more often desexualized and caricatured as powerless, infantile, and socially compliant" (Ellison, 1996, p. 49). When presented as animals or possessed by their animal nature, all women become objects of the gaze. Given colonial constructs of the exoticized woman of color, however, these depictions are more complicated. Thus "domination may be either cruel and exploitative with no affection or may be exploitative yet coexist with affection" (Hill-Collins, 2000, p. 144). Whether women are represented "and treated as wild animal or domesticated pets depends to a great extent on racist norms" (Ellison, 1996, p. 49). Furthermore, "this over-reliance and easy association of black women" often shown as doubles of black panthers, "with animalistic hypersexuality ... is [a] persistent problem" (Brown, 2015, p. 133). These portrayals thereby teach men that women, particularly women of color, are creatures to be tamed and controlled and, if they succeed in catching them, have bodies they are entitled to. Roche (1988) argues that doubling "indicates profound unease on the part of a patriarchal society with aberrations from the social norm, with the behavior of women and children who do not conform."

Advertising Analysis

French author Colette (2003) wrote, "Two tricks over the years have taught me how to conceal my tears. That of hiding my thoughts, and that of darkening my mascara" (qtd. in Simon, 2002, p. 4). The kohl-rimmed eyes of cats have long served as inspiration for female beauty. There are cat-eye glasses, feline print footwear, and leopard inspired clothing. The classic look can be traced to ancient Egypt where kohl-rimmed eyes imitated those of cats:

> The actual design of the embellishment of the female Egyptian eye included one strange element—a horizontal black line that extended back from the outer

side of each eye heading towards the ear. This highly characteristic, decorative element had a magical significance, because it was an imitation of the eye markings of the cat—an animal sacred to the Egyptians. (Morris, 2011, p. 58)

The exotic look lasted thousands of years in Egypt, among Greek courtesans, and Roman women. This display was less often seen thereafter, at least among European women, until early in the 20th century as a backlash against Victorian primness (Morris, 2011). In early black and white, particularly silent, cinema, actresses (and actors) needed to make their eyes visible and cat eye imitations were perfect examples. Theda Bara was famous for her "heavily-lidded eyes" that spurred on a cosmetics industry explosion (Morris, 2011, p. 59). Both Bara's role as Cleopatra and that of Elizabeth Taylor in the 1963 epic inspired women all over the world to imitate this cat-based look. It is seen today on the dramatically dark-rimmed eyes of Adele, Rihanna, Katy Perry, Angelina Jolie, Megan Fox, and others. The precise application of liquid eyeliner is key with a final upward sweep to create the dramatic imitation of what cats naturally come by.

Maybelline Colossal Cat Eyes Mascara

As discussed earlier, a cat-eye look in women's cosmetics has ancient origins. Furthering the feline optical allure also includes long eyelashes. The Maybelline Colossal Cat Eyes Mascara commercial opens with a face of an endangered snow leopard (white with black stripes) roaring with amplified blue eyes and very pink nose. The camera quickly cuts to an extreme close up of the eyes (also exaggerated blue) of a dark haired model The voice over asks: "want fierce feline curls? Go cat eyes!" the word "meow!" appears on the screen, and roaring is heard in the background. The announcer continues: "only our spiky applicator creates wild volume." The black mascara tube with pink stripes is shown with the words "Volume Express Cat Eyes Mascara" on it. The camera cuts back to the roaring leopard and the voice over says, "get cat eyes mascara," and quickly cuts to a scene of a skyscraper as the voice says "Maybelline New York." Then returns to the model who is applying the mascara (can those be actual lashes or fake ones?) Then another extreme close up follows a single eye, and the voice says,

"Create wild eye volume." Model and cat faces are then shown side by side to demonstrate how cat-like she looks. "Get wild eyed curls that last," another roar by the cat, the voice says "Perfect," concluding with image of the product against a black screen. The voice says, "New hyper curl cat eyes," and the theme "Maybe it's Maybelline," plays. The model is shown writhing on her back, looking directly at the camera and then seems to roar, the transformation from cat to woman to cat complete.

The version of this commercial created for the German market (Maybelline Jade) is in brown and tan tones. In this spot, the model is blond and the cats are cheetahs. An adult cheetah slinks across a room, the model, wearing imitation cheetah print, playfully hides behind furniture. Her eyes are also made up in classic cat-eye fashion with exaggerated lashes. Her eyes dart from side to side as she slyly looks around. The cheetah leaps. At the words "secret formula," she unlocks a giant safe/vault to reveal the cheetah lounging inside. Then she is shown on the floor, playing with a stripped tiger cub, who has a necklace in its mouth, and a solid white cub. She holds one of the cubs and seductively says, "meow." The next seen is the extremely blue-eyed model unfolding herself from an elegant car, holding a tiger cub who is then shown on a leash. The final scene is the blond beauty holding the blue-eyed tiger cub next to her face.

Yves St. Laurent's Opium

The imitation of what cats look like also extends to how cats behave. They have an aura of mystique, a beyond-words understanding/intuition, and a certain kind seductive energy. Those qualities combined with independence, self-sufficiency, calm, and self-assurance flies in the face of a culture that values women's dependence. "The cat's calm center, her implacable response to an uneasy world," is a reflection of those same traits within many women (Simon, 2002, p. 15). What we learn as well when we engage with cats is that nothing can be taken for granted. Furthermore, the long, lean idealized female physique is also comparable to the cat's way of moving and being. "The feline use of distance as enticement" is powerful (p. 16). When embodied by women, it can be a powerful aphrodisiac.

This ad for YSL's Opium fragrance stars 28-year-old English actor Emily Blunt. The commercial opens with a solid black screen on which is written in red Yves St. Laurent. The music, Mozart's Requiem Mass in D minor, rises. The next image is the same screen but written on it, as if a film, is Opium avec Emily Blunt. Ms Blunt is dressed in a solid black top, cut below breast level, which ends just below her bottom. Her high-heeled legs are covered with black hose. She wears a heavy gold necklace. She is walking down the hallway of a dimly lit fancy home or posh hotel. Her hair is long and her eyes are made up in class cat eye fashion. As she glides toward the camera, she casts a glance over her right shoulder. A flash of something slinky is seen, slightly out of focus. She looks to her left and we see a spotted leopard walking amongst the furniture. Looking up, the cat seems to know Blunt is coming and trots toward the camera.

Blunt enters a room, hands drawing back curtains. The camera cuts back and forth between her cat-like motion and that of the real animal. An extreme close up of her green eye looking through what appears to be a peephole. The cat, guardian of the fragrance, sees her and crouches. As Blunt enters the room the cat rises, they are eye to eye. The camera focuses on the strength, agility, and beauty of the way both cat and actor move. They are clearly locked in one another's gaze. They walk toward one another, she looking downward, the leopard meows, and reaches his or her head into Blunt's extended hand as she walks by, stroking the back of the cat. She passes the cat and sees, on display what appears to be a fine jewel—it is revealed as a bottle of Opium. The leopard looks back at Blunt who is shown reclining on a maroon and gold settee, stroking the fragrance on her throat (of course the place that would be most vulnerable were the cat to attack). The camera moves down her limp extended arm to her hand, which is holding a bottle of fragrance. A French accented voice over says in English, "Opium, Yves St. Laurent."

Conclusion

That beautiful women and exotic cats appear in commercials is not unusual, that is until we focus the lens of textual analysis on them. This chapter explores the coding of films and advertisements with women who look like cats, act like cats, and/or act as cats. The almost natural morphing of one in to the other offers a semiotically seamless view of womanhood as sexy, sexual, predatory, and powerful. On the one hand, this can be read in the preferred version as desirability. We have beautiful women who take on the appearance and affect the nature of felines. It is a nice comparison to make—that women and gorgeous animals not only have a naturally affinity for one another but can in fact become the other. At the same time, however, a negotiated reading looks behind the production veil and asks about why these choices are made—what is it about cats and women that make them objects of comparison and easy targets for control, confinement, and capture? A resistant reading interrogates these codes and, as we have done, explores the history of these representations. What makes them seem so normal and natural that we fail to notice the power dynamic? How is it gazing at women (and animals for this matter) in this way can be used as a tool for ideological control of the lives of both? The answers to these questions are complex, but the coding of women in this way, whether in film roles, to sell mascara or perfume, is no accident.

> Women, like cats, are often labeled as sneaky, slinky, mysterious, hard to read and impossible-to-please. Women are often shunted into either the Madonna or whore category, just as cats have been either revered as deities (ancient Egypt) or vilified as demons. (Salem witch trials, 1692)

The unpacking of these codes is further complicated by issues of race and ethnicity. While a full discussion of this is beyond the scope of this chapter, it bears comment. In 1933, in the midst of exotic women mania, Paramount Studios launched a search to track down "the perfect panther woman" (Adinolfi, 2008, p. 27). The actor they found starred in Island of Lost Souls (1933)—Kathleen Burke. The same year Fay Wray appeared the same year in King Kong (1933), which was the most visible example of the post-colonial exoticizing of white women with dark, dangerous figures. White women as feline-like figures are common in narratives in which White men, in the end, reign supreme by rescuing the damsel in distress. In 1903, W. E.

B. Dubois proposed that Black men must adopt a "double consciousness," a two-ness, in order to successfully navigate both the White and Black worlds straddling cultural understandings of both societies. I propose that women must also learn the ways of both worlds and women of color must adopt a triple consciousness, one being of their race, dominant culture's race (white), and that of being female. These "looking relations" (Gaines, 1986, p. 59) do not only apply to human beings. Animals also learn to live in both their world and ours simultaneously. Furthermore, the anthropocentric gaze is one in which human society takes pleasure in looking at animals also creates an active human/passive animal relationships. As is the case with animals who become human-like in anthropocentric narratives such as King Kong, Curious George, and Beethoven the dog, they are decontextualized from their natural environments thereby functioning as disguises as "they prevent us from seeing the authentic animal beneath the cultural frippery" (Malamud, 2012, p. 72). The literature of ecofeminism[1] shows us how the exploitation of women and animals is interconnected (see Chapter 1 on Intersectionality) and has harmed both. Re-presentations of women as animals or animal like, in this case in the form of big cats, exemplifies the tendency to show both as sexual objects.

> It is a smooth extrapolation to characterize Mulvey's male gaze (upon the filmed female creature) as a human gaze (upon the filmed animal creature). … the image of the animal becomes passive raw material for the active gaze of the human. (Malamud, 2012, p. 74)

In visual culture, some animals and women are prized for their cuteness and even their sexiness. Appropriating catness in to definitions of femininity might bring something to the human being but takes away from the animal, the real animal, whose conditions of being are blurred by their serving as a prop for human action in the movies and commercials. As Mulvey (1975) pointed out more than thirty years ago, with women in visual culture, what matters is what she provokes, not who she is. This has barely changed. The same can be said of the erasure of the real animal who function as "supporting cast" for human drama (p. 76).

What happens if the real animal, for example, the highly endangered tiger (Figure 8.2) who appears in many of the mascara ads, is made invisible through marketing and advertising?

Figure 8.2: Tiger.
Source: Used by permission iStock/Getty Images.

Note

1. Ecofeminism is defined, by Carol J. Adams (2017) as: "A dynamic political theory that identifies how oppressions are interconnected." Adams' work in particular focuses on intersections of gender, sex, and species (http://caroljadams.com/about-ecofeminism/).

References

Adams, C. J. (2017). *Ecofeminism*. Retrieved from http://caroljadams.com/about-ecofeminism/

Adinolfi, F. (2008). *Mondo exotica: Sounds, visions, obsessions of the cocktail generation.* Durham, NC: Duke University Press.

Arnold, R. (2001). *Fashion, desire, and anxiety.* London: I. B. Taurus.

Bamberger, J. (2011, June 2). How to write about Sarah Palin and Michele Bachmann without invoking a "cat fight." *Poynter.* Retrieved February 6, 2013 from http://www.poynter.org/latest-news/top-stories/134342/how-to-write-about-sarah-palin-and-michele-bachmann-without-invoking-a-catfight/

Baudelaire, C. (1857/1952). Les Fleurs du mal (The flowers of evil). In R. Campbell (Ed.), *Poems of Baudelaire.* New York, NY: Pantheon.

Berg, A., & Schaffer, J. (Writers), & Ackerman, A. (Director). (1997, May 15). *The season of George [Seinfeld].* Season 8, Ep. 22. Los Angeles, CA: Castle Rock.

Berger, J. (1972). *Ways of seeing.* New York, NY: Penguin.

Bhabha, H. (1994). *The Location of culture.* New York, NY: Routledge.

Bierce, A. (1906/2000). *The devil's dictionary.* Retrieved February 5, 2013 from http://dd.pangyre.org/w/woman.html

Blakeley, K. (2009, October 15). Crazy cat ladies. *Forbes.* Retrieved February 3, 2013 from http://www.forbes.com/2009/10/14/crazy-cat-lady-pets-stereotype-forbes-woman-time-felines.html

Brown, B. R. (2012, March 15). Lecture six: Fetishism and popular culture: Umberto Eco's Casablanca. Cultural Studies: Introductory Lectures. Retrieved January 29, 2013 from http://culturalstudieslectures.blogspot.com/2012/03/fetishism-and-popular-culture-umberto.html

Brown, J. (2015). *Beyond bombshells: The new action heroine in popular culture.* Jackson, MI: University Press of Mississippi.

Burkert, W. (1982). *Structure and history in Greek mythology and ritual.* Berkeley, CA: University of California Press.

Carroll, R. (1988). Something to see: Spectacle and savagery in Leonora Carrington's fiction. *Critique, 39*(2), 154–166.

Colette, S. G. (2003). Quoted in Simon, C. (2002). *Feline mystique.* New York, NY: St. Martin's.

Collard, A. (1989). *Rape of the wild.* Bloomington, IN: Indiana University Press.

DeMello, M. (2015). Foreword. In K. Kirkpatrick & B. Faragó (Eds.), *Animals in Irish literature and culture.* New York, NY: Palgrave.

Ellison, M. M. (1996). *Erotic justice: A liberating ethic of sexuality.* Louisville, KY: Westminster John Knox Press.

Estes, C. P. (2003). *Women who run with the wolves.* New York, NY: Random House.

Evans, M. (2001). *Feminism: Feminism and modernity.* New York, NY: Taylor & Francis.

Fletcher, A. (1995). *Gender, sex, and subordination in England, 1500–1800.* New Haven, CT: Yale University Press.

Foucault, M. (1977). *Discipline and punish: The birth of the prison.* New York, NY: Pantheon.
Gúzman, I. M., & Valdivia, A. (2004). Brain, brow, and booty: Latina iconicity in US popular culture. *The Communication Review, 7,* 205–221.
Hall, S. (1973/1980). Encoding/decoding. In S. Hall (Ed.), *Culture, media, language: Working papers in cultural studies, 1972–79* (pp. 128–138). London: Hutchinson.
Hamel, F. (2003). *Human animals.* Whitefish, MT: Kessinger Publishing.
Hendricks, R. (1978/2004). *Classical gods and heroes.* New York, NY: HarperCollins.
Hill-Collins, P. (2000). *Black feminist thought: Knowledge, consciousness, and the politics of empowerment.* New York: Psychology Press.
Irigary, L. (1984). *Éthique de la différence sexuelle.* Paris: Mimut.
Jardine, L. (1983). *Still harping on daughters: Women and drama in the age of Shakespeare.* New York, NY: Harvester Press.
Jung, C. G. (1964). *Man and his symbols.* New York: Doubleday.
Kaplan, A. (2002). *Women & film.* New York, NY: Routledge.
Kristeva, J. (1982). *Powers of horror.* New York, NY: Columbia University Press.
Krzywinska, T. (2006). *Sex and the cinema.* New York, NY: Wallflower Press.
Kurzweil, E. (1986). Michel Foucault's history of sexuality as interpreted by feminists and Marxists. *Social Research, 55*(4), 647–663.
Malamud, R. (2012). *An introduction to animals and visual culture.* New York, NY: Palgrave.
Mathis-Lilley, B. (2016, October 7). Trump was recorded in 2005 bragging about grabbing women "by the pussy." *Washington Post.* Retrieved from http://www.slate.com/blogs/the_slatest/2016/10/07/donald_trump_2005_tape_i_grab_women_by_the_pussy.html
McKee, A. (2003). *Textual analysis.* Newbury Park, CA: Sage.
Michelet, J. (1904). *The sorceress: A study in middle age superstition.* Paris: Charles Carrington.
Morris, D. (2011). *The naked woman.* New York, NY: Random House.
Mulvey, L. (1975). Visual pleasure and narrative cinema. *Screen, 16*(3), 6–18.
O'Connor, S. (2015). Hares and hags: Becoming animal in Eilís Ní Dhuibhne's *Dún na mBan trí Thine.* In K. Kirkpatrick & B. Faragó (Eds.), *Animals in Irish literature and culture* (pp. 92–104). New York, NY: Palgrave.
Onstad, K. (2011, June 18). Why are passionate women always compared to cats? Meow! *Globe and Mail.* Retrieved February 3, 2013 from http://www.theglobeandmail.com/life/relationships/why-are-passionate-women-always-compared-to-cats-meow/article625397/
Regula, (1995). *The mysteries of Isis: Her worship and magick.* Woodbury, MN: Llewelyn.
Rodríquez, L. I. (2009). Of women, bitches, chickens, and vixens: Animal metaphors for Women in English and Spanish. *Cultural Language and Representation, 7,* 77–100.
Rogers, K. M. (2006). *Cat.* London: Reaktion Books.
Ruiz, A. (2001). *The spirit of ancient Egypt.* New York, NY: Algora Publishing.
Simon, C. (2002). *Feline mystique.* New York, NY: St. Martin's.

Smelik, A. (1999). Feminist film theory. In P. Cook & M. Bernink (Eds.), *The cinema book* (2nd ed., pp. 353–365). London: British Film Institute.

Terry, J. (2000). "Unnatural acts" in nature: The scientific fascination with queer animals. *GLQ: Journal of Lesbian and Gay studies, 6*(2), 151–193.

Warner, M. (1994). *From the beast to the blonde: On fairy tales and their tellers*. New York: Farrar, Strauss, & Giroux.

Williams, A. (1995). *Art of darkness: A poetics of gothic*. Chicago, IL: University of Chicago Press.

Zorich, Z. (2008, November/December). Fighting with Jaguars, bleeding for rain. *Archeology, 61*(6). Retrieved February 1, 2013 from http://archive.archaeology.org/0811/etc/boxing.html

Chapter Nine

Nevermore

Ravens in *Game of Thrones*

Dark wings, dark words.

—(*Game of Thrones*)

We watch, we listen, and we remember. The past is already written. The ink is dry. Three-eyed raven.

—(*Game of Thrones*)

For we all of us, grave or light, get our thoughts entangled in metaphors, and act fatally on the strength of them.

—(Eliot, 1872)

"Quoth the raven, 'Nevermore.'" This phrase is likely the most often heard raven reference in English literature. It comes from Edgar Allen Poe's 1845 poem "The Raven" in which a distraught lover, mourning the death of his beloved Lenore, hears a tapping at his "chamber door." When curiosity gets the better of him he opens the portal, a raven enters his room and perches on top a bust of Pallas, which sits above the door frame[1] (see Figure 9.1). The narrator invokes the talking bird's reputed prophetic skills in order to ask questions about whether or not he will be reunited with his love, even in death. To each and every question the bird responds with only one maddening word: "Nevermore." The mythological characteristics and notoriety of the raven are called forth (the "ghastly grim and ancient raven," with "grave and

Figure 9.1: "Not the Least Obeisance Made He." Gustave Doré illustration for the 1884 edition of *The Raven*.

stern decorum") (Poe, 1845) when the increasingly agitated man gains no satisfaction from the bird's responses:

> "Prophet!" said I, "thing of evil!—prophet still, if bird or devil!—
> Whether Tempter sent, or whether tempest tossed thee here ashore,
> Desolate yet all undaunted, on this desert land enchanted—
> On this home by Horror haunted—tell me truly, I implore—
> Is there—*is* there balm in Gilead?—tell me—tell me, I implore!"
> Quoth the Raven "Nevermore."

Public Domain

What Poe drew upon in this poem was an ancient sense of the Raven, built from Western mythology, lore, folk and fairy tale, that constructed the bird in to a symbol of darkness, evil, prophecy, and foreordination. Crows and ravens are common narrative devices used in television programs (*The Following*) and movies to indicate danger and invoke a sense of doom and are "among the most vivid and widely employed animal symbols" (Lawrence, 1997, p. 9). Raven's behavior and cries were taken as prescient by ancient Romans and inspired the poem by Poe. The bird served as a companion to the title character in Charles Dickens' *Barnaby Rudge*.

Perhaps no other Northern Hemisphere animal (other than the wolf) is more deeply steeped in myth than is the raven. In some cultures, the bird is revered, signifying strength, power, serving as companion and advisor to gods and to saints. In others Raven is despised and feared as an omen of evil and carrier of the souls of the dead, often unjustifiably blamed for thievery, and sometimes hunted and killed as vermin. There is evidence of psychological interchangeability of ravens and crows. Savage (1997, p. 9) notes "an American hunting magazine urged its readers to take up crow shooting as a cure for cabin fever" because the birds eat what is rotting, hence cleaning up the potentially dangerous departed. The poet Spencer describes Raven as

> A cursed bird too crafty to be shot,
> That always cometh with his soot-black boat

To make hearts dreary,—for he is a blot
Upon the book of life.

This chapter uses conceptual metaphor (CMT) (Lakoff & Johnson, 1980) and conceptual blending (CBT) theories (Joy, Sherry, & Deschenes, 2007) to unpack the use of Ravens in the first season of HBO's *Game of Thrones* (*GoT*). CMT examines the linkages, typically in language, of one thought to another. More importantly, however, CMT investigates metaphor as essential to human thought (see Gibbs, 1994). In this study, the concept of Raven is linked as a *visual* metaphor to re-presentations in popular culture in general and *GoT* in particular. The impact of re-presentations on species is discussed in terms of the ongoing contribution to the stereotype of the birds as only and forevermore dark and foreboding.

The focus of this chapter is on the first season of *GoT* while also referencing the first book and later seasons, as the raven is a constant figure throughout.[2] While the book uses crows the television series substituted ravens. Many writers use both birds interchangeably when discussing crows and ravens, I argue that the raven is worthy in his/her own right, to be considered as such. If, in the 20th and 21st century, "people are influenced more by crows than ravens" (Marzluff & Angell, 2005/2007, p. 110), it is particularly interesting that the creators of *GoT* chose Raven over Crow. It may be because, as Cornell ornithologist and bird artist George Miksch Sutton (1936) wrote the raven is "wary and solitary in nature," and as a "bird of the wilderness [one] that few people ever saw" (Heinrich, 2002, p. xvi).

The first section of this chapter is a brief description of real ravens. The second section discusses the role and function of mythology and how Ravens figure into many mythologies. The final section reviews re-presentations of ravens in popular culture, concluding with an analysis and discussion of their use in *GoT*.

The Real Raven

Ravens (*Corvus Corax*) are members of the family *Corvidae*, which includes crows, magpies, jackdaws, and jays. This bird is found in the

Figure 9.2: Raven.
Source: Used by permission iStock/Getty Images.

Northern Hemisphere, most particularly in North America, Europe, and Northern Asia.[3] There are approximately ten species of birds in the world called Raven, two of which live in North America (Young, 2014, p. 247) (see Table 9.1).

Not as social as crows, ravens are part of communities and are extraordinarily playful. "If corvids are the most playful of birds, young ravens are said to be the most playful of corvids" (Savage, 1997, p. 71). They are also inventive and highly intelligent. One story holds that, "a raven that heard repeated explosions being set off by a highway crew is reported afterwards to have shouted out "Three, two, one, kaboom!" (p. 80). Distinct characteristics of the raven are that they are excellent navigators, seasonal migrators, builders of nests who have complex and sometimes dramatic courtship rituals, and grieve the loss of their mates. Ravens are faithful to these mates and helpful with offspring, have feathers that re-grow, and vary in coloring. They "generally live as couples or small families in remote, often mountainous areas,

Table 9.1. Raven Facts.

Scientific name:	Corvus corax
Weight:	1.5-4.4 lbs.
Wingspan:	3.3-4.9'
Conservation status:	least concern (population increasing)
Habitat:	Northern Hemisphere.
Diet:	Eat almost anything including carrion, eggs, grasshoppers, beetles, fish, wolf dung, berries, pet food.
Nesting:	Primarily built by females; in trees, on cliffs or structures such as power/telephone poles, bridges, billboards.
Incubation Period:	20-25 days
Nestling Period:	28-50 days
Fun fact:	Rate in intelligence with dolphins and chimpanzees.

Source: http://mentalfloss.com/article/53295/10-fascinating-facts-about-ravens

though even they occasionally congregate to form groups of hundreds and even thousands" (Sax, 2003, p. 25) and in the wild can live up to 40 years (Savage, 1997, p. 104). That they tend to isolate, are big (the size of a large hawk) makes them mysterious and powerful symbols. Further adding to their allure, ravens often accompany packs of wolves, play "tag" with them, and eat the remains of what the wolves have killed. They "work cooperatively with cougars, hawks, and other predators who are more adept at killing" (Young, 2014, p. 247). Ravens also have a keen, insightful intelligence. In *Mind of the Raven*, Bernd Heinrich (2002, p. 356) writes, "I conclude that ravens are able to manipulate mental images for solving problems. They are aware of some aspects of their private reality, seeing with their minds at least some of what they have seen with their eyes."

In 1905 R. Bosworth Smith wrote that ravens are "among the boldest, the cleverest, the most wary, the most amusing, the most voracious … . The rarest, and that in an ever accelerating degree, of its kind" (p. 76). Smith wrote not as a scientist, but as an educator whose love of birds prompted him to observe them tirelessly. As early as 1905 he saw a decline in the population of the birds, pointing out "he is passing away from the whole of the interior districts of England, where, a generation or two ago, his solemn croak could so often be heard" (p. 81).

The Symbolic Raven

Mythology is where, at least until modern times, people sought and found answers to the big questions of life such as where do we come from, what is love, what happens when we die? Myths are the stories we tell ourselves about ourselves (Merskin, 2011, p. 4). The term is misused in contemporary culture, typically paired with ideas that are untrue such as Top 10 Diet Myths. In reality, myths are the greatest of truths, indeed myth is "the penultimate truth, of which all experience is the temporal reflection. A mythical narrative is of timeless and placeless validity, true nowhere and everywhere" (Coomaraswamy, 1996, p. 6). As a result, myths are not "detached stories. They are imaginative patterns, networks of powerful symbols that suggest particular ways of interpreting the world. They shape its meaning" (Midgley, 2004, p. 1).

When symbols lose their fluidity, and begin having concretized meanings, they become signs. In Christian mythology, for example, the snake becomes the equivalent of danger, temptation, and the fall of Eve. As a result, reptiles in general and the snake particular are afforded few to no positive associations. Whereas signs are "consciously invented" (Fontana, 1994, p. 8) consisting of " ... terms, names, or even pictures that may familiar in daily life, yet that possess specific connotations in addition to their conventional obvious meanings" (Jung, 1964, p. 20), a symbol reaches deeply into the human unconscious, arises, and is expressed spontaneously. We are aware of its presence and power, but symbols are impossible to fully articulate Furthermore, "certain kinds of symbolism constitute a universal language, because the images and their meanings offer in similar forms—and carry similar power—right across cultures and centuries" (Fontana, 1994, p. 10).

Animals who take center stage in myths are those who are central to a particular culture. In any story of human beings, animals are also present. At times, we use animals as stand ins for ourselves, letting them act out roles for which there are human equivalents. The meanings vary by culture. We anthropomorphize in order to give them our voices, emotions, thoughts, and behaviors so that they are relatable. These stories impact human behavior toward one another and toward animals. There are five characteristics to which mythical creatures are found, based on the following traits or forms: (1) birds and beasts, (2) human/animal composites, (3) creatures of darkness, (4) fairies, and (5) giants. This is a much wider range of evil dark characters in world mythology than good. The same animal can also be viewed differently in different cultures.

Ravens are the first birds to be written about in the Bible (Young, 2014, p. 249) and appear in two episodes of the Old Testament

> Forthwith from out of the ark a raven flies, And after him, a surer messenger, a dove. The ravens, with their horny beak, Food to Elijah bringing ev'n and morn, Tho' rav'nous, taught to abstain from what they brought.

It was a Raven who was sent to Cain to provide instruction on how to dispose of the body of his murdered brother, Abel. In a Babylonian story of the great flood that pre-dates the Bible it was Raven who found dry land. Ravens are also included in the Koran. Second or Third Century BCE Celtic helmets from Romania bore the image of a raven with hinged wings that would flap upon entering battle.

The ancient Romans regarded the Raven as the highest form of birds and believed the Raven's cry (*cras*) to be the Latin word for "tomorrow," considering it a sign of optimism and hope. In Greek mythology, ravens are associated with prophecy and the God Apollo. One story tells of Apollo sending a white raven to spy on on his lover Coronis, who he suspected was unfaithful to him. When the bird returned with the news it was true, Apollo scorched the bird's feathers, turning them black.

In Norse mythology, for example, the god Odin was accompanied by two ravens, Hugin (Thought) and Munin (Memory). The birds were released at dawn and would return to tell Odin what they had learned. In this mythological system, Ravens symbolize both good and evil. "As symbols of Odin's mind and thoughts [they] symbolized his power to see in to the future. As symbols on the battlefield, they represented Odin's welcoming to his palace, Valhalla, the spirits of slain human heroes who died in battle" (Daily, 2009, p. 84). The Viking flag bore the symbol of the raven. In ancient Persian religion the raven is said to be an incarnation of Verethragna, "the god of victorious battles," hence their feathers were worn as talismans (Sax, 2003, p. 53).

Raven is Bhutan's national bird who guards important deities. According to Jewish beliefs, Ravens are unclean because they eat carrion but to Zoroastrians, "the birds are pure because they remove dead things from the earth" (Young, 2014, p. 250). In ancient times Linnaeus wrote, "He will banquet with the beasts" (qtd. In Smith, 1905, p. 98). An omnivorous bird, the raven's diet "ranges from a worm to a whale" (p. 93).

Raven legends and lore persist throughout Europe, although the origins are nested in a disturbing past. In England, for example, it was believed that ravens foretold the coming Plague in London. As Christopher Marlowe (1589–1590/1850, pp. 262–263) wrote in Act II of *The Jew of Malta*: "The sad presaging raven, that tolls the sick man's passport in her hollow beak, And in the shadow of the silent night Doth shake contagion from her sable wings."

There are always six ravens in permanent residence at the Tower of London.[4] A version of the Tower story tells it that, despite hatred for the birds, because of their eating of carrion during plagues and wars, during the London fire of 1666 six of the birds were nevertheless allowed to live at the Tower of London. This was due to royal astronomer Sir John Flamstead's prophecy, told to King Charles II, that if all the ravens were killed, the British kingdom would fall. As a result, since the 17th century to today, Ravens have resided at the Tower and are protected by royal decree (their wings are clipped so they do not leave, assuring continued reign of the monarchy). Today the big birds hop along in a field near the White Tower. Scholar Boria Sax went to great effort to verify the story of King Charles in an effort to separate fantasy from reality. Whether or not there actually was an official proclamation matters little, for what is evident is the significance these resident birds have for British citizens past and the present. The birds have staff caretakers who are specific members of the Tower Guards, known as Raven masters, who feed the birds blood soaked biscuits, sheep hearts, and pig livers (Young, 2014, p. 248). The English singer Kate Bush draws on this legend in the 1978 title track of her "Lion Heart" album: "Our thumping hearts hold the Ravens in, keeping the Tower from tumbling."

Ravens also figure in the settlement stories of ancient Iceland. It was, by way of ravens, that the Vikings located to the large island. The story is told that

Landnámabók, Flóki Vilgerðarson took three ravens to help him find his way. Thus, he was nicknamed Raven-Floki (Icelandic: Hrafna-Flóki). Flóki set his ravens free near the Faeroe Islands. The first raven flew back on board. The second flew up in the air and then returned to the ship. However, the third flew in front of the ship and they followed its direction to Iceland. He landed in Vatnsfjörður in the Westfjords after passing what is now Reykjavík. One of his men, Faxi, remarked that they seemed to have found great land—the bay facing Reykjavík is therefore known as Faxaflói. A harsh winter caused all of Flóki's cattle to die—he cursed this cold country, and when he spotted a drift ice in the fjord he decided to name it "Ísland" (Iceland). (http://www.bevaraweb.com/ravens.html)

In such tales, ravens (and crows) are associated with death and being eaten after death by crows. The birds wait at the gallows, perch in tree branches awaiting the inevitable slaughter on battlefields, and serve as avatars signaling forthcoming death. For example, it is believed that "if one [raven] croaks near the house of a sick person, that person does not have long to live" (Sax, 2003, p. 69). A raven's speech is "one of the most sepulchral sounds in nature" (Smith, 1905, p. 92). Its caw both foretold optimistic times (Roman) or death (English), and in between is the belief that the raven's call is a sign of a procrastinator "who would complacently put off making his peace with God, not realizing that he could die at any moment" (p. 71).

Some Native American tribes have clans whose totem animal is Raven. For example, according to Hopi (U.S. desert South West), the tribes were created by Grandmother Spider. The story goes that after the Sky Spirit Tawa, created the world and all of its inhabitants, Grandmother Spider remained on Earth with the animals and the people. It was up to her to sort everyone out. She divided people in to groups such as Zuni, Dine', Pueblo, Comanche, and Ute and from thereafter they knew their names. She also named the animals. But they were all in the underworld and Grandmother Spider knew the darkness of the four caves was not a good place for them to remain. Mourning Dove flew out ahead to find places for the people to live. One animal led each group of people out of the darkness and in to the world. Thereafter, the people were known as the people of the crow, the Antelope clan, and the clan of the Raven (see Caduto & Bruchac, 1997).

For some tribes, Raven is the clan name and creator of the people. Whereas to people of the desert southwest it is coyote, to many tribes in the Pacific Northwest (including Tlingit, Haida, Tsimshian, Kwakiutl, Salishan, and Nisgaa-Gitksan) and northern Athabaskan tribes (Tanaina), raven is also a trickster, a clown, and a maker of mischief. His calls are full of information. He makes rivers flow only one direction to make travel tricky, and "it was believed that Raven's greatest trick of all was to give each male animal testicles, so that he might be entertained by the silly games and preoccupations they constantly engaged in" (Marzluff & Angell, 2005/2007, pp. 112–113). Raven is imaged on a variety of items such as bentwood boxes, art forms, and carved in to totem poles. For the Zuni, a tribe in the American South West, raven (*kotollo-ah*) and crow (*kalashi*) are associated with dark rain clouds, and "keeping with the birds' unpredictable nature, however, they can either bring clouds or drive them away" (Bahti, 1999, p. 68).

Today, in the Pacific Northwest region of the United States, for example, members of Kwakiutl (Kwakwaka'wakw) Raven clan on Blake Island in Puget Sound, perform important dances, dressed in full raven costume. Three dancers, each representing a different "cannibal," or *hamatsa*, dance (Marzluff & Angell, 2005/2007, p. 108) present as Raven, How How, and Crooked Beak.

Previous sections of this book discuss what anthropologists, psychologists, linguistics, and others have said about the power and importance of symbolizing values, attitudes, and beliefs. What these schools of thought share is the deeply psychological process of associating unrelated concepts with real living animals who then become symbolic stand-ins for ideas, emotions, and ways of being, i.e. metaphors. A question posed by early anthropologists such as Radcliffe-Brown (1977/2004) and Lévi-Strauss (1962) is "why this particular species?" Crow, raven, eagle, and eagle hawks represent something that doves, turkeys, and sparrows do not.

These can be unpacked through two theories: Conceptual Metaphor and Conceptual Blending.

Conceptual Metaphor Theory

A metaphor, as commonly understood, is "an implied comparison between two things of unlike nature that nevertheless have something in common" (Corbett & Connors, 1999, p. 479) or "understanding or perceiving of one kind of thing in terms of another kind of thing" (Lakoff & Johnson, 1980, p. 5).

A *Conceptual* metaphor is "not just a figure of speech but a thoroughly embodied activity, generated by thought and imagination" (Joy et al., 2007, p. 40). Identifying the psychological nature of the act of conceiving of something recognizes the deeper level activity of association. We know that, for example, when Shakespeare wrote "Juliet is the sun" this was not meant literally, rather, it referred to aspects of who she was, her personality, her way of being in the world that was warm and happy. Similarly, everyday expressions that are metaphoric about romantic relationships include "Our marriage is on the rocks," "We're at a crossroads," or "We're going opposite directions" (Croft & Cruse, 2004; Kovecses, 2002, 2006; Lakoff & Johnson, 1980, 1999). These concepts bring together unelated ideas (conceptual metaphors) to form a single expression that makes sense within a particular culture. Many of these follow systematic psychological patterns of association. The scope of the abstract conceptual domain can include emotions (Kovecses, 2000), science concepts (Brown, 2003), cultural ideologies (Goatly, 1997) and others. As such, conceptual metaphors are not merely tools to make language more colorful, rather they operate at a fundamental psychological level in associating understood ideas with others. The conceptual domain from which metaphorical expressions originated is the source domain. What is formed through this association is the target domain (Lakoff & Johnson, 1980). A target is "the object to which attributes are ascribed" (van Mulken, van Hooft, & Nederstigt, 2014, p. 334). Lakoff and Turner (1989, p. 51) describe basic conceptual metaphors as

> Part of the common conceptual apparatus shared by members of a culture. They are systematic in that there is a fixed correspondence between the structure of the domain to be understood (e.g., death) and the structure of the domain in terms of which we are understanding it (e.g., departure). We

usually understand them in terms of common experiences. They are largely unconscious, though attention may be drawn to them. Their operation in cognition is almost automatic. And they are widely conventionalized in language, that is, there are a great number of words and idiomatic expressions in our language whose meanings depend upon those conceptual metaphors.

Can there be similar linkages, or mappings, through the use of images rather than words? Can images shape thinking in the same way words do? Absolutely. Visual metaphors "involve[e] an interaction between external visual metaphors and the user's internal knowledge representations" (Ziemkiewicz & Kosara, 2008, p. 1269). Logos, for example, used in advertising and branding, function as visual metaphors. Joy et al. (2007, p. 41) use Prudential Insurance Company as an example. The logo, dating back to 1891, is of a huge rock. The associative qualities of the rock are how the insurance company wishes to be identified: stable, strong, and enduring. What does a rock have to do with insurance? Nothing.

As discussed in earlier chapters, images of animals similarly function as metaphors. Their appearance in advertisements, movies, and on greeting cards brings something more to the re-presentation by imbuing the associated product or narrative with greater complexity than time or space allow, functioning on both cognitive and emotional levels. This associative practice enables us "to 'map across' behavioural domains, taking patterns learned in one and transferring them to other, novel domains" (Mithen, quoted in Hirschman, 2007, p. 230) as animal anthropomorphism. Naming a car after a big cat, for example, such as Jaguar, invokes the qualities associated with the cat and suggests the car also has them. Comprehension of the information requires that the viewer understands the conventions and that "viewers and makers share expectations and implicit rules" that vary from culture to culture.

The second theory, Conceptual blending (CBT) is a model of meaning construction that takes the analysis deeper and "occurs at the moment of perception and creates new meanings out of existing ways of thinking" (Joy et al., 2007, p. 39; see also Fauconnier & Turner, 2002). CBT is used to analyze visual communications such as advertising where words and images of everyday life are brought together to construct meanings. Whereas conceptual metaphor theory identifies the process by which people make meaning by moving from the source to a target domain, blending adds the dynamic of individual interpretations to the process based on "an individual's unique representation[al]" repertoire (p. 39). Emojis of a dove with an olive branch belies the original story behind the bird. Julian Barnes (1990, p. 24) retelling of the tale of Noah's Ark story has this in mind.

> You have elevated this bird, I understand, into something of symbolic value. So let me just point this out: the raven always maintained that *he* found the olive tree; that *he* brought a leaf from it back to the Ark; that Noah decided it was "more appropriate" to say that the dove had discovered it. ... The dove ... began sounding unbearably smug from the moment we disembarked. She could already envisage herself on postage stamps and letterheads.

Cultivating Cues

A bird's eye view means the ability to see far and wide, and a bird as the vantage point of a "privileged position that gives it a superior and panoramic view of reality, an overview" (Colin, 2000, p. 446). Thus birds not only have sight, but also insight to reality as well as the deeper aspects of consciousness as well as the unconscious.

Colors matter as well, or fur or feathers. Anthropologist Marshall Sahlins noted, "colors are in practice semiotic codes" (2013, fn28). Ravens are black birds who, by the very nature of cultural constructions of colors, suggest something different than do birds who are white.[5] Savage (1997, p. 9) describes them as: "Black as shadows, they rustle unseen in the treetops. Eerie as night, they swoop overhead with a hiss. Dark as death, they land in hoarse-voiced squabbling flocks to feed on rotting carcasses." In a Vietnamese story, "Why the Raven is Black,"

> In the olden days, the raven and the peacock were close friends who lived on a plantation in Vietnam. One day, the two birds decided to amuse themselves by painting each other's feathers. The raven set willingly to work and so surpassed itself that the peacock became, as it is today, one of the most beautiful

birds on earth. Unwilling to share its glory even with its friend, the mean-spirited peacock painted the raven black. (Savage, 1997, p. 70)

Animals who are black experience a kind of prejudice based solely on the color of their feathers or fur. Black dogs, for example, are said to be passed over more often for adoption than are dogs of other colors because of unfounded fears based purely on color. Black cats have long had mystical and magical associations and some believe are at greater risk of being abused during Halloween, thus some animal shelters will not adopt them out around this time (Knibbs, 2014). For Ravens, it is also the blackness, of black beak, eyes, claws, toes "that the inside of his mouth and his tongue itself are also black. It is easy to see how country folk, struck by the completeness and intensity of his sable coat, might well conclude that he must be black inside as well as out—be black, that is at heart" (Smith, 1905, p. 87).

Ravens in Popular Culture

Literature and poetry are filled with Ravens who learn to imitate human language nearly as well as parrots. "In fable," writes Bosworth Smith (1905, pp. 79–80), "the raven is among birds what the fox is among animals, the most adroit, the most unknowing the most unscrupulous among them all." Furthermore, the raven "is a bird whose historical and literary pre-eminence is unapproached" (Smith, 1905, p. 80). Ravens appear in many Shakespearean plays such as *Hamlet, Macbeth, Othello, As You Like It,* and the *Twelfth Night*. One of Aesop's fables (qtd in Gibbs, 2002) talks about trust:

> The raven seized a piece of cheese and carried his spoils up to his perch high in a tree. A fox came up and walked in circles around the raven, planning a trick. "What is this?" cried the fox. "O raven, the elegant proportions of your body are remarkable, and you have a complexion that is worthy of the king of the birds! If only you had a voice to match, then you would be first among the fowl!" The fox said these things to trick the raven and the raven fell for it: he let out a great squawk and dropped his cheese. By thus showing off his voice, the raven let go of his spoils. The fox then grabbed the cheese and said, "O raven, you do have a voice, but no brains to go with it!"

So far we've explored the use of Ravens in mythology and popular culture, in particular the significant role they play in the psyche for expressing ideas and concepts associated primarily with foreshadowing doom, death, and communicating bad news. The next section is an analysis of a specific media text, Home Box Office's (HBO) *Game of Thrones*, and how and why Raven functions within this fantasy television show.

Game of Thrones

GoT is an HBO television series inspired by the book "A Song of Fire and Ice" written by American George Martin (www.hbo.com/game-of-thrones/about/). The description of the weekly (Sunday) show on the HBO web site reads:

> Summers span decades. Winters can last a lifetime. And the struggle for the Iron Throne continues. It stretches from the south, where heat breeds plots, lusts and intrigues, to the vast and savage eastern lands, where a young queen raises an army. All the while, in the frozen north, an 800-foot wall of ice precariously protects the war-ravaged kingdom from the dark forces that lie beyond. Kings and queens, knights and renegades, liars, lords and honest men … all play the "Game of Thrones."

Beginning first as a series of five books, this adult fantasy literature (AFL) was first published in 1996. AFL differs from children's fantasy literature (CFL), which relies on fantastical characters, magic, and paradisiacal, in that it

> Takes its readers into unchartered territories and, unknown and unexplored realms; where the children's fantasy world is strangely asexual, where romance replaces passion, where food is a substitution for sex and friendship is glorified instead of love, the adult fantasy novel focuses on taboo subjects such as incest, where sex and lust replaces romance and there are graphic descriptions of sex and violence. (Krishnamurthy, 2013, pp. 86–87)

GoT, the television program, premiered on April 17, 2011 and was created by David Benioff and D. B. Weiss. Viewership was huge for the first episode (3 million viewers) and has grown steadily ever since (5.4 million viewers in 2013) (Windolf, 2014). In 2017 "an average of more than 23 million Americans watched each episode .... When platforms like streaming and video on demand are accounted for" (D'Addario, 2018, p. 68). It is also "the most pirated show" (p. 68). The multi-Emmy award winning program "airs in more than 170 countries" and is filmed in locations such as Northern Ireland, Croatia, Iceland, Spain, Malta, Morocco, Scotland, and the United States (p. 68). Scholars have studied *GoT* in terms of gender and power (Clapton & Shepherd, 2017; Gjelsvik & Schubart, 2014), sacred fantasy (O'Leary, 2015), sound (Neil, 2015), religious aesthetics (Wells-Lassagne, 2014a, 2014b), rape culture and feminist fandom (Ferreday, 2014), Machiavellian fantasy (MacNeil, 2015), disability (Donnelly, 2016; Lambert, 2015) and hospitality and violence (Stanton, 2015). In 2014 *Vanity Fair* magazine made *GoT* the cover story, with photography by Annie Leibovitz (Windolf, 2014) and, in 2015 an entire issue of the journal *Critical Quarterly* was dedicated to studies of the show.

It is impossible to describe this epic fantasy drama in a few words or even a few paragraphs for it has all the complexity of characters, names, and familial lines as does a Russian novel. The characters are many and the labyrinthian nature of relationships spans time, space, and multiple dimensions. In a nutshell, the story takes place on two continents, Essos and Westeros, and in seven kingdoms. The program details the civil war in progress between the Seven Kingdoms, with the leaders of each vying for the ultimate victory: The Iron Throne. Not only does the story line follow the trials and tribulations of the many different family members and leaders, presenting their collective and individual challenges, but does so against a backdrop of an impending winter to beat all winters and terrifying threats from legendary characters and peoples.

From the very first episode, animals and/or animal symbolism are central metaphorical techniques in *GoT*. In fact, "a sudden image ... a huge wolf, found dead in the snow," is reputed to be the inspiration for Martin's entire undertaking (Garcia & Antonsson, 2012, p. xii). While wolves, dire wolves[6] more specifically, are the first animals viewers meet (in addition to horses) in *GoT*, the raven follows closely behind. Raised in rookeries in Westeros, ravens are the harbingers of forthcoming trepidations and tragedies as well as the carriers of messages.

The vast majority of the time that messages are brought by raven, they carry bad news.

The character whose has the most immediate relationship with the crows, in particular a three-eyed crow, is Brân, "whose name in Welsh means 'crow' or 'raven'" (Sax, 2003, p. 61). Brân (played by Isaac Hempstead-Wright) is the young son of Winterfell patriarch Eddard Stark. Crows and Ravens are important figures throughout the *GoT*. "This portrayal is consistent with beliefs about the supernatural nature of Ravens, their being black in color, and highly intelligent. Ravens are also bringers of truths, no matter how feared, and what they carry is considered the legitimate word on a matter. For example," until the raven arrives with the news of Eddard Stark's death, not everyone could know it" (p. 137).

There has been significant controversy among readers and viewers as to whether or not the series has stayed consistent with the books. Hard core fans hold the television series writers to task in this regard. For example, Brân is seven years old at the beginning of the books and nine in the television series. Nevertheless, the first season is said to have stayed quite true to the book in terms of characters, tone, and themes in this "drama that combined elements of the heroic epic with a moral scale that covered the range from the saintly to the monstrous" (Garcia & Antonsson, 2012, p. x). While much of the story pivots on political intrigue, espionage, truth, morality, betrayal, and darkness, there remains a magical something else running throughout the stories. The human characters seem real, but inevitably something always happens to remind us we're not in Kansas anymore.

The primary tropes of *GoT* are family and families vying for power. The constant battles, literal and figurative, for territory, possessions, people, and place are fueled by intrigue, secrecy, betrayals, and violations. Based on CMT, *GOT* contains a "hybrid mix" of elements in *GoT* that viewers look forward to every season. The third element is the focus of this chapter:

1. Families (and interfamilial issues)
2. Geographic and seasonal dangers (i.e. in the fort to the North)
3. Malevolent, magical forces harnessed by enemies and friends.

Among the magical forces are Ravens, in particular a three-eyed Raven who reminds viewers of the magic inherent in the show, magic that "takes a long time to come in to play" (Gardner, 2014, p. 174) which is a bit unusual for epic fantasy tales. Viewers accept that young Brân's life is sustained for months as he lays immobilized following his terrible fall from a castle tower. The appearance of the three-eyed Raven in dreams is more providential than magical. The implications of the bird in real life (and eventual transformation in to a part human), are foreshadowed throughout the series, a role ravens often play as visual metaphoric markers.

Analysis

Season 1, episode 1, "Winter is Coming," is, like many first episodes of new series, shocking. This foundational episode introduces the context of the shot, the plots, the characters, and the highly visual nature of the costumes and context. Throughout the series, but particularly in this first episode, colors (or the lack of color) is stark, as in the contrasts of black, white, and bits of gray creating uncertainty and a sense of vulnerability. The program opens with three horseman riding through a tunnel at the end of which a gate is opened out of what will become known as The Wall. The riders are heavily clothed in black. They enter a completely white world of snow and ice. Black horses, black capes, the men are Raven-like in their movements. They are, as viewers will come to know, members of a military order called Night's Watch, who guard the northern boundary of the Seven Kingdoms. The Night's Watch, with all their secrecy and allure, are a band of mostly ner do wells, criminals and misfits who are entrusted with security of the northern boundary from that which lies beyond. They are a dark, secretive society with a strict code of conduct.

In the forest the riders stop and dismount. One crawls on his belly through the snow to peek over a drift in to an encampment. What he sees is all that remains of what appear to be men, women, and children whose sliced and diced torsos and body parts have been placed strategically in a circle. Those who appear dead are thought to be Wildings, people who were kept out by the wall and stereotyped (much like

Native North Americans) as uncivil "cruel men ... salvers and slayers and thieves. They consorted with giants and ghouls, stole girl children in the dead of night, and drank blood from polished horns" (*GoT*, 1:11) (Old Nan, qtd. in Zontos, 2015, p. 103), but as we learn, the bodies are in fact of something quite different.

As the three knights inspect the scene, one is beheaded by a tall mysterious being, but by who? Zombie-like creatures who travel faster than light or sound pursue the remaining two, decapitating one, leaving the other gazing upward as he kneels in the snow. So begins the first episode. We are then transported to green pastures where heraldic looking horsemen near the kingdom of Winterfell chase down the survivor of the forest attack. The penalty for desertion from the Night's Watch is, after all, death.

In another scene, Young Brân practices his archery, under the gaze of his parents and half brother, Jon Snow. The two Stark girls, Sansa (Sophie Turner) and Arya (Maisie Williams) of the Winterfell ruling family, embroider indoors. The scene moves outside where the youngest girl, Arya, outdoes her brother in archery accuracy. The scene switches back to that of the captured deserter who is beheaded, but not before he swears to have seen White Walkers (zombies). 10-year-old Brân is forced to watch, for this "justice" is in keeping with a strict code of honor within the Watch and the family.

Animals are also introduced in the next scene, in the snowy forest, where the Stark brothers Rickon (Art Parkinkson) and Robb (Richard Madden), Brân, and half-brother Jon Snow, along with their father, Eddard, find the carcass of a huge deer and the corpse of a dead mother Dire wolf,[7] whose puppies are whimpering and circling around her. The order is given to kill them but Jon Snow intercedes (much to the relief of most viewers), saying "Lord Stark, there are five pups, one for each of the Stark children. The dire wolf is the [symbol] of your house. They are meant to have them." The pups are saved and become the companion of each of the Stark boys and girls. A smaller runt wolf pup is revealed and given to Jon Snow.

The camera then cuts to outside the tower and to a bird's eye view of a raven flying in for a landing on the wall. What message might this bird bring? It is a raven from King's Landing telling those of Winterfell that the mad king, Jon, is dead, and that "a fever took him." Along with that, the raven brings more news, the new King, Robert Baratheon (Mark Addy) will be coming to Winterfell with his much younger Queen (Cersei Baratheon played by Lena Headey). Brân watches from atop the wall, and is scolded for climbing so high, yet tells of their approach. His mother asks for his word, which he gives, that he will no longer climb the towers. The wolf headed helmets are worn by arriving king's party who are greeted by the Stark family. Father Eddard is asked to be Hand of the King, and soon thereafter leaves Winterfell.

Despite his promise and his mother's admonitions, Brân climbs the wall to get a view of his father's departure to join the king. At the top he is surprised to discover twin Lannister brother and sister, Jaime and Cersei Lannister, who, we learn, have an incestuous relationship. When Cersei tells Jaime that he should be The Hand of the King, he says, "That's an honor I can do without. Their days are too long and their lives are too short." Brân hears huffing and puffing and looks in the window to see the twins having sex. Jamie pulls the boy in the window. "Quite the little climber aren't you, how hold old are you boy?" "Ten," says Brân. In the blink of an eye, Jaimie turns away while pushing the boy out the window saying "The things I do for love."

In the book, as Brân is pushed out the window Martin (1996/2016, p. 85) writes that "Somewhere off in the distance, a wolf was howling. Crows circled the broken tower, waiting for corn."

The book also goes in to greater detail about the prescient nature of Brân's fall, how as he descends he hears repeatedly the word "fly," coming from a crow, to which he replies he cannot. "The voice was high and thin. Brân looked around to see where it was coming from. A crow was spiraling down with him, just out of reach, following him as he fell. 'Help me,' he said. *I'm trying*, the crow replied, *Say, got any corn*?" (p. 161). Brân reaches into his pocket and the crow urges him to try to fly; he says he can't but asks "how if you don't try?" The crow tells him "there are different kinds of wings" ... "Every flight begins with a fall" (p. 162). Brân is told he must live because "winter is coming" (p. 163). Before he hits the ground Brân notices this is no ordinary crow as, "it had three eyes, and the third eye was full of a terrible knowledge" (p. 163).

In Episode 2 "The Kingsroad" Brân remains in a coma. His mother, Catelyn Tully (Michelle Fairley) suspects that her son didn't simply fall, but was pushed from the tower window. She gathers her sons and advisors around her and says that she must be the one to speak to the Lannisters about this. She is told to send a raven, but replies that she will go in person because you "cannot trust a raven."

Jaime and Cercie are clearly worried that Brân, having survived the fall, will reveal their sordid secret and send an assassin to kill him. The murderer fails, and is killed by Bran's protective wolf, Summer.

In Episode 3 "Lord Snow," Eddard Stark rides to become the King's Hand and attends a meeting of the Small Council. The Stark daughters travel with him. Brân is in his bed, having just awakened from his coma. A crow caws and lands in the window. An elderly lady sitting with him says "don't listen to him, crows are all liars."

In another scene, commander of the Nights Watch says that "the raven came for Ned Stark's son" (meaning Jon Snow) as he pulls a paper out of his pocket. "Good news or bad?" he is asked by Tyrion Lannister (Peter Dinklage). "Both," he replies.

Episode 4, "Cripples, Bastards, and Broken Things," opens with a Raven flying in to the courtyard at Winterfell. Brân is mobile and walking (he's been paralyzed by the fall) so viewers know he must be dreaming. He is shown aiming his bow at something when the Raven lands and immediately lifts off, inviting Brân to follow. Raven leads Brân in to the family crypt and lands on a stone wolf head, the Stark family symbol. Brân suddenly opens his eyes, aware now it was a dream. "The Little Lord's been dreaming again," says the elderly woman caring for him.

It is not until Episode 6, "A Golden Crown," that Ravens appear again. This time as messengers. There is a war brewing between the Starks and the Lannisters over Cat's abduction of Tyrion Lannister, the dwarf son of patriarch Tywin Lannister (Charles Dance). Tyrion is accused of trying to murder Brân. A message could be sent between families about the situation, and telling them that Eddard Stark has been imprisoned. Thus it is said to "Send a raven and put an end to it."

The scene then changes to Brân in the Stark's courtyard, again following the three-eyed Raven to tomb, a place so cold we see the bird's breath. The bird has taken him a bit further in this time, then suddenly Brân awakens, sensing something is terribly wrong for his father.

In the meantime, Tyrion Lannister is to fight a guard as part of a trial held at Cat's sister's (Lysa Arryn, played by Katie Dickie). Because of his small stature, a substitute is needed for him. He selects his brother Jaime but is told there is no time to "send a raven for him."

In Episode 8: "The Pointy End," a Raven has been sent to the Night's Watch with news that King Robert Baratheon is dead. Dozens of Ravens fly out of king's castle at the moment of his passing.

In Episode 9, "Baelor," a Raven bearing a messages takes off from a tower, cawing as he or she flies, but is intercepted, shot through with an arrow by Jon Snow. A companion reads the note, which says there will be a war. Faced with the knowledge that his entire family is in danger Snow must decide whether to remain with the Night's Watch or face desertion charges (the penalty for which is death) should he decide to help them. As Snow feeds raw meat and carrion to caged Ravens, he speaks with the blind Keeper to decide what the most honorable choice is, he asks what his father would do? But it is too late to help his father, who, unbeknownst to Jon, has been beheaded by the twisted young son of Jaime and Cersei, Joffrey (Jack Gleeson), who is heir to the throne. In this final episode "Fire and Blood," Eddard Stark has been killed. A Raven is sent to Winterfell bearing the news. Brân foresees this in a dream in which the three-eyed Rave tells him "to come with me so I did, my father is down there ... with wilding girl."

Discussion

Ravens in general function in *GoT* as messengers. The words strapped to their legs are nearly always as dark as their feathers. The first season is the three-eyed raven's introduction. In ensuing seasons there is less attention to this bird than at first, but comes round again as the series progresses revealing interesting twists and turns.

This chapter is an examination of how Ravens are used as symbols signifying darkness, both psychological and social and how they are used as plot devices. As literal messengers of what is to come, the birds' mythological status transcends any single culture, but functions within stories and popular culture as a narrative device. What is the relationship between the re-presented raven and real Ravens?

On a collective level Ravens are not threatened, at least not in sheer numbers. Raven populations were heavily impacted, and their range reduced during white Euro colonization of the American West when buffalo herds were decimated as their carcasses were a major food source for the birds (Young, 2014, p. 249).

The use of ravens in media content as harbingers of darkness and death or as key characters as in *Game of Thrones* is consistent with CMT and CBT. Identification of the metaphor of "raven" brought by CMT accompanied by individual associations blended in to that image as predicted by CBT suggest the Symbolic ripeness of Raven (and crow) in *GoT*. While the emphasis on this study is Element Three of the "hybrid mix," all components, family, geographic and seasonal dangers, and malevolent, magical forces, are combined in this popular show. The birds present as real but also serve, as so many animals do, as messengers of symbolic meaning as well. Long association with darkness, death, battlegrounds, the image of Raven is not change, but rather concretized in *GoT*, missing an opportunity to also show their cultural and symbolic complexity and potentially influencing how human beings engage with real birds in the world.

Notes

1. Pallas is another name for the Greek Goddess Athene and the Roman Goddess Minerva. Athena is the goddess of wisdom.
2. The books use crows whereas the television series substitutes ravens.
3. "Common Raven populations increased across the continent between 1966 and 2014, according to the North American Breeding Bird Survey. Partners in Flight estimates their global breeding population to be 20 million with 18% living in Canada, 9% in the U.S., and 3% in Mexico." https://www.allaboutbirds.org/guide/Common_Raven/lifehistory
4. When visiting the Tower of London in 2015 I was told that in fact eight ravens are kept, just in case something happens to any one of them.
5. There are, however, white ravens.
6. Dire wolves (*Canis* dirus) are the prehistoric ancestors of contemporary gray wolves (*C lupus*). They lived during the Pleistocene era 250,000–10,000 years ago.

They were much larger than today's wolves, averaging around 200 pounds, not quite as large as they are shown on *GoT*, however. According to a biomechanics specialist "the dire wolf had one of the largest canine bite forces of any living or extinct animal in the carnivore group" (qtd. In Montanari, 2016).

References

Bahti, M. (1999). *Spirit in the stone: A handbook of southwest Indian animal carvings and beliefs*. Tucson, AZ: Rio Nuevo Publications.

Barnes, J. (1990). *A history of the world in 10 ½ chapters*. New York, NY: Vintage.

Brown, T. (2003). *Making truth: Metaphor in science*. Champaign, IL: University of Illinois Press.

Caduto, M. J., & Bruchac, J. (1997). *Keepers of the animals: Native American stories and wildlife activities for children*. Golden, CO: Fulcrum.

Clapton, W., & Shepherd, L. J. (2017). Lessons from Westeros: Gender and power in *Game of Thrones*. *Politics*, *37*(1), 5–18.

Colin, D. (2000). *Dictionary of symbols, myths, and legends*. London: Hachette.

Coomaraswamy, A. (1996). *Hinduism and Buddhism*. New Delhi: Munshiram Manoharlal.

Corbett, E. P. J., & Connors, R. J. (1999). *Classical rhetoric for the modern student* (4th ed.). New York, NY: Oxford.

Croft, W., & Cruse, A. (2004). *Cognitive linguistics*. New York, NY: Cambridge University Press.

Daily, K. N. (2009). *Norse mythology A to Z*. New York: Chelsea House.

D'Addario, D. (2018, July 10 & 17). How they make the greatest show on earth. *Time*, pp. 66–85.

Donnelly, C. E. (2016). Re-visioning negative archetypes of disability and deformity in fantasy: *Wicked*, *Maleficent*, and *Game of Thrones*. *Disability Studies Quarterly*, *36*(4).

Eliot, G. (1872). *Middlemarch*. London: Penguin Classics.

Fauconnier, G., & Turner, M. (2002). *The way we think: Conceptual blending and the mind's hidden complexities*. New York: Basic Books.

Ferreday, D. (2014). Game of Thrones, rape culture, and feminist fantasy. *Australian Feminist Studies*, *30*(83), 21–36.

Fontana, D. (1994). *The secret language of symbols: A visual key to symbols and their meaning*. San Francisco, CA: Chronicle Books.

Game of Thrones. (2011). D. Benioff & D.B. Weiss (executive producers), television series. Ongoing USA: Home Box Office.

Garcia, E. M., & Antonsson, L. (2012). Foreword. In H. Jacoby (Ed.), *Game of Thrones and philosophy: Logic cuts deeper than swords* (pp. ix–xii). Hoboken, NJ: John Wiley & Sons.

Gardner, L. (2014). Review. *Game of Thrones*. *International Journal of Jungian Studies*, *6*(2), 171–177.

Gibbs, L. (2002). *Aesop's fables* (L. Gibbs, Trans.). Oxford: Oxford World Classics.

Gibbs, R. W. (1994). *The poetics of mind: Figurative thought, language, and understanding.* Cambridge: Cambridge University Press.

Gjelsvik, A. & Schubart, R. (2014). *Women of ice and fire: Gender, Game of Thrones, and multiple media engagements.* New York: Bloomsbury.

Goatly, A. 1997. *The language of metaphors.* New York, NY: Routledge.

Heinrich, B. (2002). *Mind of the raven.* New York: HarperCollins.

Hirschman, E. C. (2007). Metaphor in the marketplace. *Marketing Theory, 7*(3), 227–248.

Joy, A., Sherry, J. F., & Deschenes, J. (2007). Conceptual blending in advertising. *Journal of Business Research, 62,* 39–49.

Jung, C. G. (1964). *Man and his symbols.* New York, NY: Doubleday.

Knibbs, K. (2014, October 31). Shelters ban black cat adoption on Halloween to prevent abuse. *Gizmodo.* Retrieved from http://factually.gizmodo.com/shelters-ban-black-cat-adoption-on-halloween-to-prevent-1652829811

Kovecses, Z. (2000). *Metaphor and emotion.* New York, NY: Cambridge University Press.

Kovecses, Z. (2002). *Metaphor: A practical introduction.* New York, NY: Oxford University Press.

Kovecses, Z. (2006). *Language, mind, and culture: A practical introduction.* New York, NY: Oxford University Press.

Krishnamurthy, S. (2013). A feast for the imagination: An exploration of narrative elements of the text and hypertext of *Song of Ice and Fire* by George R. R. Martin. *Nawa: Journal of Language & Communication, 7*(1), 86–97.

Lakoff, G., & Johnson, M. (1980). *Metaphors we live by.* Chicago, IL: University of Chicago Press.

Lakoff, G., & Johnson, M. (1999). *Philosophy in the flesh.* New York, NY: Basic Books.

Lakoff, G., & Turner, M. (1989). *More than cool reason: A field guide to poetic metaphor.* Chicago, IL: University of Chicago Press.

Lambert, C. (2015). A tender spot in my heart: Disability in *A Song of Ice and Fire*. *Critical Quarterly, 57*(1), 20–33.

Lawrence, E. A. (1997). *Hunting the wren: Transformation of bird to symbol.* Knoxville, TN: University of Tennessee Press.

Lévi-Strauss, C. (1962). *The savage mind (La pensée sauvage).* Chicago, IL: University of Chicago Press.

MacNeil, W. (2015). Machiavellian fantasy and the game of laws. *Critical Quarterly, 57*(1), 34–48.

Marlowe, C. (1589–1590/1981). The Jew of Malta. In M. Kelsall (Ed.), *Christopher Marlowe* (pp. 131–154). New York, NY: Brill.

Martin, G. M. M. (1996/2016). *A Game of Thrones.* New York, NY: Bantam Spectra.

Marzluff, J. M., & Angell, T. (2005/2007). *In the company of crows and ravens.* New Haven, CT: Yale University Press.

Merskin, D. (2011). *Media, minorities, and meaning: A critical introduction.* New York, NY: Peter Lang.

Midgley, M. (2004). *The myths we live by.* New York, NY: Routledge.

Montanari, S. (2016, May 4). Are the dire wolves from *Game of Thrones* real? *Forbes*. Retrieved from https://www.forbes.com/sites/shaenamontanari/2016/05/04/are-the-dire-wolves-from-game-of-thrones-real-animals/#2a56c01b18db

Neil, V. (2015). Wall of sound: Listening to *Game of Thrones*. *Critical Quarterly, 57*(1), 71–85.

O'Leary, P. (2015). Sacred fantasy in *Game of Thrones*. *Critical Quarterly, 57*(1), 6–19.

Poe, E. A. (1845). *The raven*. Boston, MA: Richard G. Badger & Co.

Radcliffe-Brown, A. (1977/2004). *The social anthropology of Radcliffe-Brown*. New York, NY: Routledge Kegan Paul.

Sahlins, M. (2013). *Culture and practical reason*. Chicago, IL: University of Chicago Press.

Savage, C. (1997). *Bird brains*. San Francisco, CA: Sierra Club.

Sax, B. (2003). *Crow*. London: Reaktion Books.

Schwab, A. P. (2012). "You know nothing, Jon Snow": Epistemic humility beyond the wall. In H. Jacoby (Ed.), *Game of Thrones and philosophy* (pp. 142–153). New York, NY: Wiley.

Smith, R. B. (1905). *Bird life and bird lore*. London: John Murray.

Stanton, R. (2015). Excessive and appropriate gifts: Hospitality and violence in *A Song of Ice and Fire*. *Critical Quarterly, 57*(1), 49–60.

Sutton, G. M. (1936). *Birds in the wilderness: Adventures of an ornithologist*. New York: Macmillan.

van Mulken, M., van Hooft, A., & Nederstigt, U. (2014). Finding the tipping point: Visual metaphor and conceptual complexity in advertising. *Journal of Advertising, 43*(4), 333–343.

Wells-Lassagne, S. (2014a). Religious aesthetics in *Game of Thrones*. *TV/Series, 5*, 4–18.

Wells-Lassagne, S. (2014b). Adapting desire: Wives, prostitutes, and small folk. In A. Gjelsvik & R. Schubart (Eds.), *Women of ice and fire: Gender, Game of Thrones, and multiple media engagements* (pp. 39–56). New York, NY: Bloomsbury.

Windolf, J. (2014, March 24). The gathering storm. *Vanity Fair*. Retrieved from http://www.vanityfair.com/hollywood/2014/04/game-of-thrones-season-4

Ziemkiewicz, C., & Kosara, R. (2008). The shaping of information by visual metaphors. *IEEE Transactions on Visualization and Computer Graphics, 14*(6), 1269–1276.

Chapter Ten

Fables and Foibles as Global Economic Concepts

Animals on the Covers of *The Economist*

Animal fables are not about animals, but rather transpose human social relations onto the animal world in order to narrate and comment on human behavior.

—Palmeri (2006, p. 83)

Fairy tales are more than true: not because they tell us that dragons exist, but because they tell us that dragons can be beaten.

—Gaiman (*Coraline*, 2002)

So watchful Bruin forms, with plastic care Each growing lump, and brings it to a bear.

—Alexander Pope

Bears are bold, lions are brave, eagles are fearless, and foxes are feisty. As has been demonstrated in previous chapters, re-presentational animals are a "familiar part of all cultures" because they are easy to relate to, can provide a humorous diversion from serious topics, and attract attention quickly (Feldhammer, Whittaker, Monty, & Weickert, 2002, p. 160). However, what an animal stands for in our imaginations has little to do with *actual* animals but rather is a manifestation of our ideas (mythological, folkloric, stereotypical) projected on to them. This projection is evident in the covers of magazines designed to grab potential reader's attention immediately, especially in hopes of newsstand sales. For generations, animals-as-metaphors have functioned as tools of propaganda, symbols of national identity, global reputation, and/or enmity in the eyes of other countries. These dynamics come together when one examines the covers of international business publication such as *The Economist* where giant dragons stand in for China, camels for Middle Eastern nations or policies, tigers for India, and eagles for America.

The focus of this chapter is a study of *Economist* covers that include animals (1997–2017) demonstrating how animals figure prominently on the covers as illustrations of complex economic and global concepts. The goal is to analyze the frequency with which particular species are used and which concepts and issues they represent. I suggest this is yet another re-presentation that contributes to the disconnect between animals' lived experiences in the world, some of whom are endangered. As such "interpretation renders invisible the animal subjects who initially seem so vivid" (Palmeri, 2006, p. 983). Meisner and Takahasi's (2013, p. 255) study of *Time* argues that "Scholars of environmental communication acknowledge the importance of visual representations in shaping perceptions and actions in relation to environmental affairs." It makes sense that the same could be said of re-presentations "shaping perceptions and actions" related to animals. Therefore, using their study as a model (p. 260), the following research question(s) guide this study:

1. Which animals are presented on the covers?
2. What issues, stakeholders, and/or actions are re-presented?
3. Which aspects of the animals are presented?
4. How are the aspects of the animals re-presented?

This chapter adds to literature on magazine covers in general and to the rarer analyses of visual communication and magazine covers in environmental communication literature in particular. This under re-presentation might be due to their everyday nature, the difficulty in gauging impact because of varying means of distribution (newsstands versus home delivery), and readership. However, these popular culture artifacts are important because they "not only offer information about what's inside a particular issue, they also provide significant cultural cues about social, political, economic, and medical trends" (Johnson, 2002, p. 8). This chapter draws on Baker's (1993/2001, p. 33) concept of the "status of *the animal as image*" (ital. orig) and the nature of the meanings and allusions proffered by re-presentations in popular media and culture. This visual material, "the rhetoric of the image" (p. 33), is a tool with which one can critique re-presentations that is not method driven, rather employs mythology, symbology, and cultural studies to tease out subtle meanings. This includes shared symbols related to gender, politics, stereotypes on the basis of race, gender, sexuality, as well as amplifying social norms (see also Cerulo, 1984; Leath & Lumpkin, 1992; Pompper, Lee, & Lerner, 2009). The first section discusses animal images for purposes of propaganda and marketing. The second reviews literature that has examined magazine covers generally and business publications in particular. This is followed by a discussion of *The Economist*—its origins, intent, and audience. Finally, covers that include animals are analyzed with an eye to what they say about human political issues and how that serves as projection on other nations and erasure of real animals.

Animal Tales

The fable is "an instructional story ... has traditionally featured anthropomorphic portrayals of animals" (Miles & Ibrahim, 2013, p. 1864). Besides moral tales told to children about differences between right and wrong and the importance of obeying parents, fables can also be used as frameworks for analyzing how and why animals are used to signify economic and political issues in ways that are removed from real experiences. This is known as "marketing-oriented fabular anthropomorphism" (Miles &

Ibrahim, 2013, p. 1862). It "focuses on the way in which fables use animals to depict messages about the consequences of categorization and differentiation in human society" (p. 1862).

As discussed in earlier chapters, symbols (as opposed to signs) are multi-dimensional indicators of a way of seeing the world. They offer a format for thinking about an emotion, quality, idea, or way of being and are both "universal and particular" (Cirlot, 1971/2014, p. xvi). Symbols have "imaginative resonance" and "complex, sometimes ambiguous meanings" (Tresidder, 1998, p. 6). Most symbols have ancient origins and function as explanatory tools for beliefs about the cosmos and human's relationship to the greater worlds. Others are psychological, inward directed, often taking an ordinary object or being and assigning meaning that goes beyond the everyday.

Animals are widely used as *national* symbols. "They are images which wield a certain power, and which may therefore be taken to matter both to those who have invested in that power and to those against whom it is wielded" (Baker, 1993/2001, p. 33). They are seen "as an 'expression' of national characteristics" (p. 33) that "symbolize human identity and values" (p. 34). Importantly, these re-presentations, like so many in popular culture, are generally taken to be unremarkable, as every day, whose meaning is assumed simply to be "this animal standing for this country, that one for that" (p. 34). But they are more than that; there is underlying each re-presentation, particularly by an outsider to the culture, hegemonic intent. They are about power, image, intention, and objectification.

During World War II animals were widely employed by Western powers to re-present themselves, their values and beliefs, and what they thought of others, in particular whoever was considered to be "the enemy." One's own animal symbol was, of course, powerful, dignified, and worth serious regard whereas The Other's animal ran from simply silly to dramatically disgusting. Both the United States and Germany used eagles to say something about themselves. But when depicting each other used them quite differently. Whereas "the national self's body" is presented as "a perfect container," (Baker, 1993/2001, p. 39) the Other, as in the case of American representations of the German eagle, for example, is rough, dark, and, "from a propagandistic standpoint

... conceptually cast in the role of the aggressor" (p. 40). Whereas the American ideal eagle is distant and idealized, the German one is brought closer and is used to impart preferred versions of enmity on the part of the image-producer of the image. Specific species as political re-presentations also carry powerful symbolic weight, so much so that laws are created to protect them, ban the hunting, killing, and display of them. Whereas, in anthropologist Mary Douglas' (1970/2013, p. 70) view, "the human body is always treated as an image of society," so is the animal body, particularly when used to re-present the nation state.

World War II marked a significant shift in propaganda communication practices from that of earlier times. Whereas prior to this time, animal representations were seen mostly in advertising, a shift to using posters to display war time information took place. The mass audience, able to receive communications almost instantaneously across vast distances, received image-based information widely, whether it was for products, services, or war time propaganda. By WWII, citizens in the West were largely consumer citizens, used to receiving magazines, newspaper, and radio broadcasts which contained less text and more visual and aural information. Thus, they were becoming trained in reading re-presentations and symbols. As such, animals were appearing as substitutes for language, and within this visual discourse "'our' side was always winning, and ... 'our' animal was always the good and noble one" (Baker, 1993/2001, p. 46)[1] (see Figure 10.1 for an example of racist propaganda).

"The British bulldog, the American eagle; as animal symbols of the national self they are already known, and they are there simply to be recognized" (Baker, 1993/2001, p. 43). The bulldog has been a symbol for Great Britain, particularly during the Churchill years of World War II, in part because Winston Churchill's "jowly face, broad body, and steadfast determination to overcome powerful Nazi forces in World War II made him an almost living embodiment of the heroic pooch" (Jenner, 2015). These symbols must be immediately recognizable to the intended audience, quickly grab attention, and carry with them information already taught. Importantly, these images carry with them no real aspects of their animalness, rather "we are able to identify with 'our' animal symbol because we have been led to overlook its animality" (p. 43).

Figure 10.1: "Tokio Kid Say." Source: Wikimedia Commons.

As was discussed in Chapter 1, animals and humans are often substituted for one another in re-presentations in general and in negative propagandist literature in particular. Just as apes and crows have been used interchangeably with African Americans, so animals such as rats, bats, wolves, as well as insects have been used to demonize, shame, and stereotype whoever is defined as the enemy. Such portrayals do nothing to support human rights nor regard of certain species of animals. The media play an important role in the perpetuation of this practice. For example, "there is a crucial correlation between mainstream news media's readiness to repeatedly characterize opponents as insects or animals and what happened at Abu Ghraib, in which the metaphor of the animal is made horrifyingly literal" (Steuter & Willis, 2009, p. x).

In their detailed exploration of the role of metaphor in the waging of wars and human suffering, Steuter and Willis (2009, p. 69) argue that "there is a connection between the remarkably consistent and sometimes overlapping metaphorical frames that figure the enemy-Other as animal and disease, and some of the most horrifying practices that have surfaced in the war on terror."

In post 9–11 speeches, then president George W. Bush used animal references when speaking about "terrorists," using phrases such as "The terrorists may burrow deeper into caves" and other entrenched hiding places and phrases that suggested "The enemy was a dirty, dehumanized animal that scurried to caves and dark places" (Merskin, 2005, p. 379). Furthermore, "Bush ... spok[e] of 'smoking them out of their holes,'" drawing on symbolic associations with rodents. Defense Secretary Donald Rumsfeld spoke of "drying up the swamp they live in" an odd choice of metaphor considering the desert landscape from which the attackers originated (Steuter & Willis, 2008, p. 71). Thus, in this type of discourse, metaphors associated with hunting, tracking, exterminating, and trapping come to seem a normal and natural way of thinking of Others as dirty, diseased, and disposable. This languaging removes any imaginative possibility from thinking about them as individuals with lives, families, dreams, and desires and concretizes these ideas into signs, thus making it easier and seemingly logical to be rid of them. "They" become beasts and monsters, whereas "we" are heroes and guardians.

In his analysis of political animals Baker (1993/2001) first critiques a late 1980s photograph whose meaning remains relevant and tactics still employed in British politics. In a newspaper photograph, then chairman of the ruling Conservative Party is shown posing with a bulldog named Duke, who is also used in posters along with other dogs (the poster was designed by the advertising agency Saatchi & Saatchi). In the poster, three dogs are posed, each representing economic growth (or lack of) in other European nations compared with Britain. A tiny white French poodle wears a beret and onions on a string. Next to him/her is a German shepherd who wears a Tyrolean hat and has a stein of beer at his or her feet. Both dogs deferentially gaze at the third dog, the largest, which is the bulldog, a long time symbol of Great Britain who wears no decorations, only a Union Jack tag on the collar. The point of the poster is to use dogs as emblems of nationhood. But neither the poodle nor the shepherd is that nation's national symbol, whereas the bulldog has been for Britain. What matters, according to Baker (1993/2001), is not whether or not the symbols are realistic or dignified, in fact "as a physical animal it is effectively invisible: a mere vehicle for the transparent transmission of a symbolic meaning" (p. 37). The bulldog is not anthropomorphised in the same ways the others are—not human accoutrements. While the bulldog is serious, the others seem silly. This single example offers several themes that are useful when considering the subject of this chapter:

1. "In a political context ... pictorial animal symbolism has traditionally worked by means of an opposition centered on the contrasting depictions of the rival animal's bodies."
2. It offers consideration of the stability of these re-presentations over time in popular culture.
3. It raises questions about how serious animals are taken when used as "vehicle[s] for the transmission of symbolic meanings." (Baker, 1993/2001, p. 37)

Economic and political interests are at the heart of most nation's and many individual's views of the environment in general and animals in particular. "The media play a pivotal role in giving consistency to what society considers important" (Soares, 2015, p. 224). Studies on visual communication of nature issues in general are rare, but growing field. Some scholars look to the early days of the environmental movement in the United states (Schoenfield, 1983), but more often these are studies of newspaper coverage such as *The Washington Post, Lost Angeles Times*, and the *New York Times*.

Covering Communications

Magazine covers are an important form of communication as they are often the first point of contact potential audiences have with a publication. Concepts must be immediately understandable and accessible to a global audience. Content on these covers are thereby "pictorial metaphors" (Forceville, 1994, p. 1) drawing on widely shared political, economic, cultural, and religious beliefs. Covers "are a prominent vehicle to visually communicate about nature and environmental affairs to the public" (Meisner & Takahasi, 2013, p. 256). In their study of the covers of the weekly news magazine *Time*, Meisner and Takahasi (2013), found that the re-presentation of "environmental affairs," which includes issues, such as global warming, and problems (excessive fossil fuel burning) as well as players in the scenario and actions that address the problems.

Time magazine has been widely studied, perhaps because it is one of the most widely circulated American mainstream magazines and because of "its dominance as a news vehicle in the arena of public discussion" (Scott & Stout, 2006, p. 2). The covers have been examined in terms of religion (Scott & Stout, 2006), ability to influence public opinion on China (Perlmutter, 2007), and the impact of their "person of the year covers" on setting the agenda for who or what is important in the world and the gendered nature of agendas (Christ & Johnson, 1985, 1988).

There are few studies of animals on publication covers. In a study of depictions of images of insects, most portrayals are negative, but nature magazines tend toward more positive presentations (Moore, Bowers, & Granovsky, 1982). Dead animals in hunting magazines were the focus of Kalof and Fitzgerald's (2003) research that looked at these visual re-presentations. In Meisner and Takahasi's (2013) study of environmental issue coverage on the covers of *Time* the researchers noted that "the most common ways the issues are represented is with animals, sources of pollution, and humans" (p. 266). When animals were used some were shown as "suffering" (e.g., oil-soaked bird) or dead (e.g., skeleton fish). Most of the time, however, when animals were used they were "unharmed examples of the species at risk" (p. 266). A contradiction was noted. When species shown were/are endangered they were not presented as dead, even if they were/are imperiled. Rather the "covers used healthy-looking exemplars ... to illustrate the issues" (p. 267). They concluded that *Time*'s covers lack "affective force" which could make the story more powerful (p. 272).

Business Journalism

Certainly less "sexy" than celebrity and tabloid pubs, business magazines also have lower circulations. However, drawing on Benedict

Anderson's concept of "imagined community," Soares (2015) suggests that "news reports are important not just in the delivery of information, they are tools for the construction of 'particular images of self, community, and nation" (p. 224).

Business magazines, particularly those published outside of the United States, are rarely studied (Claussen, 2015, p. 248; Soares, 2015, p. 225). When they are, "the favored news magazines for academic research are *Time, Newsweek,* and *U.S. News & World Report*" (Soares, 2015, p. 227). Even during times when business is booming and economies are strong, in-depth pieces about aspects of business are often viewed as tedious. During the booming 1990s, *The Economist* (2004) (discussed in the next section) stated that business journalism was

> ... about getting rich, [but] watching share prices crumble was less fun, and being misled by bulls was costlier than being misled by bears ... The reality of business—a touch, often tedious slog—and of investing may not be compelling enough for television.

According to Claussen (2015, p. 252), "Professional, industry, trade, corporate, and other magazines not primarily for consumers account for the majority of magazines published in the United States." Yet this is an understudied category perhaps due to the fact that they are less sexy, less sensational, and less conspicuous than are consumer targeted publications. How to spice things up a bit, without losing respect as a vital organ of news? This is a dilemma faced by financial institutions, attorneys, accountants and others trusted with money and information. One way these "serious" magazines draw attention to themselves is through captivating covers. A magazine that globally reports on economics and politics, British born and based *The Economist* plays a powerful role in re-presenting issues to an elite audience, who has among its members, those in positions to impact policy and practice. "For advertising purposes, *The Economist* can be seen to be an up- market, homo-social, masculine place" (Wörsching, 2009, p. 223).

The Economist

The Economist was founded in 1843 as a newspaper in the early years of Victorian Britain, "to campaign for free trade, laissez-faire and individual responsibility ... [and] its principles and methods remain relevant 150 years later' (Edwards, 1993, p. 3). More than half the nearly 1.5 million circulation is in North America, followed by 14% in Continental Europe, a mere 17% in the United Kingdom, 10% in Asia/Pacific, 1% Middle East/Africa, with not more than 1% in Latin America (http://printmediakit.economist.com). Today, despite appearances, the now glossy weekly continues to consider itself a newspaper as the founders viewed the intention and function of this publication. In the preface to a history of the publication Edwards (1993) writes

> New papers often fail because they lack a clear identity: about *The Economist* there was no confusion. Its purpose was to further the cause of free trade in the interests of national and international prosperity: its voice was the highly distinctive voice of James Wilson, who announced himself in the prospectus (in the guise of "ourselves") as having "very strong opinions, formed after long observation, experience, and reflection, and which the further observation of every day tends only to make stronger." (pp. 1–2)

Economist founder James Wilson was a decided believer in the *laissez-faire* view of economies—"a belief that the public good is best served by leaving individual to look after themselves, since government interference in economic affairs tends to upset the balances of wealth-creation" (Edwards, 1993, p. 6). This no doubt influences what appeared and appears on the cover. "Wilson's *Economist* was to be perhaps the most influential disseminator of this doctrine, through the prism of which is examined and pronounced on the topical issues of the day" (p. 6). This agenda-setting function thus delivers to the business community and its wealthy audience (average household net worth is $1.6 million) what it believes to be of the utmost importance. Today about 6% of *The Economist's* total audience is digital (48,000 subscribers in 2012). Although this business magazine has a long history, it aims to be viewed as progressive in terms of its availability and ideas.

The front covers of *The Economist* metaphorically illustrate a timely, relevant, and illustratable problem, phenomenon, or personality in the global marketplace. Despite its glossy appearance, the publication considers itself a newspaper, in part, "because to be different—and especially, quirky—is an advantage in a competitive media world, a trait shared with the publication's other idiosyncrasy, that of anonymity for its writers" (Emmott, 2015, p. xiii). Bill Emmott was editor-in-chief of the *Economist* from 1993 to 2006 (p. 626). Geoffrey Crowther, who served as editor (the longest serving editor of the 20th century, 1938–1956), saw the rise of *Newsweek* (1933) and *Time* (1923) as current affairs journalism, and wanted to retain the idea of British "sensibility" about "serious" news, thus "he believed in [values that] were most closely linked to newspapers, at least in Britain, at the time: seriousness, reliability, and analysis" (p. xiii). A study of *Der Spiegel* and *The Economist* revealed "discourses of nature and sport are conceived to assert global hegemonic masculinity" thereby supporting the magazine industry goal of reaching a global audience (Wörsching, 2009).

As a decidedly British publication it is no surprise that animals figure prominently in *The Economist's* re-presentations of other nations and global issues. There have indeed been claims on the part of the English that they "exhibit[t] an exceptional devotion to animals" (Carson, 1972, p. 43). Whether or not "exceptional", there is no doubt that "animals have long figured prominently in the public display of 'being British'" (Baker, 1993/2001, p. 67). Self-presentation as a global power as well as portrayal of Great Britain's colonializing past through presentation of the nation has a long history.

Cortés de Los Ríos' (2010) study of image schemas critiqued *The Economist's* covers and concluded that the economy is typically framed as a natural, versus human made, institution. For example, the December 6, 2008 cover headline reads "Where have all your savings gone?" and shows the image of a man looking into a black hole in the ground, which she refers to as an "apocalyptic metaphor" (p. 83).

Which specific species are used as symbolic stand-ins for human beings? According to Brown's (2010) study of mascots "the closer the creature is to humankind, the more likely it is to be adopted as a brand mascot" (p. 217). Animals such as bears, in part because they can stand on two legs, and, in Brown's (2010) study, the most popular animals are "bipedal ... with binocular (forward facing) eyes, particularly those that tend to sit on their haunches in an upright posture" (p. 217). This type of anthropomorphism is, as the term implies, more about humans than other animals. In a world saturated with images, brands, and increasingly visual communication it is a creative strategy increasingly useful for quick reader/viewer comprehension with little need for text to convey a message. This practice is widely seen and studied in advertising (Kennedy & McGarvey, 2008; Lancendorfer, Atkin, & Reece, 2008; Lloyd & Woodside, 2013; Spears, Mowen, & Chakraborty, 1996) but less so when it concerns the covers of magazines who similarly are there to sell, albeit the publication, at least on newsstands, to draw readers in to the content. Importantly, the privileging of certain images over others or by image makers over others, is relevant when symbolizing different nations: "Animals used in marketing (whether for simple mascots or as more developed characters in allegorical narratives) can be seen as embodiments of *difference* above and beyond any symbolic function based upon cultural symbolic associations" (p. 1864).

As discussed in earlier chapters, metaphors, fables, and tales are tools for sharing stories, making associations between often dissimilar objects or beings. They "depend for their power on shared cultural and experiential knowledge that allows an audience to transfer characteristics from a source to a target domain. Marketing's use of animals needs to connect into established cultural symbologies or, at least, popular contemporary experience" (Miles & Ibrahim, 2013, p. 1864). Animals as political symbols are found throughout different cultures and have specific meanings each one. However, through propaganda such as posters, created either by the source culture or projected on to the culture by others, it can be positive, negative or both. Positive self-image is usually generated on behalf of one's own country. For example, the United States re-presents aspects of self-identified patriotism as best reflected by the eagle, as national bird, who stands for the idea of the country. While rumor has it that Benjamin Franklin advocated for the turkey, this isn't quite accurate, rather, initial designs for the presidential seal, more *resembled* a turkey, which he preferred to what he considered the unsavory nature of the Bald Eagle:

> For my own part I wish the Bald Eagle had not been chosen the Representative of our Country. He is a Bird of bad moral Character. He does not get his Living honestly. You may have seen him perched on some dead Tree near the River, where, too lazy to fish for himself, he watches the Labour of the Fishing Hawk; and when that diligent Bird has at length taken a Fish, and is bearing it to his Nest for the Support of his Mate and young Ones, the Bald Eagle pursues him and takes it from him.

> I am on this account not displeased that the Figure is not known as a Bald Eagle, but looks more like a Turkey. For the Truth the Turkey is in Comparison a much more respectable Bird, and withal a true original Native of America ... He is besides, though a little vain & silly, a Bird of Courage, and would not hesitate to attack a Grenadier of the British Guards who should presume to invade his Farm Yard with a red Coat on. (Stamp, 2013)

The choice of the eagle as good, for example, and the turkey or the vulture as bad, is not informed by actual animal behavior, but what they seem to be.

> Each of these birds is so closely identified with their respective qualities of nobility, fierceness, and protectiveness on the one hand and with rapacity, sinister appetite, and sly, scavenging greed on the other that it is hard to recall that these characteristics are not natural but assigned. (p. 111)

The same is likely to apply to political symbols as well, certainly characteristics by which a nation likes to envision qualities such as strength, courage, and ferocity.

The present study uses Meisner and Takahasi's (2013) study of *Time* as a guide when considering how *The Economist* covers use of animals or elements of nature (for example trees) intentionally or not contribute to environmental discourse which "concerns itself with the problematic relationship between humans and the rest of nature, ... [and] is a subset of the discourse of nature which concerns itself with what nature is, how it works, and what it means to humans" (p. 257).

Method

Using Google image search for *Economist covers* as well as the magazine's online archive (1997–2016 @ http://www.economist.com/printedition/covers) all covers that included animals were identified. Each cover was coded for the presence of animals, headline, and category, employing, but also refining Meisner and Takahasi's (2013) categories for nature imagery, "as victim/patient," "animal as problem," "animal as resource," "animal as research subject," "animal as human analog and/or companion," "animal as exemplar of fitness," and "animal as just itself," i.e. having no particular characterization that is anthropomorphic. There were 98 such covers over the span 1996 to July 2007.

Research Questions

Drawing on Meisner and Takahasi's (2013) study of Time, the primary questions guiding this textual analysis and critical inquiry study are:

1. Which animals are presented on *The Economist* covers?
2. What issues, stakeholders, and/or actions are re-presented?
3. Which aspects of the animals are presented?
4. How are the aspects of the animals re-presented?

Findings

Which Animals Are Presented on the Covers?

For the twenty-year period 1996–2017 the top five animals most often seen are dragons (8), Tigers (7), Brown Bears (7), Pig/Piggy bank/dinosaurs, and bulls (6 each), eagle (5), elephants (4), and pandas (4). Other species are shown on Table 10.1. The following section focuses on the symbolism of the top three most re-presented beings: the dragon (China), tiger (India), and the bear (Russia). While world mythologies fill volumes on these species, which is beyond the scope of this chapter, each is briefly discussed as it most relates to how the symbol is used based on the culture that produced it (Western/UK).

The mythical dragon is used most often on *The Economist* covers as a re-presentation of China. Whereas many of the species, real or imagined, have one or two re-presentations over the years, it is China-as-a-dragon that appears most often. A complete study of all the covers and all of the issues would reveal whether or not China is presented as the cover story more often than other nations but as this chapter focuses on animals these were the only covers examined. Dragons are not, perhaps, and never were, real in the sense they are created but they still hold animalistic associative places in the imagination. Certainly there is a reptilian nature to the imaging.

Table 10. 1. Species Re-presented.

Species	Number	Issues/Stakeholders/ Actions	Aspects
Dragon	11	China/Asia/Mgmt./ Pollution	Ferocity, deception, power
Tiger	8	India/Asia Mgmt.	Speed, power, secrecy
Brown Bear	7	Russia (5); Wall Street (1)	Ferocity, power,
Pig/Piggy Bank	6	Japan, U.S. Finance, Savings, Credit	Vulnerability, toy-like
Vultures	6	Foreign threats to White House	Dangerous, dirty
Dinosaur	4	End of eras; Detroit; Cheap oil	Fragility, faded power, irrelevance
Horse	4	France (1); US (2); 1 world finance	Power, persistence, loyalty
Panda	4	China/Hollywood; America's fear of China; India;	Gentle power
Elephant	4	India (3); US (1)	Power, steadfastness,
Eagle	4	U.S.	Power, Charisma
Bull	4	U.S. Wall Street	Power, Tenacity
Fish	3	Fat = Saddam Hussein; Fish farming	Passivity, slowness
Shark	4	American economy	Sneaky, dangerous, powerful
Ducks	4	Consumer satisfaction	passivity
Sheep	2	Cloning	Passivity
Wolves	2	Russia and the US	Power lock
Dove	2	Peace	Beauty, steadfastness
Butterfly	2	Asia	Delicacy
Black bird	2	Germany	Nobility, power
Lion	2	The west—confused; Ancient image-eating bull = Iran	Power, former power

FABLES AND FOIBLES AS GLOBAL ECONOMIC CONCEPTS 249

Species	Number	Issues/Stakeholders/Actions	Aspects
Mammoths	2	Endangered public companies	Mammoths
Hawk	1	Arab Nations	Strength, sight
Hybrid fish/bird	1	Global mergers gone wrong	mergers
Donkey	1	American Education	Toy, passive
Dog	1	US – following G. W. Bush	Loyalty
Fat Bird	1	World debt	Sluggish
Camel	1	Middle East	Passivity
Flies	Multiples	Spies	Sneaky
Snake	1	Belgium	Sneaky
Scorpion	1	Belgium	Dangerous
Goose	1	Emerging world- hatching	Curiosity
Rooster	1	France	Proud
Gorilla	1	Big Media struggles w/ Digital	Taking over
Jaguar	1	Ancient- At Bay Capitalism	Power
Snail	1	American economic slowdown	Slowness
Whale	1	Corporations	Large
Macaw	1	"World's Lungs"	Grace, mystique
Octopus	1	Leviathan = The State	Taking over
Underwater creatures	Multiples	Corporations	Taking over
Cat	1	India	Curiosity, self-assurance
Bird	1	European Economy	Dead
Tortoise	1	U.S.	Slow economy

What the dragon means to the people of China and what it means to non-Chinese people are no doubt very different interpretations. For both Eastern and Western cultures, dragons are "the reptilian embodiment of primordial power," according to Tresidder (1998, p. 67). It "is probably the most universal of all mythical creatures" (Willis, 2000, p. 64). Furthermore, as one of the most ancient representations as what constitutes "a dragon" is fairly widely defined (sometimes serpent, sometimes snake, sometimes the worm). Thus, dragon "stands for 'things animal' *par* excellence" (Cirlot, 1971/2014, p. 86), it is "a ferocious and untamed (but not necessarily evil) beast which embodies in many cultures the elemental forces of chaos and cosmic order" (Willis, 2000, p. 64). For Chinese, the dragon has "all-embracing cosmic significance" and is a symbol for "rhythmic life" (p. 87), good luck, and strength. It brings both rain and typhoons. Ancient Sumerians viewed the animal as "adversary," and demonic, and above all else primordial, particularly to those in Western cultures. Given that *The Economist* is an English-language speaking, Western publication the way they present dragons reflects Judeo-Christian views of what the animal represents in the collective imagination. According to Tressider (1998, p. 68), "Christianity was the primary influence behind the evolution of the dragon into a generalized symbol of adversarial evil" linking dragons to reptiles and thus emissaries of the Devil. Guardian of hidden treasures in myth and lore, dragons represented the underworld, darkness, and were emblems of warriors, "appearing on Parthian and Roman standards" as well as carved on to the prows of Viking ships, in the legends of Siegfried, Perseus, Cadmus, Herakles, Sigurd, and Apollo. Patron saints such as St. George and the Archangel St. Michael battle dragons. Some have wings, some breathe fire, some live in water, others on land, some have a single head while others are polycephalic. The dragon's tail can be a powerful destructive instrument and legend holds it feeds on animals and humans alike. Pliny, Pascal, and Galen wrote of the dragon having characteristics of strength, vigilance, "with exceptionally keen eyesight, and it seems its name comes from the Greek word *darken* ('seeing')" (Cirlot, 1971/2014, p. 87). Modern psychology defines the dragon symbol as "something terrible to overcome,' for he who conquers the dragon becomes a hero" (Jung, qtd. in Cirlot, 1971/2014, p. 88).

The dragon is also "a symbol of imperial sovereignty" (Rowland, 1973, p. 66). This fits well with the presentation of the dragon-as-China when used on *The Economist* covers, ranging from a bloated smoke spewing dragon (8/21/04) for "China's Growing Pains," as "Angry China" (5/3/08), "The World's Worst Polluter" (8/10/13), and "What China Wants," with the dragon holding a globe. Showing competition with India (as a tiger) the headline reads "New masters of management" (4/17/10).

The second most often used animal re-presentation to signify economic concepts is the tiger. Shakespeare used the tiger "as a symbol of inhumanity and ferocity," royal houses employ the tiger in family crests and as emblems (Rowland, 1973, p. 152). The tiger is often used "to symbolize energy," as it was in the US for the ESSO brand of gasoline ("Put a tiger in your tank"), but in Asia re-presentations are typically more benign (pp. 149–150). Used by the West to symbolize India, the tiger is a fearsome creature who lurks in the darkness of jungles, ready and able to pounce at any moment. It is said that the tiger who is found in India, first became known to Europeans through the invasion of Alexander the Great's campaigns (Biedermann, 1994, p. 344).

Along with the dragon, the tiger is both a "wild beast and [a] tamed animal" (Cirlot, 1971/2014, p. 343), or certainly tamable animal. The tiger is associated with the wine god Dionysus, wind god Zephyr, but can also be a mother figure. The first tiger "appeared in Rome in A.D. 19 as a gift to Augustus from an Indian delegation" (Biedermann, 1994, p. 344). The big cat also symbolizes "strength and valour in the service of righteousness" (p. 343) and is part of many Asian and Hindu myths. Viewed through the lens of Jungian psychology, the tiger has archetypal significance, which varies "according to the relative status of the animals within the hierarchy: for instance, the tiger struggling with a reptile stands for the superior principle, but the converse applies if it is locked in combat with a lion or a winged being" (p. 343).

On the covers of *The Economist*, tigers were shown without other animals and in active postures. The July 19, 1997 cover was a drawing of a tiger's paw, scratching its way down a wall that was used to represented the headline "SE Asia loses its grip." Other times, the tiger is in competition with the dragon representing China: "India v. China"

(6/21/03) and the blurry photograph of a running lion and the headline "How India's Growth Will Outpace China's" (10/02/10). For example, the cover of the June 24, 2017 issue has an illustration of India's Prime Minister Narendra Damodardas Modi riding a giant tiger. Riding crop in hand, the jewel colored cat leaps over a lily filled pond and the headline reads: "Modi's India: The illusion of reform."

The March 30, 2013 cover again re-presents India as a Tiger, but only as reflection/aspiration of an ordinary orange domestic cat's vision of him/herself looking in the mirror. The headline: "Can India become a great power?" suggests only India has such a view of itself as an economic power. A third example is the October 2, 2010 cover shows a blurry image of what appears to be a photograph of a real tiger, running at a break neck pace. The headline reads: "How India's growth will outpace China's." Were China also represented on that cover, keeping with the Jungian view, no doubt the dragon, or more likely the panda (see below) would be shown over powered by the tiger.

The third most re-presented animal on the magazine covers was the bear, most often as a moniker of Russia. The Eurasian brown bear has appeared in multiple images and activities such as drama, cartoons, articles, and propaganda:

> the bear was the majestic and luminous god of storms and sunshine in ancient myth; the gentle friend or prince in disguise in the folktale; the honey-loving dupe in the fable; the docile disciple of saints in legend; the progenitor of the magic hero in saga; the ferocious monster which was chained, baited, and blinded in Merry England. (Rowland, 1973, p. 31)

The meaning of the bear varies widely across cultures. From a Jungian psychological perspective, bears in dreams can mean "the embodiment of the dangerous aspects of the unconscious" (Biedermann, 1994, p. 33). The brown bear has long been used by Russians (adopted in the 19th century) to symbolize the nation as well as being a "national symbol, a marketing tool, a wonder of nature, an unspoken fear, and a prize for hunters" (Barton, n.d.).

The bear appears in Russian coats of arms and, is part of a tradition of using them as entertainers, amongst which is the famous Mishka, who was symbol of the 1980 Moscow Olympics (Pyykkö, 2012, p. 248).

In terms of the "political bear," "the bear is the symbol of the so-called Putin's party, the Edinaia Rossiia ('United Russia')" (p. 248).

The Economist covers that use the bear to stand in for/as Russia include March 1, 2009 bearing the headline "Welcome to Moscow" in which the head of a giant brown bear fills the space. His/her mouth is open, teeth bared with a happy, unsuspecting looking American President Obama walking up a series of red, white, and blue stairs in to the beast's gaping jaws.

The panda bear stands in for China. This is a 20th century substitution for the dragon (Songster, 2004). While in Chinese culture this animal is regarded as a symbol of peace and friendship, Western re-presentations are less warm and fuzzy. There is no doubt that the black and white bandit-looking being is adorable, at the same time, this one dimensionality masks the fact that the panda is a bear.

According to some sources, the panda has replaced the dragon as a re-presentation of China. China, when representing itself has been known to send giant pandas to other nations as a gift as "*the* national treasure of China" (Songster, 2004, p. 15). This state gift giving has "had a direct and depleting effect on the wild panda population" (p. 15). Re-presentations on *The Economist* covers don't emphasize sameness but rather substitute difference for a King Kong type being who scales the Empire State building ("America's Fear of China," 5/19/07).

What Issues, Stakeholders, and/or Actions Are Re-presented?

For all of the covers, stakeholders are readers, advertisers, and the global economic community. Depending on the cover story, individuals and/or nations have a stake in the re-presentation (see Table 10.1). In some cases, the animals used are also those embraced by the re-presented nation (Russia's national symbol is the bear; China self-portrays as a dragon and celebrates the dragon in mythology and ceremony). At the same time, the stereotypical nature of these images (Tigers as only fierce; Sharks as only menacing) do little to serve animal or human communities whose natures are not reflected by these one dimensional portrayals. Bears are hunted, held captive for entertainment, and tigers are in tremendous peril. Little to nothing is gained for them by the use of their likenesses in these ways. On the other hand, the covers are tidy tools for presenting troubling globally impactful issues, such as China as a major polluter, that keep the animal front and center.

How Are and Which Aspects of the Animals Are Presented?

Using Meisner and Takahashi's (2013) categories for nature imagery as a coding scheme, animals as fantastical beings are presented on the covers primarily as drawings, illustrations, and other purely symbolic/objectified forms. None of the categories is mutually exclusive. Only five of 90 covers were actual photographs. Two were tigers (peeking through bars and running), one of a bear on Wall Street, another of a Hawk with an Arab man, and finally, an eagle signifying America.

In terms of aspects of animals that were re-presented, the emphasis was on power, tenacity, and ferocity (see Table 10.1). In the case of dragons this was demonstrated by smoke spewing, imposition of size, and threat. Bears were also shown as large, imposing, ferocious with teeth bared, or, in the case of the bear as economically wounded Russia, as humbled. In the one non-Russian bear cover, the August 8, 1998 issue carries the headline "Grin and Bear It" and features an illustration of a brown bear who is wearing sunglasses on the lens of which show a rapidly declining chart of economic vitality of Canada.

Another cover draws on imaging of threats and fear by re-presenting telecommunications as a snake. While it can be argued that a curled telephone cord naturally resembles a snake, there's more than that going on. In animal-as-enemy propaganda imagery the enemy is often re-presented as snake. For example, a 2006 Cox and Forkum editorial cartoon is labeled "Islamic Republic of Iran" and shows a rearing cobra. The snake/hydra symbol has powerful mythological and ideological associations (see Miel's "Terrorism as Snake-Hydra" cartoon as analyzed in Steuter & Willis, 2009, p. 112). Little vipers are spawned from the body of the "mother" terrorism. In Christian cultures, the connection between the serpent as evil is so complete that it is a form of what Mumby and Spitzack (1983, p. 162) call "metaphoric entrapment," wherein it "becomes so tied up with a particular metaphoric structure that alternative ways of viewing the concept are obscured, or appear to make less sense. Immigrants are similarly re-presented as invading swarms etc" (see also Santa Ana, 2002). This confinement through re-presentation can have significant consequences in terms of regard and treatment of real beings: "the framing of problems often depends upon the metaphors underlying the stories which generate problem setting and set the direction of problem solving" (Schön, 1979, p. 138).

Conclusion

Over time, there has been a shift from the naturalized meaning of the animal as political symbol, i.e. "nationalist values" have lost "ground to corporate and multinational considerations in many parts of the world" (Baker, 1993/2001, p. 61). Transformation and change are natural in the process of human symbolic communication, and that in and of itself isn't bad. However, "in the end the symbol's function outweighs its form, and the form can be shed like a skin if necessary" (p. 62). If the skin that is shed is animal, this symbolic loss is often of the real animal, obfuscating fundamental needs and replacing them with commercial goals. For example, although the eagle remains a symbol of the United States, and figures in the economic visual discourse of *The Economist*, what is absent is knowledge of the conditions real eagles, and other raptors, face in the world, even when protected by law. This is particularly so as "Mickey Mouse has achieved the status of a 'national symbol in America'" and as such demonstrates that "just about anything will do as a national symbol" (p. 62). Thus, not only is something lost when imagery takes over from imagination and real experiences but more so where living, breathing beings are concerned. Audiences are further distanced from what actual animals experience in terms of care, consideration, and lifeways as the meanings extracted and representations employed thus the image/brand "need owe *nothing* to the characteristics of the animals it employs" (p. 62). That so many of the "animals" have been rendered empty, lifeless in connection to real beings this analysis reveals the truly postmodern nature of these re-presentations. As Carol Adams (2016) posits, "there has been a shift in relation to animals and what prevails now is a cultural concept of animals" (p. 351).

Whereas something of "the real" remained even in the circumstances of the absent referent. Today that is no longer true.

Reasons for using animals on the covers in these ways is consistent with goals of political propaganda. The dragon, for example is a purely mythical, imaginary, fabulous creature, who comes to stand in for a nation and a people. But, as South (1987, p. ix) points out, "in a sense all fantastic beings are 'invented' or 'made up' (that is, they do not actually exist in nature), but, in inventing them, people have usually drawn upon natural forms ... exaggerating or distorting features of real creatures." The use of animals is also consistent with Cortés de Los Ríos (2010) study wherein "the economy is often framed a natural, rather than [human]made institution or system" (as described in Claussen, 2015, p. 248).

There are real world implications to use of animals as symbols in a world rapidly detached and disaffected from and by the natural world. Early chapters presented research that demonstrates the importance both to humans and to animals of experiencing them directly. Animals used on the covers of magazines to sell newsstand copies and ideological concepts are a far cry from cultivating compassion for their experiences. The emphasis is on their use, because they are *used* in these ways. What *The Economist* could do is investigative stories in to the treatment of real animals in the global economy. In addition, paralleling an entire nation and its citizens with acts of fearsome dragons and terrifying tigers is a form of visual oppression. For the animal, fetishizing results in real suffering as "the totemic symbol of Russia is the bear, and the Russians were not averse to making their symbol into rugs and garments" (Hellie, 1999, p. 55).

What these re-presented animals have in common is all being predator species. Yet so are human beings. It is far easier, however, to accept, in fact promote, destructive, threatening, or darker behaviors or intentions using animals as indicators of our own natures than present issues as they are. In addition, in an effort to generate interest in the less-than-sexy-content that makes up business news, *The Economist* no doubt relies on these dramatic renderings as a unique visual identity. Professional communicators nevertheless have a responsibility to ethically present other nations and peoples as well as not stereotype members of other species. To do otherwise is to colonize minds as well as nations. Evans (1987, p. 55) reflects on this as well:

> As the world shrinks to ever smaller proportions, the monsters that once inhabited charted realms are either driven inward—emerging as the repressed urges of our psychological selves—or reinvented on a larger scale; it is a fair guess that mankind's oldest and greatest monster—the dragon—will continue to play its terrible part in our imagination.

Note

1. For a discussion of political cartoonist Chris Riddell, whose animal drawings capture both traditional and transitional sense of animals as nations, such as the British Lion, Chinese Dragon, and the Russian Bear, see Baker (1993/2001, p. 56).

References

Adams, C. (2016). *The Carol J. Adams reader: Writings and conversations, 1955–2105*. New York, NY: Bloomsbury.

Baker, S. (1993/2001). *Picturing the beast*. Champaign, IL: University of Illinois Press.

Barton, T. (n.d.). Of Russian origin: Medved. Russiapedia. http://russiapedia.rt.com/of-russian-origin/medved/

Biedermann, H. (1994). *Dictionary of symbolism: Cultural icons & the meanings behind them* (J. Hulbert, Trans.). New York, NY: Meridian.

Brown, S. (2010). Where the wild brands are: Some thoughts on anthropomorphic marketing. *The Marketing Review, 10*(3), 209–224.

Carson, G. (1972). *Men, beasts, and gods: A history of cruelty and kindness to animals*. New York, NY: Charles Scribner's Sons.

Cerulo, K. A. (1984). Social disruption and its effects on music: An empirical analysis. *Social Forces, 62*(4), 885–904.

Christ, W. G., & Johnson, S. (1985). Images through *Time*: Man of the Year covers. *Journalism Quarterly, 62*(4), 891–893.

Christ, W. G., & Johnson, S. (1988). Women through *Time*: Who gets covered? *Journalism Quarterly, 65*(4), 889–897.

Cirlot, J. E. (1971/2014). *A dictionary of symbols* (2nd ed.). London: Routledge & Kegan Paul.

Claussen, D. (2015). Business journalism in magazines: Wrestling with economic issues. In D. Abrahamson & M. R. Prior-Miller (Eds.), *The Routledge handbook of magazine research* (pp. 244–258). New York, NY: Routledge.

Cortés de Los Ríos, M. (2010). Cognitive devices to communicate economic crisis: An analysis through covers in *The Economist. Ibérica, 20,* 81–106.

Douglas, M. (1970/2013). *Natural symbols.* New York, NY: Routledge.

Edwards, R. D. (1993). *The pursuit of reason: The Economist, 1843–1993.* Boston, MA: Harvard Business School.

Emmott, B. (2015). Foreword. In D. Abrahamson & M. R. Miller (Eds.), *The Routledge handbook of magazine research: The future of the magazine form* (pp. xiii–xiv). New York, NY: Routledge.

Evans, J. (1987). The dragon. In M. L. South (Ed.), *Mythical and fabulous creatures: A source book and research guide.* New York: Greenwood.

Feldhammer, G., Whittaker, J., Monty, A.-M., & Weickert, C. (2002). Charismatic mammalian megafauna: Public empathy and marketing strategy. *Journal of Popular Culture, 36*(1), 160–167.

Forceville, C. (1994). Pictorial metaphor in advertisements. *Metaphor and Symbolic Activity, 9*(1), 1–29.

Gaiman, N. (2002). *Coraline.* Middlesbrough: Quality Books.

Hellie, R. (1999). *The economy and material culture of Russia, 1600–1725.* Chicago, IL: University of Chicago Press.

Jenner, G. (2015, September 4). What is the significance of the British bulldog? *History Revealed.* Retrieved from http://www.historyrevealed.com/article/animals/what-significance-british-bulldog

Johnson, S. (2002). The art and science of magazine cover research. *Journal of Magazine and New Media Research, 5*(1), 1–10.

Kalof, L., & Fitzgerald, A. (2003). Reading the trophy: Exploring the display of dead animals in hunting magazines. *Journal of Visual Studies, 18*(2), 112–122.

Kennedy, P. F., & McGarvey, M. G. (2008). Animal-companion depictions in women's magazine advertising. *Journal of Business Research, 61*(5), 424–430.

Lancendorfer, K. M., Atkin, J. L., & Reece, B. B. (2008). Animals in advertising: Love dogs? Love the ad! *Journal of Business Research, 61*(5), 384–391.

Leath, V. M., & Lumpkin, A. (1992). An analysis of sportwomen on the covers and in the feature articles of Women's Sports and Fitness Magazine. *Journal of Sport & Social Issues, 16*(2), 121–126.

Lloyd, S., & Woodside, A. G. (2013). Animals, archetypes, and advertising (A3): The theory and practice of customer brand symbolism. *Journal of Marketing Management, 29*(1/2), 1–21.

Meisner, M. S., & Takahasi, B. (2013). The nature of *Time*: How the covers of the world's most widely read weekly news magazine visualize environmental affairs. *Journal of Landscape Architecture, 7*(2), 255–276.

Merskin, D. (2005). Making enemies in George W. Bush's post-9/11 speeches. *Peace Review: A Journal of Social Justice, 17,* 373–381.

Miles, C., & Ibrahim, Y. (2013). Deconstructing the meerkat: Fabular anthropomorphism, popular culture, and the market. *Journal of Marketing Management, 29*(15/16), 1862–1880.

Moore, W. S., Bowers, D. R., & Granovsky, T. A. (1982). What are magazine articles telling us about insects? *Journalism Quarterly, 59*, 464–467.

Mumby, D. K., & Spitzack, C. (1983). Ideology and television news: A metaphoric analysis of political stories. *Central States Speech Journal, 34*, 162–171.

Palmeri, F. (2006). The autocritiques of fables. In F. Palmeri (Ed.), *Humans and other animals in eighteenth-century British culture: Representation, hybridity, ethics* (pp. 83–100). Burlington, VT: Ashgate Publishing.

Perlmutter, D. (2007). *Picturing China in the American press: The visual-portrayal of Sino-American relations in Time magazine*. Lexington, KY: Lexington Books.

Pompper, D., Lee, S., & Lerner, S. (2009). Gauging outcomes of the 1960s social equality movements: Nearly four decades of gender and ethnicity on the cover of the *Rolling Stone* magazine. *Journal of Popular Culture, 42*(2), 273–290.

Pyykkö, R. (2012). Official and unofficial symbols of Russia and their use in media. In A. Koskensalo, J. Smeds, A. Huguet, & R. de Cillia (Eds.), *Language: Competence, change, contact* (pp. 239–252). Berlin: LIT Verlag Münster.

Rowland, B. (1973). *Animals with human faces: A guide to animal symbolism*. London: Allen & Unwin.

Santa Ana, O. (2002). *Brown tide rising*. Austin, TX: University of Texas Press.

Schoenfield, C. (1983). The environmental movement as reflected in the American magazine. *Journalism Quarterly, 60*, 470–475.

Schön, D. (1979). Generative metaphor: A perspective on problem-setting in social policy. In A. Ortony (Ed.), *Metaphor and thought* (2nd ed., pp. 136–164). Cambridge: Cambridge University Press.

Scott, D. W., & Stout, D. A. (2006). Religion on *Time*: Personal spiritual quests and religious institutions on the cover of a popular news magazine. *Journal of Magazine and New Media Research, 8*, 1–17.

Soares, I. (2015). Covering public affairs: The arena of newsmagazines. In D. Abrahamson & M. R. Prior-Miller (Eds.), *The Routledge handbook of magazine research: The future of the magazine form* (pp. 224–243). New York, NY: Routledge.

Songster, E. E. (2004). *Panda nation: Nature, science, and nationalism in the People's Republic of China*. (unpublished manuscript).

South, M. (1987). *Mythical and fabulous creatures: A source book and research guide*. Westport, CT: Greenwood.

Spears, N. E., Mowen, J. C., & Chakraborty, G. (1996). Symbolic role of animals in print advertising: Content analysis and conceptual development. *Journal of Business Research, 37*(2), 87–95.

Stamp, J. (2013, January 25). American myths: Benjamin Franklin's turkey and the presidential seal. *Smithsonian*. Retrieved from http://www.smithsonianmag.com/arts-culture/american-myths-benjamin-franklins-turkey-and-the-presidential-seal-6623414/

Steuter, E., & Willis, D. (2009). *At war with metaphor: Media, propaganda, and racism in the war on terror*. Lexington, KY: Lexington Books.

Tresidder, J. (1998). *Dictionary of symbols*. San Francisco, CA: Chronicle Books.
Willis, R. (2000). *Dictionary of world myth*. London: Duncan Baird Publishers.
Wörsching, M. (2009). Gender and images of nature and sport in British and German news magazines: The global and the national images in advertising. *International Journal of Media & Cultural Politics, 5*(3), 217–232.
Young, W. (2014). *The fascination of birds: From the albatross to the yellowthroat*. New York, NY: Dover.

Index

A

Absent referent, 47, 136, 159, 256
Accumulation theory, 15
Advertising, xvi–xvii, 26, 62, 86, 91, 104–105, 143, 147–151, 181, 185, 192, 195, 201, 217, 237, 239, 242, 245
Affectivity, 63
Agency, xxi, 14–15, 35, 63, 119
Agreement on the Conservation of Polar Bears (1973), 142
Althusser, Louis, 37
Animal, defined, xxv fn. 1 and 2, xxv, 7
Animals and
  Agency, xv, xviii, xxi, 14–15, 35, 63
  Beliefs about, xiv, 14, 20–21, 37–38, 42, 44, 93, 103, 147, 166, 183, 213, 215, 222, 236, 240
  Color, 152, fn. 2, 218–219, 222
  Companionship, 5, 62,
  Defined, xxii
  Divide, xvi, xxii, 5–6, 8–, 20
  Fables, 122, 219, 233, 235–236, 245, 252
    Defined, 235
  Law, xiv, 6, 10, 16, 22, 28 fn. 2, 44, 166, 237, 255
  Others, xiv, 13, 16, 18, 25
  Rights, xvi, fn. 3 xxiv, 95, 120, 166, 172, 238
    Define, xiv fn. 3
  Utility, xiv, xviii, xxii, 3–5, 38, 40, 103
Animal Apperception Test (AAPT), 62
Animal Media Studies, xix, xxi–xxii, 27, 33, 40–42, 95
Animal turn, 40–41
Anomie, 61
Anthropocentrism, xiv, 40, 68–69
Anthropocene, 149
Anthropomorphism, xx–xxi, 46, 96, 106, 171–173, 217, 235, 245
Attachment, 62, 70, 74

B

Bear(s), 37, 48, 86, 91, 98, 164, 233–234,
    242, 244, 247–248, 252–257
    Polar, 86, 104, 106, 124–125,
        135–152,
Belsky's Process Model, 64–65
Bentham, J., 10,
Berger, John, 6, 87, 96, 190
Biophilia
    Defined, 60–61
    Hypothesis, 60
Books,
    General, 54, 71, 91, 150,
    Children's, xxii, 72, 96, 113–131,
        136, 149

C

Canada, 138, 142, 152, 159, 160, 228, 254
Cat(s), xiv, xxii, xxv fn.2, 5, 11, 15, 40–41,
    48, 55, 58, 67, 94, 98–100, 118, 129,
    130, 168, 179–201, 217, 219, 249,
    251–252
Cat People (1942), 180, 190, 193
Charisma, 137, 146–147, 150
Charismatic mega fauna, xxiii, 44,
    147–148
Child development, xxii, 49, 64–65, 71,
    114
China, 234, 241, 247–248, 250–254
Coca–Cola, xxiii, 86, 150–151
Coloniality, 163
Colonialsm, 140, 153 fn. 5, 165
    Settler, 158, 164–165,
Colonization, 13, 139, 164, 228
Condensation symbol, 137, 150
Codependence, 63
Conceptual Blending Theory, 208, 215,
    217
Conceptual Metaphor Theory, 208,
    215–218

Content
    Manifest 124
    Latent 124
Continuity, 63–64,
Crow(s), xxiii, 91, 207–209, 214–215, 222,
    225–226, 228, 238,
Cultural Studies, 34, 40, 43,
    190–191, 235
Curtis, Edward, 140, 169

D

Descartes, René, 9–10
Decoding, 36
Disney, xxiii, 48, 86, 158, 169, 170–171,
    173–176
    Formula, 171
    True Life Adventures, xiii, 158, 170
Disnification, 169
Documentary, xxiii, 140, 169–171, 174
Dragon, 233–234, 247–248,
    250–254, 256
Dreaded comparison, 6, 20
Dualism, 23, 44, 46
Durkheim, E., 61, 93

E

Eagle(s), xx, 100, 102, 146, 159, 163, 165,
    215, 234, 236–237, 245–246, 248,
    254–255
Ecofeminism, 43–44, 200, 201 defined
    fn. 1
Ecological thought, xvii
Economist, The, xxiii, 233–235, 242–244,
    246–247, 250–253, 255–256
Empathy, xix, 21, 46, 57, 63, 67, 68, 71,
    73–74, 77, 94
    Critical, 40
    Entangled, xix, xxii,
Encoding, 36

F

Fable, 122, 219, 233, 236, 245, 252
  Defined 235
Feline mystique, 188
Femme Sauvage, 185
Feral feminine, 179, 185, 187, 189, 192–193
Films/movies, 16, 27, 37, 54, 59, 71, 78, 85–87, 103–105, 147, 150, 170, 174, 181, 190, 194, 200, 207, 217
Flaherty, Robert, 140, 169
Foucault, Michele, 97, 180
Fourth educator, 57, 77
Freud, Sigmund, 56, 59, 93, 194
Frisson, 190
  Defined 194

G

Game of Thrones, xxiii, 86, 205, 208, 220, 228
Gender, xvii, xxi, xxiii, 16–17, 19, 23, 27, 34, 43–44, 48, 90, 98, 113–117, 120, 122–131, 140, 149, 172, 201 fn. 1, 221, 235, 241
Goffman, Erving, 27, 87
Goodall, Jane, xv, xvii
Great Chain of Being, 8–10

H

Haraway, Donna, 48
Hegemony, 35–37, 48, 98
Heterotopia, 97
Human zoo, 13, 140
Humane Education, 76–78

I

Ideological State Apparatus, 36

Image to Imagination, 143–144
Internet, 48, 91, 102–103
Intersecting Axes of Privilege, Domination, and Oppression, 21–22
Interspecies Model of Prejudice, 20
Intersectionality, 19, 43, 115, 200

J

Johnson, Mark, 97, 208, 216, 235
Journalism, business, 241–242
Jung, Carl, 194, 211, 250–252

K

Knut the polar bear, 136, 146, 152

L

Lakoff, George, 97–98, 208, 216
Language, xvi–xvii, xxiii fn. 1, 7, 12, 26, 40–41, 57–58, 60, 73, 97–100, 104, 114, 158, 160, 175, 182–184, 208, 211, 216–217, 219, 237
  Zoological references in, 12, 17, 25, 99–100, 182–184, 191
Last chance tourism, 148
Latent content, 124
Latent orientalism, 144

M

Magazine(s), xvi, 27, 105, 121, 136, 237, 240–242, 244
  Business, 241–243
  Covers, xxiii, 183, 234–235, 240–241, 245
Magritte, René, 97, 107
Manifest content, 124

Manifest Destiny, 164–165
Marketing–oriented fabular anthropomorphism, 235
Maslow's Hierarchy of Needs, 24
Metaphor, xx, 8, 14, 39, 71, 96–97, 99, 136, 150, 180, 182–184, 205, 208, 215–218, 221, 223, 228, 234, 238–240, 244–245, 254–255
  Defined, 216
Mirror Neuron, 70
Misogyny, 43, 182
Misothery, 43
Monstrous, The, 12, 222
Muybridge, Eduard, 91
Myth, Mythology, 137, 149, 163, 165, 184–186, 188, 194, 206–208, 211–212, 220, 228, 234–235, 247, 250–254, 256
  Defined, 184, 211

N

National Geographic, xv–xvi, 171, 180,
Neoteny, 96, 146, 160
Newspaper(s), 16, 18, 48, 105, 121, 237, 240, 242–244

O

Oedipus & the Sphinx, 186–187, 193

P

Panda(s), 146, 247–248, 252–253
Pet(s), 5, 11–12, 14, 27, 38, 40, 44, 45, 54–55, 58, 62–63, 69–71, 73, 74–76, 77, 87, 103–104, 113, 122, 152, 168, 195
  Abuse, 73–76
  Defined, 27
Petroglyph, 88–90, 96
  Defined, 88

Photography, 61, 102, 169–170, 185, 221
Pictograph, 90
Poe, Edgar Allen, 206–207,
Poetry, 121–122, 188, 206–207, 219
Polar Bear(s), xxi, xxiii, 86, 104, 135–152
Power, xvii, xix, 8, 15, 17, 20, 26–27, 34–36, 40, 44, 46, 57–58, 75, 98, 101, 104, 139, 147, 150, 166, 174, 180–182, 188–192, 199, 211, 215, 221–222, 236, 245
Prairie Dog(s), xxiii, 157–176
Propaganda, 14, 16, 234–235, 237, 245, 252, 254, 256

R

Raven(s), xxiii, 90–91, 205–208, 211, 213–228
Racism, 22–23, 44, 93, 164
Radio, 102, 105, 237
Representation, defined, 35
Repressive state apparatus, 37
Rewilding, xvii–xviii
Rock art, 88, 90, 92, 96
Russia, 138, 247–248, 252–254, 256–257

S

Semiotics, xviii, 45, 126, 135–136, 147, 149, 159, 182, 199, 218
Sentinel species, 139
Settlers (Euro), 158–159, 164, 166
Settler colonialism, 158, 164–165, 174
  Defined, 164
Sexism, 22
Shamanism, 91–92
Signifying practices, 27
Snake(s), 4, 8, 23, 73, 173, 211, 249–250, 254
Social Support Hypothesis, 60, 62
Speciesism, 22–23, 43–44

Stereotype, 17, 27, 42, 71, 73, 103–104, 115–116, 120, 123–125, 130, 143–144, 189, 208, 223, 235, 238, 256

Symbol(ism), xx–xxiii, 4, 15, 17, 27, 35, 38–39, 43, 45–49, 59, 70–71, 75, 87, 93–96, 101–104, 114–117, 136–137, 143, 144, 146–149, 150, 152, 163–165, 180–185, 188, 192, 207, 210–212, 215, 218, 221, 224, 226–228, 234– 235, 236, 237, 239–240, 244–247, 250–256

Symbolic annihilation, 103

T

Television, xv–xvi, xxiii–xxiv fn. 4, 27, 54, 62, 65, 71, 85–87, 102–103, 120–121, 124, 147, 150, 168, 170, 189, 207–208, 222, 228, 242

Textual analysis, xviii, xxiii, 115–116, 126, 180, 191, 198, 247

Tiger(s), 4, 100, 116, 129–130, 146–147, 180, 197, 201, 234, 247–248, 251–254, 256

Totem, 92–93, 214–215, 256
  Definition, 92

True Life Adventures, xiii, 158, 170

U

Utilitarian interest(s), xvi, 38, 40, 103

V

Vanishing motif, 172–173
Vanishing Prairie, 159, 170–171
Varminting, 166–167

W

"Winter is coming," 223, 225

Wolf, Wolves, xix, xviii, xix, 4, 91, 98, 100, 103, 106, 116, 129, 142, 146, 152, 163, 165, 183, 207, 210, 221, 224–226, 238, 248,
  Dire, 86, 221, 224, 228 fn. 6, 229